A HAND WEAVER'S NOTEBOOK

SHARON ALDERMAN

 INTERWEAVE PRESS

Photography by Joe Coca
Cover Design by Signorella Graphic Arts
Back Cover Photograph by John Schaefer
Illustrations by Ann Sabin
Production by Marc McCoy Owens

Library of Congress Cataloging-in-Publication Data

Alderman, Sharon D.
    A handweaver's notebook : swatch collections from Handwoven
magazine / Sharon Alderman.
        p.   cm.
    Includes index.
    ISBN 0-934026-57-2 : $18.00
    1. Hand weaving.   2. Textile fabrics.   I. Handwoven.   II. Title.
TT848.A6497   1990
746.1'4--dc20   90-38089
                                                                    CIP

This book is dedicated to the readers of HANDWOVEN.

ACKNOWLEDGMENTS

I'd like to acknowledge the personal help and friendship of the following individuals without whom this book would not exist: Bonnie Phillips, Kim Pedersen, Janet Wolf, Bonnie Mangold, and Donita Mason.

CONTENTS

Preface

The first issue of HANDWOVEN, fall/winter 1979, had just been published. Those of us who had had a hand in producing it were justifiably pleased and looking forward to the spring/summer 1980 issue.

In early November, Linda Ligon, HANDWOVEN's publisher and original editor, called to tell me about an idea she had: What would I think about publishing collections of handwoven fabric swatches, coordinated fabrics for clothing? They would come out twice a year: fall/winter and spring/summer. They would not be made into actual garments; we would present the fabrics and let our readers go from there.

I told her I thought it was a very good idea; moreover, I would like to be the one to do it. As it turned out, that was exactly what she had in mind.

I still think it is a good idea.

In the following pages you will find some general ideas about the designing process, the first twenty Swatch Collections, their photos, their instructions, and the stories that lie behind their creation.

Over the last ten years, new yarns have become available and others have been discontinued. Although I have always tried to choose yarns that seem likely to be around for a long time, some of these are no longer available. In such cases, we have tried to suggest alternatives which are available—at least this year!

I hope that you will find this book useful. I particularly hope that you will be encouraged to try your hand at designing. It is generally brain-cudgeling and frequently exasperating, but it is always the most exciting, rewarding work possible!

Sharon Alderman
September, 1990

DESIGNING: SOME GENERAL IDEAS, SOME SPECIFIC OPINIONS

Designing is a personal matter, as you will see; it comes right out of one's life. Where else could it originate? Besides the experiences that trigger my ideas, I have some basic notions about designing good, sound, beautiful cloth.

The cloth I design must function and must be beautiful. I begin with its function—how will it be used? I am happiest when I know what the cut of the garment will be; that is the only way I can be sure I will design cloth of the appropriate weight, drape, and scale. When I designed the fabrics in this book, I had images of garments in my mind or sketches that told me whether the fabric had to be firm or soft, lightweight or hearty, dainty or rugged. Designing toward an end directs my work.

These collections have appeared twice a year: fall/winter and spring/summer. This seasonal rhythm has strongly influenced fiber selection, the first decision I make about a fabric. For warm weather, I choose cotton, linen, and ramie or combinations of those fibers. For cool weather, wool, silk, mohair, alpaca, and cotton, either alone or in combination. I have decided to weave luxury fabrics; to me, that means natural fibers. My inclination is to design and wear elegant, understated fabrics. I like subtlety and the surprise in the cloth that shows up on close inspection. Inevitably, my personal taste shows up in my work. How could it be otherwise and still be mine?

Fiber selection

When I think about the function the fiber performed when it was part of a living organism, it is easier to see what it can do for me. The protein fibers—wool, silk, mohair, cashmere, alpaca, camel down, and angora—all served as insulation, holding heat next to the body. All except silk were coats that kept the skin of the animal dry. Silk, spun by the silkworm, became a stiffened tent in which the worm was sheltered as it pupated. Cellulose fibers conduct heat along their length, the opposite of being an insulator. The best conductor is linen, followed by ramie and cotton. Fabrics made of linen, ramie, or cotton help keep us comfortable in warm weather by carrying the heat away from the body.

Our skin is always releasing water vapor, winter or summer; fabrics which absorb that water vapor are comforting. Fabrics made of unabsorbent fibers feel clammy in cold weather and sticky in hot weather. Nylon, polyester, and some rayons are not absorbent; neither are plastic bags. The most absorbent fiber is wool, followed by silk, linen (which releases moisture quickly so that it stays dry), and cotton.

Highly resilient fibers resist wrinkling because when they are creased they smooth out without having to be pressed. A resilient fiber, particularly if well spun and woven into a firm structure, resists tearing: when a resilient fabric I am wearing is snagged, it stretches a bit, allowing me the time to realize that I've gotten caught on something; a nonresilient fabric is more likely to rip when snagged. Because handwoven fabrics are often coarser than commercial fabrics and thus more likely to snag, resilience is important.

Resilience also helps protect a fabric from damage due to abrasion: the fabric gives just a little rather than being worn away. The most resilient fiber is wool, followed by silk. Cotton, ramie, and linen are not resilient; they are more likely to retain wrinkles and do not stretch. The yarn style (see below) of a given fiber makes a big difference: combed, mercerized cottons wrinkle far less than less processed cottons. The structure of the fabric (a firm twill wrinkles less readily than plain weave) is also a factor, and the use of a lining in a garment further cuts down on wrinkling.

Yarn style

Yarn style is nearly as important to a fabric's utility as the fiber itself. Yarns made of the same fibers but spun differently can behave very differently in the finished cloth.

WOOL

The most obvious example of the influence of yarn style is the difference between woolen and worsted yarns. I can tell which is which even without labeling: a woolen-spun yarn is spun with oil which I can usually smell, and when I untwist a piece, the fibers are relatively short. When I break a worsted yarn, a sort of watercolor-brush-end forms because the fibers are longer and combed so that they are aligned.

Worsted yarns are usually more expensive—combing adds another process to their manufacture and therefore to their cost—but one style is not inherently better than the other. They simply do different things. When I want a fabric with a clear surface, no fuzziness, and a crisper, cooler feel, I choose worsted yarns. When I want a yarn that fluffs when it is washed (I used this prop-

woolen   *worsted*

erty in Swatch Collection #14) and fills in the holes between the yarns, I choose woolen-spun yarns. Woolen-spun cloth is well suited for windproofing, for hearty, less formal jackets and overcoats. To me, worsted fabrics look and feel a little more refined and elegant.

COTTON

Cottons are also spun with and without combing. Combed cottons are usually mercerized, too, making them smoother, more lustrous, stronger, and less likely to retain wrinkles. Mercerization (hot lye is used; it is **not** a home process!) makes the cotton fibers, which resemble flattened, twisted ribbons when ripe, plump out and resume a cylindrical shape. They are stronger and more light-reflective after mercerization.

The analogy to the woolen/worsted pair is quite close: uncombed cottons are spun from shorter fibers. When I want a fabric with a soft, velvety surface—like old, well-worn cotton jeans—I choose uncombed, unmercerized cotton. When I want a silky, refined cotton, particularly if I am showing off an intricate structure, I choose mercerized cotton.

Some combed, mercerized cottons are "gassed"—passed rapidly over a tiny gas flame to singe off the ends of the protruding fibers. Such highly processed cottons are so smooth and shiny that they can be confused with spun silk. In my experience, they wrinkle a lot less than regular mercerized cottons, even when woven plain weave.

mercerized

SILK

The silk yarns I can buy as a handweaver are mostly spun or noils. Noils yarns are made from the short bits: short fibers, knots, little lumps, tangled fibers. They are not light-reflective, tend to feel powdery and dry—not "silky"—and tend to be weaker. Although I have used some noils yarns for warps, others pull apart with only moderate tension or abrade away in the reed as they are woven. The only way to tell for sure which will serve as warps is to weave a sample.

Spun silk is smooth and feels "silky". It is made up of moderately long fibers twisted together but has not been reeled. The fibers may be several inches long, producing a smooth, strong, lustrous yarn.

Reeled silks are rarely offered to handweavers. The only exception I have found is tram silk. Tram silks are reeled from the cocoons, doubled and redoubled but hardly twisted at all. They are strong because the fibers are continuous and very shiny because light reflection is not broken by the twist, but they tend to abrade and look scuffed if woven with floats or used in a place of high wear such as cuffs or over elbows.

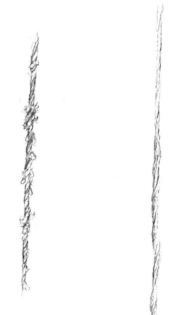

noil   *spun*

LINEN

Linen, the name given to spun flax fibers, is spun in two main styles, analogous to silk. Stem-long fibers are twisted to make line linen. Wet-spun line linen is the smoothest and strongest; dry-spun line linens are more textural but also strong. The short parts, broken fibers, and jumbled bits of flax combed out in the making of line linens are saved and spun into tow linen, analogous to noils silk. Line linens are lustrous, particularly after repeated laundering, shed little lint (after the initial washes), and are strong. Tow linens vary considerably; some have fibers as long as 6" and make passable warps. Others resemble spun barn sweepings. The latter make weak, harsh, prickly cloth. Tow linens are usually used for their textural contrast.

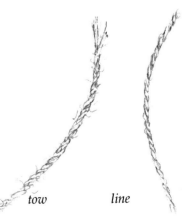

tow   *line*

BLENDS

Yarns composed of a blend of fibers vary a lot. I prefer to use blends made up of fibers that have something in common. For example, I prefer a blend of silk and wool—both are protein fibers, prefer acidic conditions, prosper with a little water vapor—to a blend of linen and wool—linen is cellulosic, prefers basic conditions, and must be kept dry. My concern is that the conditions that favor one fiber destroy the other. I consider each blend individually and carefully. I am not interested in making a wool cloth that will mildew or a linen cloth that the moths will eat!

I have noticed that yarns made of fibers of similar diameter look and feel good. I have seen and handled blends made of fibers dissimilar in diameter in which the coarser fiber sticks out of the yarn and is shed from it as it is used. I'd rather use yarns that stay together so that the cloth is the same years after it was woven. My aim is to make fabrics that last for many years, and I base my decisions about fiber blends on that aim.

I am still thinking about fiber blends. Viyella® fabrics, for example, are spun of a blend of very fine wool and cotton fibers. Ordinarily, blends of protein and cellulose concern me, but the luxury of the resulting cloth in this case is very seductive. I will continue to think about blends and engage in internal debates from time to time about them.

FANCY YARNS

a three-element fancy yarn

Fancy yarns are made of practically any fiber and are often blends. They provide visual and tactile contrast in the cloth when they are combined with plain yarns or can be used for the whole face of the cloth (I used a cotton/flax blend that way in Swatch Collection #1).

Most fancy yarns are made up of three elements, but a few are two-ply. Common two-ply fancies are made of two threads, the weight of one or both of which differs along their length. Two singles yarns in different colors may be plied to make a ragg or marl yarn. A two-ply yarn may be comprised of two fibers: a fine noils silk thread and a fine cotton, for instance.

Most fancy or novelty yarns are composed of three parts: a core thread; an effect thread that loops, zigzags or forms knots or seeds across the core; and a binder thread that wraps the first two securely together to prevent shifting of the loops, knots, or seeds. Chenille yarns are actually woven of two yarns (warp yarns) which twist around each other leno-fashion to hold short pieces of yarn (the weft) in place; when they are removed from the loom and cut, they twist and become round and velvety, resembling the caterpillars for which the French named them.

The fiber content of the elements in novelty yarns varies. A loop or brushed mohair may have a wool core, a mohair effect thread, and a nylon binder, for example. The binder thread is usually fine, so that it is unobtrusive, and must be strong.

When I use novelty yarns—any yarns for that matter—I make sure I know their fiber content so that I can finish the cloth properly. I learned the hard way once when I combined a fiber with a low melting point with one which required ironing at a moderately high temperature. When I finished the cloth, the more plastic fiber melted to the iron and made gooey strings when I lifted the iron away from the face of the cloth. Most finishing incompatibilities are not so dramatic, but I have remembered that lesson.

In general, novelty yarns are best suited to fabrics not subjected to a lot of abrasion. The fibers in them are not tightly spun into the yarn but sit on the surface, more or less unprotected. Fabrics with dramatic novelty yarns on their surface are more likely to pill and look unkempt in time. Just the same, one of my favorite jackets has a lovely novelty yarn on its surface; I de-pill it regularly and love it in spite of the extra maintenance required. I don't avoid the use of fancy yarns, but I think carefully as I plan the cloth, always keeping in mind that I want the cloth to be functional and beautiful over time.

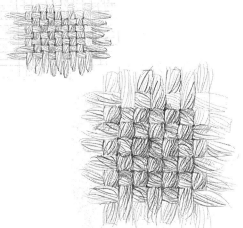

for a lightweight fabric, use a thin yarn

GRIST

The grist or size of a yarn is a part of its style. When I want a lightweight fabric, I usually use a thinner yarn. A heavier yarn woven into the same interlacement produces a heavier fabric—it's that simple. Opening up the sett and beating more gently is not the solution; that approach produces a limp, unappealing fabric. There is a range of setts at which a given yarn in a particular structure produces good cloth, but it is not very wide; it's a mistake to rely on sett to make a sheerer, lighter cloth.

A combination of yarns of various diameters all spun in the same way from a given fiber produces a textural variety in the cloth (see Swatch Collection #3). I often challenge myself to take a yarn I think I know and use it so that its qualities are revealed in a new way.

a thicker yarn produces a heavier fabric

The way a cloth will be used determines the fiber content and suggests the most appropriate yarn styles; to some extent, use also suggests the best structure.

Structures vary in the hand and draping qualities they bring to the cloth. The firmest—and sheerest—fabric that can be woven with a particular yarn, excluding tricky, weaver-manipulated weaves like leno, is plain weave. The warp and weft yarns intersect with the plane of the cloth at every opportunity, producing a great deal of friction within the structure. This friction and the lack of floats hold the cloth firm and make it resistant to snagging.

When an end (or pick) passes over more than one pick (or end), a float is formed in the cloth. A two-end (or two-pick) float is as short as they get. A cloth composed of two-end/-pick floats is thicker and has a higher thread count (ends per inch plus picks per inch) than plain weave. The more threads an end or pick floats over, the thicker and denser the cloth is. There is a limit, however, to this trend; my experience has shown that three-end/-pick floats are pretty stable in the cloth (if slippery yarns are used, they must be set closer), but floats of four, even **with** closer sett and firmer beat, collapse and become ropy unless supported another way. I can force four-end/-pick floats to lie flat (in a 4/4 twill, for example) by inserting a plain-weave shot (a finer yarn will cause less distortion of the twill line) between the twill shots. In 4/4 twill, the weft floats will be maintained by this approach, but the warp floats are cut by the plain-weave shots. If I am attempting to make the cloth heavier and thicker and it is still too thin with three-end/-pick floats, then I use two threads as one throughout, a heavier yarn, or a double-cloth structure.

As floats grow longer, the fabric becomes thicker and will be spongier, particularly if woven of a resilient fiber like wool. Look for the fabric suggestion "mohair" on the pattern envelope when you have a spongy fabric.

Structure

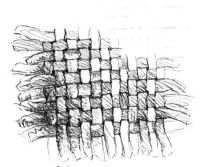

plain weave

a shot of thin weft between shots of 4/4 twill

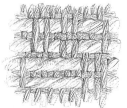

2/2 twill

a three-element fabric

Spongy fabrics are cuddly and comforting to wear, but they require simple cuts—no intricate seaming or little pieces.

A 2/2 twill has two-end and two-pick floats. This structure has a higher thread count than plain weave and, because its internal friction is only about half that of plain weave, it is softer, drapes more gracefully and, as noted above, wrinkles less than plain weave.

When cloth is woven with three elements—a warp, plain-weave weft, and a pattern thread, it handles and is sett like plain weave but is thicker. Overshot, summer & winter, and crackle are familiar structures of this type. The cloth tends to be slightly heavy because of the pattern weft that runs selvedge to selvedge. Visually, these fabrics look coarser than their plain-weave foundation. The eye tends to overlook the plain-weave structure and notice the pattern wefts instead. (That is the point, after all!) Even though the fabric's supporting structure may be fine, it is visually coarse so I avoid cutting small pattern pieces out of such cloth. Pocket flaps, pointed collars, gussets, and other details are overwhelmed by all but the tiniest overshot or summer & winter patterns.

How I work

a plowed field suggests corduroy

crested wheat grass suggests dornick twill

In time, all this information has become almost instinctual, because it has become so much a part of my "knowing" that I can draw on it any time. **It is absolutely necessary to study and bring the information in, but once it is understood and is a part of you, it flows out almost effortlessly.** When I reached that state of ease, designing became one of the highest kinds of fun. I love setting myself the challenge of designing just the right fabric for a particular application and seeing how well I can meet it. I love figuring out a solution to a problem I have set myself that I have never seen before.

Being a designer is both a blessing and a curse. (Clearly the fun of it outweighs the curse for me!) It means that as I look at the landscape, a building, a plant, or cloud formations, I am always wondering how I might turn what I'm admiring into a structure for cloth.

When I saw plowed fields on a drive just at sunset in Alberta a few autumns ago, I was struck by the light slanting over the furrows and how much it suggested a rich, thick corduroy. That corduroy showed up in Swatch Collection #8. In Chicago, I was admiring architectural details in the buildings downtown and thought of block structures. The details of the structure of crested wheatgrass (*Agropyron cristatum*) suggest dornick twills to me. The curvaceous shapes that clouds make when there are strong winds high in the sky (lenticular clouds) make me think of undulating twills or honeycomb structures.

Everything I see touches off ideas. This means that my work is never far from my mind—I can't turn it off. Nevertheless, I have come to love the shivers of anticipation as some connection is made between what I see and what I could weave. The leap that makes those connections is as quick as an electrical spark and sometimes as startling.

Those sparks of inspiration are just the beginning, of course. The next steps are far more workaday. I sketch the structural features I want the cloth to have, the placement of colors, and the scale and then flip through my "mental Rolodex" to see what structures would allow me to create a cloth that looks like that.

When I was designing the stripe in Swatch Collection #17, I wanted a fine stripe that grew wider and narrower, wider and narrower. I didn't want floats on the back so I couldn't leave warp ends floating; I knew that I had to weave the fine, contrasting stripes into the fabric at all times. I needed to figure out how to compress those warp ends and release them alternately. Woolen-spun threads bloom and fluff up when allowed to float for a distance (see Swatch Collection #14), but I was using cotton, which doesn't behave this way. The illusion had to be maintained by the structure.

I knew that if two threads are interlaced as if they were one, they take up less room. If they interlace oppositely, so that the weft passes between them with every pick, they spread out a bit. My first try used this information: the contrasting—and slightly heavier—warp ends rose and fell together to compress the pair of them and then were woven plain weave to spread them out. The effect was apparent only at a very intimate viewing distance. I needed larger expanses of color where the stripes were bolder so I changed the structure from plain weave to 1/2 basket; that is, each thread was lifted for two picks while its neighbor was down, then vice versa. The stripes—after being washed—were just the right size. If I had needed more emphasis, I'd have tried a 1/3 basket but the plain weave begins to distort beyond that. If that hadn't worked, I was prepared to double the number of contrasting ends to two per heddle and work through the sequence again. This experimental approach to structure is interesting, sometimes frustrating, always time-consuming, but usually very productive.

When I wanted to weave corduroy, I experimented with several ground structures (page 47) to see which gave the fullest, fluffiest rib. I turned to the engineering library at the University of Utah to see what I could find out about the structure of corduroy and then experimented on the loom. By reading about how corduroys were produced in industry, I was able to adapt commercial methods to the handloom.

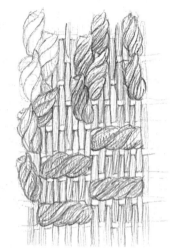

corduroy weave

Sometimes the rough sketches I make will work only if I combine structures in one cloth. I may need a fairly featureless ground cloth into which I drop another structure. The ground might be plain weave, if the fabric is to be lightweight, or twill if I need something heavier. The stripe or grid that is added to the ground cloth might be warp-faced in the warp direction and weft-faced in the weft direction (see Swatch Collection #18) and based on twill. If there is just a stripe in the warp direction (as in the cotton fabric in Swatch Collection #20), then the ground cloth can be threaded on just two shafts; the 3/1 twill requires four more shafts. When there are twill stripes in the weft direction, too, then the ground must be threaded on four (plus four for the warp stripes) to weave twill all the way across the web.

When I combine structures, I make a rough sketch first. Then I write down how many shafts each section of the cloth will require and, finally, figure out the way those threads must be lifted to make the sheds necessary to weave it. The trick is to approach this analysis in the simplest possible way. In the case of the twill stripe on a plain-weave ground, I figure out what shafts must rise to make plain weave and work that out **as if the twill did not exist;** then I move to the shafts that control the twill warp stripes and consider them alone **as if the plain weave did not exist.** Finally, I combine the sheds so that all the shafts that need to be lifted for each pass of the shuttle are noted and translated into treadlings.

stripes of plain weave and twill

When I have perfected the structure, I weave and evaluate the sample cloth. The fabrics in these collections were all designed to be worn (many can be used in other ways as well). An apparel fabric must be firm enough to hold its shape but soft enough to allow the body inside it to move without undue restriction. A clothing fabric must be stable enough to withstand normal wear; it is not appropriate, for example, to design a cloth for garments that you can put your fingers through. Cloth that snags easily can cause grief, too, but it is not necessary to design each fabric so that you could wade through thorny bushes to storm Sleeping Beauty's castle wearing it: a jacket for outdoor pursuits requires snag resistance but an evening jacket does not.

As I begin the design process, I think about the demands which will be put on the fabric and define it carefully. As further requirements or new ideas come to me, I add them to that definition. I am willing to alter. In fact, I count on the work itself to stimulate new and better ideas.

Color

Color is probably the first thing I notice about a cloth. It is color I see from a distance, long before I am close enough to tell what the structure is or what kinds of yarns and fibers are in the cloth. Although it often comes first in my designing process, in this discussion color follows fiber choice, yarn style, and structure, because it can be used to enhance all three. Color can suggest coolness and crispness (see Swatch Collection #19) or warmth and softness. Color can be used to make a brushed wool look even softer and more inviting to the touch, or it can give a crisper appearance to linen or a smooth-finished worsted wool.

Color can make the most pedestrian structure look rich and appealing. It can add the illusion of a third dimension to more complicated structures, (see the mohair/wool coating in Swatch Collection #14). Structures may be highlighted or enhanced by the strategic location of color. The waffle weave in Swatch Collection #18 is further defined and deepened by the placement of color in the centers of the squares. The purple worsted overcheck in Swatch Collection #4 is made using a slightly lighter value of the two winy colors for the overcheck to emphasize it and suggest that the threads are slightly bigger and lie higher in the cloth than they actually do.

In fact, the colors are probably the most important aspect of these collections for me. I always begin with the colors. When I have figured out which colors I will use, then I can begin to see the fabrics in my mind and work toward ways to produce them at my loom.

The ideas for the colors come from many places. I note many sources in the chapters which follow. My ideas for colors and combinations of colors often come from the natural world. When I travel to speak and give workshops, I take color charts and a notebook with me. When I see something that elicits the "ahhh response", I make notes of what I have seen. On my mind right now is a January sunset in which the sky was a soft apricot with striations of grayed blue-violet clouds. I make little sketches, note the time, place, and date, and write down the color numbers/names in my notebook. If I find an object (a leaf, a feather), I add it to my notebook, or draw it if it is something I may not or cannot take with me. I am often disappointed in color film, so I prefer making notes as messages to my future self who will weave what I am seeing.

Sometimes the colors come from a phrase overheard, a fragment of a novel or poem, or a phrase that pops into my head. Sometimes the colors come from music I listen to; the melodies or orchestration may call colors to mind. Sometimes as I look back over a years' worth of work, I can trace where I have been and what has been happening in my life. It all seems to show up in front of me on the loom.

sketch with color notes

a leaf or a feather are kept in my sketch book

When I get back to my studio, I get out yarn sample charts and see what yarns are available in the colors I want to use. When I see the yarns, I can begin, with the colors firmly in mind, to see how I want the colors arranged in the cloth, and then the structures begin to fall into place.

I often work out stripes by sketching them first with pencil on paper, then, after proportions have been worked out, by cutting strips of colored paper (magazine ads are a good source) and translating the drawn stripes into color. Strips of paper are ideal because I can overlap them if I need to make them thinner and can thus fine-tune what I have in mind. If I were working with crayons or gouache, I'd have to make a whole new sketch each time I altered a stripe. After I have assembled the paper stripes in a way I like, I wind a lightweight strip of cardboard with the yarns, which shows me the way the light plays on the surface of the yarns. I make a series of wrappings, sometimes, working from one to the next by hanging the first one on the wall and looking at it hard, for a long time. I think about what I like and what I don't and base the next wrapping on that information. I often work through four or five wrappings before I find the yarn end color orders I will use. I use the yarn order of the wrapping for the warp and weave a preliminary sample. The washed sample tells me how the yarns look interlaced, how the sett works, what sort of hand and drape the fabric will have, and whether it will wrinkle.

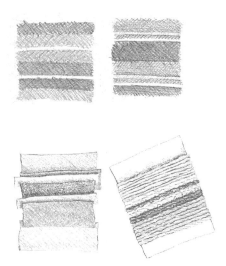

I design stripes with sketches . . . then strips of paper . . . then yarn wrappings

The Design Process

A requirement of each fabric shown in this book was that it had to coordinate with the other fabrics in its collection. Coordination means more than being compatibly or similarly colored. Frequently motifs (see Swatch Collection #19) or structures (#20) have been repeated to tie the fabrics to each other visually or structurally. The scale of the patterns must be compatible with their intended use. The scale of a repeating motif may vary throughout a collection: smaller for blouses or tops, larger for skirts and dresses, and largest for jackets and coats.

I suspect that approaches to designing may be as various as pathways to learning. Some of us learn well by reading, some do better when we hear the material, some learn best with a demonstration or diagram, and others when physical activity is involved. I see images of the fabrics I want to make and transform them into cloth via rough sketches, threadings and treadlings, and finally samples.

Clearly, the more experience you have in this process, the more natural it seems. It is never exactly easy although it is exciting and rewarding. The more yarns you have handled, woven, and washed, the more you understand what they can do. The more structures you have woven and manipulated, the easier it is to move from a rough sketch to a structure possibility. Sometimes more than one structure may do (think of the ways to make stripes, for example): your experience will help you narrow the possibilities and decide which to explore first.

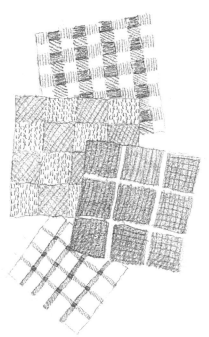

a repeated motif of squares ties this collection together

I almost never sit down to design a cloth by thinking, "I think I will weave some Bedford cord today." Approaching a design problem by boxing it in at the very beginning limits my design processes. Instead, I look at a rough sketch of what I want to have happen in the cloth and consider the ways that it might be accomplished.

Suppose that I wanted to design a cloth with stripes in it. How might I go about it? There are so many ways to create striped cloth!

The use of yarns similar in size, color, and spinning style but made of different fibers can, if they are arranged in stripes, create a cloth in which fuzzy

The design process—challenging, joyful,
frustrating and exciting—uses every visual
medium: colored paper, drafts, pencils,
sketches, yarn, doodles, and natural objects.

alternates with smooth, shiny with dull, velvety with smooth, or looped with plain. I have woven stripes of the same fiber and spinning style except one stripe was spun with an S-twist and its neighbors Z-twist. The difference in the way the light plays on the surface of the cloth is subtle but very interesting.

If the fibers used in a fiber-based stripe shrink differently, a seersuckery fabric can be produced. The stripe which shrinks less buckles in the cloth (see Swatch Collection #1). This effect is built into the cloth itself and is enhanced by not pressing the fabric. In industry, plissé fabrics are made by printing stripes on the loomstate fabric with a substance (usually a strongly alkaline paste on cotton) that causes some stripes to shrink a lot while the untreated cloth shrinks just a little. A fiber-based seersucker works similarly.

Genuine seersucker can be woven by tensioning stripes differently. The puckery stripes are tensioned just enough to make a passable shed; the remaining stripes are tensioned normally. This kind of seersucker, a structural seersucker, does not wash out, as commercially woven plissés do in time.

I have made stripes using the same fiber throughout but using different spinning styles in the cloth. I made a series of silk scarves in which the texture of noils silk was contrasted with the smoothness of spun silk dyed the same color. A similar effect occurs with novelty yarns. I once wove a very light off-white wool fabric in which I contrasted a very fine ratiné with a fine worsted-spun yarn. The cloth was subtle and wonderful.

Stripes can be achieved by color grouping or alternation as you can see throughout this series of fabrics. I love colored stripes because they are so "weaverly". Winding a striped warp is relatively easy to do and allows the weaving to be done with one shuttle—which is efficient—and doesn't require constant measuring to ensure even stripes. Sometimes we want stripes that do not repeat at all, and that option is open to us, certainly. I like the rhythm of stripes and have experimented with them a lot. To my eye, smaller repeats seem more formal, as do even stripes—stripes symmetric around a point. Stripes with longer repeats or ones that do not repeat evenly or, perhaps, at all appear to be less tailored, more informal.

The colors of stripes dramatically affect how the stripes appear. I have woven a set of stripes in more than one colorway, preserving the relative values (the lightest color is in the same place in the repeat in all the versions, and so on). The colorways with strong value contrasts were dramatic and vibrant; the colorways using low contrast looked soft and sort of misty. It is interesting to see how the effect of the cloth is altered by such a simple manipulation. I have also emphasized stripes by bordering them with one or two end(s) of black or white or gray.

Stripes can be set into a matrix of color. Stripes set into a matrix of black seem bright, sparkling, and vibrant. Using gray or white as the matrix for the same stripe sequence and colors changes the appearance of the cloth totally.

I can think of many ways that structure can be used to form striped cloth. Color can be used to make stripes in plain weave, clearer stripes in 2/1 twill, and clearer stripes still in 3/1 twill. When I want my stripe sequence to be visually nearly unaffected by the weft, I turn to satin, a 4/1 structure without the defined line of twill.

I can make striped fabric by using Bedford cord. The cords may alternate solid colors or may be composed of blended colors. The face of the fabric is plain weave, but there are long weft floats on the back. The weft which weaves the first and third stripes floats on the back of the second and fourth stripes.

Stripes can involve color, fiber, yarn style, weave structure, denting, finishing—or combinations of these.

A stripe that looks very similar can be woven with two-block double weave. When I want to create a fabric which is reversible or cannot be lined—Bedford cords must be lined or used in an application where the back is hidden—I use double weave. However, two layers of cloth everywhere makes the cloth bulkier and requires more yarn.

I frequently construct stripes by combining structures. A warp-faced stripe (three- or four-shaft twill, five-shaft satin) can be set into a plain-weave ground. Fabric I make this way is lighter in weight than a solid twill or satin fabric, and the stripe is emphasized. Warp stripes constructed this way must be set more closely than the plain-weave ground and rise up dramatically above the ground.

When I want to make lacy stripes, I turn to the loom-controlled lace weaves. M's and O's makes a stripe of sorts if I treadle it in one block only, but the stripe made of longer floats gets mushy and soft, particularly when smooth, slippery yarns are used.

I can make wonderful stripes by threading in Bronson lace, Swedish lace, huck lace, mock leno, or canvas weaves. I prefer to use just one color, warp and weft, when I weave these fabrics because the eye is drawn to the structure, the contrast between plain weave and open areas, instead of being distracted by color blending.

Sometimes I weave stripes using three-element structures such as overshot and summer & winter by threading two blocks and weaving the whole fabric so the floats appear in the same block throughout the warp. These fabrics are heavier than plain-weave fabrics because the pattern weft adds to their weight. They are stiffer than twills because they are based on and sett for the plain-weave structure.

Within each of these possibilities, I can vary the width and rhythm of the stripes to provide even more diversity. I champion diversity!

Stripes represent just one possible motif. The ideas about stripe creation can be altered and used to approach checkerboard patterns as well.

Fabric finishing

Anything that affects the appearance and performance of the cloth is a part of the design process; this includes finishing. I wet-finish (wash) all the fabrics I weave with the exception of tapestries, which I steam and block. A gentle washing of wool preserves a clear surface; a vigorous washing can produce the tight, structure-blurred surface of felt. Brushing the fabric to raise a nap changes the appearance, the hand, and the way a fabric might be used. I think out fabric finishing before weaving the cloth. The finishing techniques used in these collections are described in detail in the instructions.

After I've planned the fiber, yarn style, structure, color, and finishing, it is time to take the design to the loom to test it. There is no substitute for seeing the sample. **The proof of the design is the cloth itself.** Always.

If the yarns shrink unevenly or bleed, I need to know that before I commit to a long, wide warp. If the structure I have planned out on graph paper shifts when taken from the loom and washed, turning the hearts and flowers into a crepey pattern in which no images are discernible, I need to know. I have also learned that just because a structure has held in one fiber doesn't mean that it won't shift and blur when woven in another fiber or yarn style.

The initial sample is just one step in the process. My first samples rarely result in a cloth that appears in HANDWOVEN. When I have woven and finished the first piece of cloth, (generally there is still warp on the loom), I handle and look at it. I've made it big enough so that I can see how it drapes, pleats, gathers, and resists wrinkling. I handle the fabric a lot. I pull it on the bias; I pull wefts in the warp direction and then pull the warps in the weft direction to be sure that the threads do not slip on each other, to be sure that it is stable. I examine the sett. In short, I see how my idea turned out. If it meets my expectations when I handle it, then I pin it up on the wall and look at it. I have found that I can judge the visual design of the cloth more accurately—and dispassionately—when it is hanging than when it is flat. If the cloth will be draped in the garment, I pin it up by one corner to see how it drapes and what the design looks like when it falls into folds.

I look at the color both in sunlight and in lamplight. I design with sunlight as my standard so I look at the fabric in natural light to judge the color interactions. If the color effects are jarring or even not **quite** right, I go back to the loom and make changes.

These evaluation processes usually produce three to five preliminary samples, sometimes more, before I arrive at the fabric I had in mind. At each step, I move nearer that fabric—or a new, better one; at each step, I compare what I have in my hand with what I have in my head. Often, along the way, I come up with a better idea and if I do, I work toward it. I try not to be seduced into stopping short of the goal I set. Just producing cloth is pretty marvelous; producing just the right cloth is far better.

I don't think it is possible to be a weaver in theory only. You must put yarns to work at your loom, experiment, test your idea. The proof is **always** the cloth itself!

A few more words

The fabrics shown in this book were produced under very specific limitations which you may not share. I always choose the yarns from dependable sources; I expect you to be able to buy them for years and years. They are all available by mail order as well as in retail shops so that weavers in rural areas have the same access to them as those in larger cities and active weaving centers. The wonderful mill-end yarn you found at a conference or at your shop doesn't appear in these collections, but if you can find it, use it!

I have designed these fabrics for weavers who are using four- and eight-shaft looms, the vast majority of HANDWOVEN readers. You will find no ten-shaft patterns or, because of the difficulty of giving succinct instructions, any fabrics requiring pick-up or techniques in which the yarns are weaver-manipulated.

I wove all of these fabrics with yarns and colors available at that moment. Frequently the color around which I had designed a collection was temporarily out of stock, on back order, or en route from a foreign country. When I ran into that restriction, I had to change the design, change the colors, or otherwise alter my plan because I had to meet a deadline. None of the colors were custom-dyed by me or anyone else.

As you do your own designing, you may choose to wait for the boat to dock with the pink you want, you may dye to obtain the perfect blue-violet, you may use the seductive, one-of-a-kind mill-end novelty you found at your yarn store, you may not mind doing a little pick-up, or you may have sixteen shafts and decide to use them all.

Working under specific constraints forces us to be more resourceful and inventive, but it is not inherently more virtuous. Use what you have and invent the rest!

SWATCH COLLECTION #1

The first Swatch Collection was designed for the spring/summer issue in 1980. The conversation which began this series took place in November 1979, and my deadline was January 15th.

I sat down with yarn samples and graph paper and thought about what I could do. At Convergence '78, I had gone to an informal seminar on personal coloring and which colors best suit an individual, and thought that I'd build the first four collections around the four coloring types. I designed this one for a person with coloring similar to mine: pink skin, blue or green eyes, and soft contrast between skin and hair colors.

I chose a clear medium blue, a clear medium green, off-white, and pale, pale clear yellow. I called in the order and waited for the yarns to arrive. When I hadn't received any of the 20/2 cottons by Christmas, I began to worry. The week between Christmas and New Year's Day, I called to see what had happened. Some of the yarns were out of stock. I called the supplier directly and explained the urgency of my situation. I said, "Please send any blue, green, and yellow you have in mercerized 20/2 cotton."

When the box arrived, I opened it expectantly and nearly wept. Inside was the blue I had in mind, a green that was grayed and sagey so that it looked dirty next to the blue, and a yellow that leapt right out of the box. I began to redesign on the spot.

I had intended to use the blue, green, and yellow together to make a plaid skirt or dress fabric. One glance told me that the yellow had to go because of its intensity. Although the other two differed in intensity (the blue was clearer and purer and the green significantly grayed), they were similar in value. That suggested to me that I could blend them in the fabric to form a third color that would bridge the gap in intensities. I didn't like the way they looked when I wound them side by side on a strip of cardboard, but I had ordered a natural-colored cotton of the same weight for another fabric in the collection and thought that if I inserted the natural between the blue and green, it would provide the visual barrier to keep them from bringing out the worst in each other.

If woven plain weave, the natural stripe would be mixed with blue or green, depending on the weft passing through it. Because I wanted to maintain an emphatic visual division, I inserted a warp-faced twill stripe with the natural. The color order was blue, natural, blue, natural, green, natural, green, natural, repeat.

I wove the cloth to square, using the same color and structural sequence (although the natural is a weft-faced stripe in the weft) in both warp and weft. I wondered if it would be more interesting to have the diagonal in the twill stripe going one way in the warp and the other way in the weft, so I wove it both ways. The diagonal moves only in one direction in the fabric I eventually chose.

The plaid is soft and pleasing. The squares of blue/green are just right and bridge the gap between the blue and green well. The weight of the cloth is suited to use as a skirt.

Plaid skirt fabric (#1, page 102)

I thought of using the fabric for pants or shorts, too, but decided that the plaid should be smaller and the fabric firmer. I resleyed the warp and wove the cloth in an allover 2/2 twill. That sample is shown here.

Seercucker caftan fabric (#2, page 102)

I wanted to make a fabric for a caftan, beach cover-up, or summer bathrobe. I had long been interested in seersucker and thought that it ought to be possible to make a fabric with stripes of different fibers that would shrink differently when washed. I had from time to time woven samples which shrank unevenly and unwelcomely when they were washed, but this time I wanted uneven shrinkage so I could capitalize on that effect.

Because I felt honor-bound to use the yellow, I wound cards with all three of the cotton colors and a fine, soft, luscious, white worsted wool. I wove many, many samples. My expectation was that the wool would shrink more than the cotton. I was wrong.

I did everything I could to felt that wool and draw it up to make the cotton stripes buckle but the reverse always happened: the cotton shrank more and the wool buckled.

The first stripes I made were half an inch wide, and the buckling was barely noticeable. Little by little, as I reduced the width of the stripes, the structure "came into focus". (I can still see all those samples hung in a row on my basement clothesline.) As the stripes grew narrower, and as I stopped trying to scrub the wool into felt, the fabric buckled into a seersuckery surface. Because heavy pressing tended to flatten it out, I just lifted it from the rinse water, shook out the wrinkles, and allowed it to drip dry. I am convinced that wool of the right grade and weight can be worn comfortably in summer, and this is one way.

Open-weave blouse fabric (#3, page 102)

I designed the third fabric, a cotton blouse fabric, to be worn with the skirt and to echo the skirt's motif of many squares. I made it entirely of the natural colored cotton so the focus was on the structure.

I wanted open spaces in the plain-weave fabric without turning to a lace structure. I knew that I could control open spacing in the warp direction by alternately cramming and skipping dents in the reed, but I needed to achieve the same spacing in the weft. I soon realized that I couldn't achieve the spacing merely by beating hard and then beating very lightly. That approach results in an uneven fabric that looks like a series of weaving errors. **(If it looks like an error, it is an error.)** Instead, I would have to insert something into the warp and then pull it out, something that was uniform in diameter and slippery so that it could be removed without damaging the cloth.

I routinely use acrylic rods as warp padding, so I went to my source for those and bought some very fine ones. I experimented with several sizes, each 1/16" larger in diameter than the previous one, and saw that they worked nicely but had two major drawbacks. The first was ease of removal from the cloth. I had in mind using only three rods and leapfrogging them as I wove; after I had woven in the third and followed it with some plain weave, I'd remove the first to use next. A 40"-wide warp requires a rod about 55" wide so that enough sticks out the side to hang onto. I didn't like having to get off my stool to pull the slightly rigid rod from the cloth. And the rods break—which taught me that I needed only two spacers!

The second drawback to acrylic rods was their availability. I live in Salt Lake City and could drive to Commercial Plastics to get what I needed, but a weaver living in a rural area or small town would not have access to them.

I needed to find a substitute, something with uniform size and slick surface, that was readily available. I found just the right material at my weaving shop: a satin rattail cord, used in those days for macramé. I cut a piece about a foot longer than the width of the warp and simply wrapped the end around my hand and pulled on it when it was time to leapfrog. It never broke, was inexpensive and was available by mail order.

I experimented with the size of the spaces produced when I inserted the spacer into a plain-weave shed versus when I inserted it into a 1/3 twill shed. The former makes a slightly larger space than the latter. This is a way to fine-tune the spacing if you can't find just the right-sized spacer.

I washed each of the samples I had made using different-sized spacers and different spacings in the reed with a full washer load of bath towels. I chose the most stable—and most modest—version, which is shown here.

Blue dress fabric (#4, page 103)

I wanted to make a solid-colored fabric for a dress. I debated between the green, whose subtlety pleased me a lot, and the blue. In the interests of a showier photograph, I chose the blue.

I wanted a pattern of alternating warp and weft floats. The mercerized cotton's soft luster is dulled when it is woven in plain weave and shown off when it is allowed to float on the surface of the cloth.

Woven with the 20/2 yarn, the figure I had worked out on paper was very tiny and nearly invisible. To magnify it, I used two threads as one in both warp and weft. The cloth is heavier that way, yet is more supple than if I had used a heavier—10/2—yarn (and because I had to meet a deadline in two weeks, there was no time to order a heavier yarn anyway).

I wanted the fabric to look the same on both sides: where the warp floats on one side, the weft floats on the back and vice versa.

Nubby jacket fabric (#5, page 103)

The final fabric in this collection combines cotton and linen. I had ordered a fancy, moderately expensive novelty yarn combining linen and cotton. It looked wonderful, and I wanted every inch of it to show. I had in mind making a fabric for a cardigan jacket that could be worn over the skirt and blouse or pants and blouse, or over the sundress. I wanted to create a smooth inner surface so that an unlined fabric would feel nice over hot, sensitive, summer skin.

The novelty yarn was too heavy to use by itself, warp and weft, so I made a warp of the same natural cotton I had used in the skirt and blouse fabrics, two ends as one. I used the novelty yarn in the weft in a weft-faced twill shed with a plain-weave shot of the doubled cotton in between. I tried putting two shots of plain weave between to lighten the fabric further and also tried inserting the novelty yarn in a broken twill order to break the twill line. I liked the weight best with one plain-weave shot between the novelty shots, and the slight twill line because it also appears in the skirt fabric.

I met my deadline. It wasn't easy, but I learned a lot.

SWATCH COLLECTION #2

I designed the second Swatch Collection for use as a fall and winter wardrobe. I wanted to include coat-, dress-, skirt-, and jacket-weight fabrics in it. As usual, I began with the colors. This time I was thinking of a friend with cool brown hair, brown eyes, and ivory skin, who wears rusty colors and browns well. I chose cotton and wool for winter.

Overchecked coat fabric (#1, page 103)

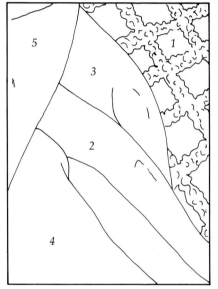

This is a cuddly woolen fabric with lots of surface texture. The novelty yarn was the most expensive yarn used in the collection, and I wanted to make sure it wàs never hidden on the back of the cloth. I decided to make the ground cloth twill, which is thicker and denser than plain weave. I wanted the novelty yarn to look as if it were just lying on the surface of the cloth.

I made samples using several colors for the ground plaid. I used white, pale oatmeal, darker tan, medium and light grayed brown, chocolate brown, a pale bluish gray, and a darker bluish gray. I wove the samples using all of the colors in both warp and weft, and looked carefully at the cloth. The white wool was the same color as the novelty yarn; the novelty yarn virtually disappeared when I used the white for both warp and weft. The chocolate brown yarns were too obvious where they held the novelty yarn in place, destroying the illusion that the novelty yarns had been pasted on. I decided against the bluish grays, although they were lovely (I used them later in another colorway of this fabric), because they turned a little lavender in the presence of the natural, creamy wool color and I wanted a browner effect. I eventually chose white (only in the warp direction), oatmeal, darker oatmeal, and grayed brown yarns for the twill ground of the fabric.

Because the novelty yarn was fluffy and big, only large-eyed heddles would accept it. It is uniform in weight, not thick and thin, which made it easier to use because it never got caught in the heddles. Sometimes I have tied special yarn heddles to accommodate yarns which don't fit through regular heddles, but it takes time to make them, and unless you make them on a wooden jig, they tend to be a little uneven, making the shed ragged. I always take into account how many will be needed across the width of the cloth before planning ambitiously. I suggest that you be sure to order your loom with the largest-eyed heddles its manufacturer provides.

I lifted the novelty yarn in the warp most of the time to keep it on the surface, or face, of the fabric. It is caught by every fourth weft, throwing it up above the twill ground structure. In the weft direction, it is caught by every fourth warp yarn, which ties it firmly to the cloth but allows it to ride on the surface.

Twill skirt fabric (#2, page 104)

I imagined the coat fabric made into a 3/4-length coat or boxy jacket and worn with a straight-cut skirt. This is the fabric for that skirt. I chose the darkest of the squares of the coat and made a twill fabric to match it. The warp is a light gray-brown crossed with darker gray-brown. I made the fabric very plain, a 2/2 twill, and a little firmer than the twill sections of the jacket fabric: the jacket's sett is 18 e.p.i. in the twill sections, and the skirt's, 20 e.p.i.

Weaving a plain-weave or regular twill fabric with one color in the warp and another in the weft is a test of one's ability to beat evenly. Any variations in beat will alter the balance between warp and weft and will show up as

color variations in the cloth. If you are still working on perfecting your beat, you might have greater success with a fabric composed of the same color in warp and weft. An uneven beat will still show—it **always** does—but not as much.

Plain-weave dress fabric (#3, page 104)

I wanted to include a very lightweight wool fabric for a dress in this collection, a dress that could be worn with the jacket or alone. I found a very fine woolen-spun singles yarn which came in a variety of grays. I wanted a warm gray, and wove samples using various grays as warp and weft. The fabric I chose for this collection, woven plain weave because that always produces the sheerest cloth with a given yarn, uses a pale tan crossed with a very pale, misty gray. The resulting fabric is lightweight and supple, but would require lining because the wool isn't soft enough to be comfortable worn next to the skin.

Overchecked blouse and dress fabrics (#4, page 104)

So far this collection was fairly monochrome. I wanted to make a fabric for a blouse to be worn with the skirt and jacket and also one for a shirtwaist dress. A rusty red cotton with an overcheck of grayed brown was my choice. Any dark color, particularly brown, is shifted toward green—red's complement— in the presence of so much red. To counteract that inevitable color shift, I chose a brown with a slightly reddish cast.

Both the blouse and dress fabric were woven plain weave, making fabrics about the weight of oxford cloth.

The dress fabric has a larger overcheck, an inch square, of brown, composed of two threads in both directions. The blouse fabric has squares half the size that use the brown threads singly; I intended it as a companion fabric for collar and cuffs to trim the dress.

Tweed coat or sport jacket fabric (#5, page 104)

The last fabric in this collection is a tweed intended for a man's sport jacket or a woman's Chesterfield coat, perhaps with a black velvet collar. I wanted to combine a dornick twill with 2/2 basket weave. When I drew the structure on graph paper and analyzed it, I was pleased to find that I could make both structures at once using only four shafts. I experimented with the relative widths of the two structures and decided to use 24 ends of twill and 20 ends of basket weave. I also liked 24 ends of twill and 12 ends of basket weave, but the version you see here was showier.

A multiple of four ends of basket weave is necessary to obtain a clean break at the junction of the basket weave and twill. Otherwise, some picks float from the basket-weave area into the twill, making a messy-looking line where the structural change takes place.

Many combinations of two colors would work well in this design, but a strong contrast in value is most dramatic. It is not necessary to use the maximum contrast, black and white; the warp here is the same pale gray used for the weft in the dress, and the weft is a dark gray.

SWATCH COLLECTION #3

The third collection (erroneously numbered 4 in the May 1981 issue) was intended for spring and summer clothing. I used cotton and rayon/flax-blend yarns to create a collection of cool, comfortable fabrics for warm weather.

The blouse fabric is plain weave with weft floats cut to make "eyelashes". The texture of the cloth after washing is like a very lightweight chenille, and the velvety surface is a pleasure to touch. I could also imagine using this fabric for a soft, comfortable summer bathrobe, constructed either side out.

The floats on the surface of the fabric are formed by a selvedge-to-selvedge weft brocade. Since the eyelashes and ground cloth are the same thread, I was able to use the same shuttle for both the ground and brocade shots in this three-shaft structure, making it speedy to weave. After weaving for about two inches, I cut all the floats before going on.

It is easiest to cut them while the fabric is stretched tight on the loom. To avoid cutting the ground cloth at the same time, I used a small pair of scissors with one pointed blade and one with curved tip. I could slip the curved tip under the floats without fear of snagging the ground cloth. Your scissor blades must be sharp right to their tips.

I set the ground cloth fairly firmly and beat it well: if the brocaded wefts are not held firmly in place, they will fall out. When I washed the softly spun cotton, the ends of the cut yarns opened, giving the cloth its velvety surface. That blooming helped to secure the yarns, too. I wove another version of this fabric using sewing thread for the weft brocade and two shuttles. I found that if I shopped carefully—I took my shuttle with me—I could find thread on spools that fit inside my boat shuttle. I used three spools together to make a generous brocade. Using three spools also gave me the opportunity to change the color subtly as I went. The ground cloth was white, and I chose three closely related colors for the eyelashes: blue, blue-blue-green, and blue-green. First I wove using just blue; then I dropped one blue spool and added one blue-blue-green, then dropped another blue, replacing it with blue-blue-green. I gradually moved from all blue to all blue-blue-green to all blue-green. The color changes in the fabric were nearly impossible to spot. What was evident was that the color at the beginning and the color at the end were different.

I built the collection around a sunny yellow-orange, with colors to the yellow and to the orange side of it. The first fabric is a textured one constructed with yarns that we don't usually think of as producing textured cloth. I used three sizes of two-ply pearl cotton in graduated sequence in a plain-weave fabric to suggest a waffle weave. Unlike true waffle weave, though, there are no floats.

Two ends of the heaviest yarn, a 3/2, outline the squares. Inside those heavy yarns, four ends of 5/2 cotton make the intermediate step, followed by six of 10/2 cotton. It's impressive to see how much texture can be achieved by such plain Jane yarns. Each size requires a different sett, of course; I sleyed them one, two, and three ends per dent, respectively, in an eight-dent reed.

You could make a subtler fabric using 5/2, 10/2 and 20/2 cotton. The size differences are not quite as dramatic, but the overall weight of the cloth is lighter. I was also interested in the interaction of three weights and three very

Eyelash blouse fabric (#1, page 104)

A waffle-weave-effect skirt fabric (#2, page 105)

closely related but different colors. If the lightest color is the heaviest yarn and the darkest the smallest, then the three-dimensionality of this fabric is further emphasized because the outlining threads seem even larger and the depressions in the cloth deeper.

Shawl fabric (#3, page 104)

Frequently, because we buy yarns by the pound or 8-ounce tube or cone, we wind up with small amounts of leftovers after a project has been completed. I designed this fabric with this in mind. The final fabric in this collection used all the yarns, the 10/2 pearl cotton; the blouse cotton, tripled; each of the rayon/flax singles; and the rayon/flax two-ply. I kept the order of the yarns in the warp constant, which makes the fabric look a little more formal and not randomly striped. (Sometimes the latter is exactly what I want, but not this time.) I used a natural-colored novelty cotton in the weft.

The sett was rather open to let the novelty weft show to good advantage. To prevent a too-dense fabric, it helps to shut the shed before nudging the weft into place. Forget the word "beat" in such cases; merely coax the weft into position.

When one uses a mixture of yarns in the warp, differential shrinkage can be a problem. If I had designed this fabric with half-inch or wider stripes of each yarn, washing would almost certainly have produced a seersucker effect. Because I used these yarns individually (I tripled the pale yellow 16/2 cotton but treated it as one end), differences in the rate of shrinkage merely add to the texture of the cloth instead of spoiling its appearance.

I had this fabric in mind for a just-barely-constructed light summer wrap. The seams require a Hong Kong or other light binding. The softness of the yarns used in it make it very comforting to tender—sunburned?—skin.

A rayon/flax suit fabric (#4 and #5, page 104)

A summer suit was the aim of the next two fabrics. The yarns are a blend of rayon and flax. The two-ply yarn, woven plain weave, is heavy enough for a jacket, preferably one without notched lapels. The color is the same in both directions and the structure is as simple as possible, but the cloth is interesting because of the slubs in the yarns. I like to use the simplest interlacement possible, plain weave, when using slubby or thick-and-thin yarns because the irregularities of the yarn then don't detract from the structure, but rather enliven it.

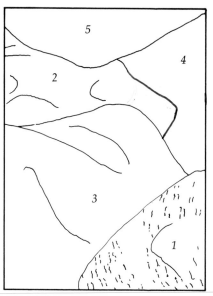

I made the skirt fabric of the same fibers, this time in a singles yarn. The plain-weave fabric is lightweight enough to use for a slightly shirred or softly pleated skirt.

I used two colors alternately in the warp, and then crossed them with the darker color. The color-and-weave effect pattern thus produced is called a **tick weave**. In sampling, I wove two versions, one crossed with the darker yarn and one crossed with the lighter. Either one worked with the jacket, but the darker version was a little more dramatic. When the darker color crossed the warp, little dots of the lighter color showed and vice versa. Using both fabrics in one garment, one to trim the other, would be interesting and easy to do, because the same warp is used throughout.

When I washed this blended fabric, it shed a lot of fuzzy fibers. The fringes of the cloth frayed dreadfully, warning me that I'd have to finish the seams carefully to avoid having a washable garment come apart. An application of Fray-Check® will help stabilize the seam allowances while you overcast or bind them, but it will not prevent their raveling or fraying when the garment is washed.

SWATCH COLLECTION #4

I designed this fourth swatch collection for a friend with dark hair, very fair skin, and bright blue eyes. I had designed the first collection for someone with light hair and eyes and ivory to rosy skin, the second for a person with dark hair and eyes and ivory to olive skin, and the third for a fair-haired, light-eyed, golden-skinned individual. According to some color theorists, everyone fits into one of these four general types.

The woman I had in mind, because of the strong contrast in her hair and skin colors, wears strong, vibrant colors well. As I was thinking about these fabrics, the colors of an autumn vineyard were much in my mind. Ripening Concord grapes display many violets and red-violets within a single bunch.

I went through my files of yarn samples looking for those vineyard colors. A relatively new set of samples for Shetland wools, unfortunately no longer available as I write this nearly eight years later, included a nice range of violets. I wanted to create fabric for an informal suit: a plain skirt and a plaid jacket. The Shetland yarns looked very "suitable" for those fabrics.

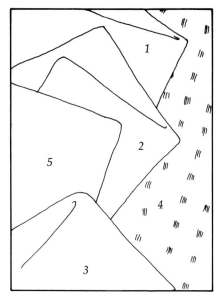

I also wanted to make a lightweight fabric for a blouse, a soft worsted wool for a dress, and a tweedy fabric for another skirt. As I looked through my sample collection, I kept those garments in mind.

The same yarn company had a lively tweed, a lavender with bright red-violet flecks in it. I chose that for the skirt.

I wanted a fine cotton for the blouse, but finding a good pale violet—dark haired, fair-skinned people also wear pastels well—was difficult. I wanted the blouse to work with the suit, so it had to be a plain color to play against the plaid. I had eliminated the idea of using silk when all I could find in a fine enough thread was a bright white, which looked too cold, and a tussah color, which looked very yellow when held near the violets. The next best alternative was a silky Egyptian cotton. A grayed violet was available in 20/2s, so I chose that.

All that remained was the worsted wool for the dress. I had woven worsted wool and made shirts from it, cozy soft shirts, and thought that a shirtwaist dress, long-sleeved and slender with no waistline but belted, either buttoning down to the hem or just partway, would be just right. I chose a variety of related colors because I wanted to make a randomly striped warp, all the colors warped in one bout and threaded as they came to hand, crossed with the middle value. I picked out four colors which reflected the rest of the collection's colors—and would work with the jacket—and called in my yarn order with a sigh of relief.

The first job in creating a collection is always to arrive at a rough idea of what I will do and to refine that to selecting specific yarns in specific amounts. Then I usually have a few days while I wait for UPS to deliver.

Ten days later, my editor called to tell me that of the worsted yarns I wanted, only one was available, the lightest, which I had intended to use sparingly just for a little "sparkle". Another source for the same yarns could produce only the darkest and the lightest.

Because all the other yarns were on their way, I had to redesign the dress fabric. I decided on a plain-weave fabric with an overcheck of two ends, where each end was two threads used as one. I found two winy colors, one slightly lighter than the other, and ordered both.

Solid skirt fabric (#1, page 106)

By this time, the Shetland wool had arrived. I had used only a little Shetland wool before and had been impressed with the soft, lofty fabric it became when washed. I started with the solid skirt fabric. To my delight, it was a success on the first try. That happens so infrequently that I was as surprised as I was pleased.

Tweed skirt fabric (#2, page 106)

From there I went to the tweed skirt fabric. I had a favorite skirt whose weight I wanted to duplicate. The first sett, 12 e.p.i., was too open, the second, 14 e.p.i., a little too open and streaky because it was an irregular dentage and didn't move around in the washing to even out and erase reed marks. (I think that the slubs and lumps of color kept the yarns from shifting in the wash.) On the third try (15 e.p.i.), the weight was just like my skirt, so I wound another warp and wove what I needed.

Plaid jacket fabric (#3, page 106)

Sometimes yarns on the sample cards look different from the same yarns on cones. I think it has to do with the order in which they are arranged on the card. That's the reason I prefer a rainbow array: it is easier to see how blue the violets are relative to each other if they are all together. I was surprised and disappointed when I looked at the three Shetland colors I had picked from the card. (I was so surprised that I compared them with the sample card and saw to my embarrassment that they were exactly what I had ordered.) The wine color which I had used for the skirt was to be the main color. The red-violet was too bright, and the pink yarn looked even lighter than it had on the card.

I had to modify the plaid I had in mind to keep it from running away with its wearer. My friend is elegant. I decided that the red-violet and pink would have to be accent colors, used with restraint. I designed a tattersall plaid and wove it in several versions, settling on one with rectangles longer in the warp direction. I chose a 2/2 twill and used just two threads of the accent colors in a field of the wine wool.

I realized, through sampling, that the accent colors would have to fall into the same two sheds every time to keep the effect uncluttered and neat. Whenever they fell into different sheds, the lines shifted in the cloth, especially where the colors in the weft intersected with those in the warp. I determined the exact number of wine picks between weft stripes that way.

After four samples, I made the warp that I used. I had made squares, elongated rectangles, and the size you see here, and had experimented with sett besides.

Blouse fabric (#4, page 107)

The blouse fabric was next. The cotton yarn I had was silky and lustrous. It had been combed, mercerized, and gassed, about as refined as a cotton weaving yarn can get. I wanted to highlight that luster by playing floats against a plain-weave ground (a lustrous yarn looks almost matte when it is woven plain weave). I could have made twill or satin stripes in a plain-weave ground, but I wanted to stay within four shafts for this fabric. Twill and satin stripes would have made the fabric heavier than I wanted, too. I made a sketch. I wanted to create floats in the warp direction to form rectangles like the ones in the jacket and those planned for the dress.

With warp floats on one side, I could have weft floats on the other side, but weft floats didn't look right to me. I decided to make the fabric look the same on both sides of the cloth by sandwiching the weft floats between warp floats. Because I had used this yarn before in plain weave, all I had to do was consult my records and find out what I had used for the sett (it pays to keep records!). I experimented until I found the number of picks it took to create the rectangles I wanted and then wove what I needed.

The dress yarns had arrived. The colors looked fine, and I had to decide which would be the overcheck. Because they had come from two manufacturers—risky because they might stretch or shrink differently—careful sampling was in order. Luckily, the darker yarn was also the softer, and nicer near the skin, so it became the body of the fabric with the lighter yarn, used four as one, making the overcheck. My original idea had called for using the yarns two as one, but that's what sampling does: it shows us what happens and then we modify our idea to obtain what we want.

I chose the same proportions I had used for the jacket and made a series of samples to check the proportions and relative shrinkages before weaving the fabric.

When I wound the bobbins for the four-threads-as-one weft, I found it best to use my fingers as a tension box. (If you have a tension box, so much the better!) I wove the yarns over and under the fingers of one hand and used the other to feed to the bobbin. If you don't control the way the yarns come to the bobbin, some will be tighter and some looser, creating loops as those tension inequities catch up with you.

By this time, I had five finished fabrics and a whole heap of preliminary samples. That is neither uncommon nor unexpected. Once again I saw that it pays to keep sample files up-to-date, to be flexible, and to keep records. I try to remember those lessons.

Overchecked dress fabric (#5, page 107)

SWATCH COLLECTION #5

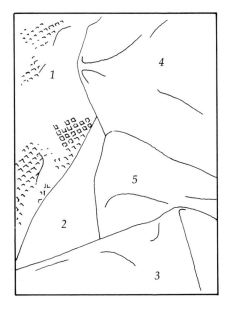

The first four collections were based on the four personal coloring types first described by Johannes Itten and embraced by color analysts, who assign each individual to a "season". According to their theories, the first collection represented summer, the second, autumn, the third, spring, and then winter. With the full cycle completed, it was time to think about what direction I would take next.

The collections to date had been full of color: blues and greens; browns, grays, and rust; yellow-oranges; and violets. I hadn't designed a collection around neutral colors, so I thought about that and considered how it would be different. If the colors were all in the same range, I reasoned, then the textures of the yarns and the cloth would be more important. I got out my yarn charts and looked for textural differences within a limited fiber and color range. I wanted to add some color because I was concerned that a neutral palette would look dull when photographed. (Most of all, I suspect, I just couldn't resist adding it.) I wanted this collection to look quiet and understated and wanted the added color to "gentle" the mixture, so I chose corals, one pale and one deep. I wanted a color most people could wear well, and had noticed that aqua and peach seemed to fit on all the personal color charts. I wanted to warm the collection slightly, which eliminated aqua.

Waffle-weave tunic fabric (#1, page 107)

The first fabric, the most textured, is waffle weave woven from silky, mercerized 10/2 natural Egyptian cotton. The first sample, set at 12 ends per inch (e.p.i.), was too open. The depth of the cells was good but the floats were too long. The second sample, set at 18 e.p.i., was better—the floats were shorter—but it still looked open and flaccid. My third try, set at 24 e.p.i., produced a fabric with depth but also sufficient stability to be practical for most uses. Cotton doesn't full or felt, so the length of the floats and the thread count (e.p.i plus p.p.i.) must be adjusted until a washed sample demonstrates that the threads will stay put.

Cloth with floats tends to be "thirstier" than a plain-weave cloth made of the same yarns. This fabric was intended for use in a tunic; the slight stretchiness the structure brings to the cloth makes it comfortable to wear. I would like to make the same fabric into a summer bathrobe or beach coverup for its soft comfort and thirst.

Thorough ironing can flatten waffle weave completely. To retain their characteristic texture, wash waffle-weave fabrics and then either tumble them for a while to shake out wrinkles or iron lightly while they're still damp to smooth major wrinkles and then shake the cloth or garment to restore the three-dimensionality and allow it to air-dry the rest of the way.

When I combined a border of waffle weave with plain weave, the waffle weave drew in more, causing the plain weave to ripple at the boundary between the two structures. I designed a pullover tunic for my daughter in which waffle weave was at the shoulders forming a yoke; the adjoining plain weave gave added fullness where her developing figure needed it **without the need for a seam and gathering extra fabric.** I liked noticing what happened at the junction between two structures and then planning a project that took ad-

vantage of that.

The natural cotton was darker on the cone and in the unwashed state than it became when washed. My experience has shown that natural cotton, linen, and cottolins all lose some color the first few times they are washed. I am always careful not to evaluate the sample I have made until it has been well washed, so I'll know what the color will be and the structure will have shifted into the most stable configuration.

Twill jacket fabric (#2, page 108)

The structure of the next cloth is dornick twill. The warp is natural gray singles linen, 10/1, the weft, a natural cottolin. The two "naturals" do not match exactly, even after washing, which was just what I had hoped.

I was asked why I crossed a linen warp with cottolin. I wanted to make a jacket or vest fabric which would wrinkle somewhat less than 100 percent linen, but I wanted the look of linen. The cottolin, because of its cotton content, is slightly less easily wrinkled.

Sometimes singles linen warps are difficult to handle. I didn't have any trouble because I was careful, but I found that it was essential to use a 10-dent reed sleyed 2 per dent rather than a 20-dent reed, in which abrasion by the reed would be destructive. I advanced the warp frequently and misted it with a plant mister because it is dry where I live and linen is stronger damp than dry. (**But never roll damp linen onto the cloth beam because it will mildew!**)

A 20/2 linen would have been simpler to handle, but the color I wanted wasn't available in that size. Also, I wanted the slight irregularities that characterize the 10/1 yarn to enhance the texture.

I noticed while I was weaving that the warp kept shedding loose flax fibers. Simultaneously, I found myself beginning to cough. I keep fresh dust masks, the inexpensive kind sold in paint supply departments, on hand all the time. Whenever I see fibers flying, I put one on to keep from inhaling the particles. I'm very particular about what I breathe!

I wanted the linen to run in the warp direction because the wrinkling would be more likely to run up and down, I thought, and the darker threads were vertical that way. If you are not willing to work with a singles linen warp, consider using the cottolin for warp and the linen as weft. The result will be somewhat different, but still attractive. There will be far fewer fibers flying around, too. (I'd still wear the dust mask, though.)

Cotton dress fabric (#3, page 108)

I designed the third fabric for a blouse or dress. It is made of 20/2 cotton, the same quality as in the waffle weave. The cotton has a wonderful, silky sheen which I wanted to show off by weaving in floats. I didn't want this fabric to be open and lacy, but I wanted a small figure woven in with a small repeat so that the cloth would suggest daintiness in both scale and color.

I used a Bronson II spot weave. If each unit in the structure is repeated at least twice before moving on to the next unit, then an open structure, Bronson II lace, is produced. (See the dark green worsted fabric in Swatch Collection #6.)

The yarn had a good twist and was mercerized, making it stronger as well as lustrous—perfect for warp. I threaded plain weave (see draft) at the selvedges, which made a neat, strong edge.

The fourth fabric is a plain-weave stripe. I combined three neutral colors, natural, light gray and darker gray, with a dark coral. By keeping the light gray stripe between the darker gray and separate from the natural, I was able to shift it toward violet. The coral stripes are very narrow because they are so strong visually. A friend looked at the fabric and told me it reminded her of rose bushes in the snow, with all the color drained away except for the rose hips. Each time I look at it, I remember that.

The weft is natural cottolin—which changes just a little in the wash—and the sett is fairly firm so that the fabric can be tailored into slacks, shorts, a vest or jacket. If you want to make a softly shirred skirt, use a more open sett; 16 e.p.i. makes a soft fabric.

Striped fabric for jacket or slacks (#4, page 108)

I designed the fifth and final fabric to coordinate with all of the others. It is plain-weave cottolin, set more open to give it more drape. The warp is the lighter, cool gray, and the weft, natural. The result is a softened gray toward the violet, matching the stripe in the fabric just above. I imagined this fabric used for a skirt, either dirndl or divided. If you plan a more tailored garment, set the warp at 20 e.p.i. and weave to square.

Taken as a group, these cotton and cotton and linen fabrics are quiet and refined. The strong textures in the waffle weave, dornick twill, and Bronson spot break up what could be visually flat surfaces. The simple plain-weave fabrics are enlivened by subtle use of color.

I learned quite a bit about working with neutrals while doing this collection. I learned that natural means different things in different fibers, which suited me perfectly, that natural colors change with washing, and that designing within a tight color palette, rather than limiting my thinking, opened new possibilities. Interesting.

Plain-weave skirt fabric (#5, page 109)

SWATCH COLLECTION #6

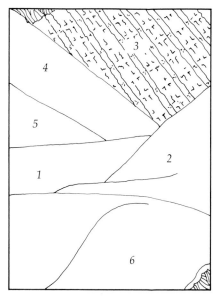

I am lucky enough to have plenty of work to do, so weaving for myself often gets pushed aside. I had just finished designing and weaving a whole wardrobe full of fabrics to illustrate *Handwoven, Tailormade,* and my editor suggested that it was time for me to design a Swatch Collection for myself. I had just been to a color analyst and had learned which colors would be most flattering to me. If you have darkening blond hair, green-blue eyes, and pinkish fair skin, this collection is made to order for you, too.

I compared the swatches of colors that had been "assigned" to me in the analysis with the yarns in my sample file. At first it was difficult to make decisions, but once I had regained my objectivity, I was on my way.

I wanted a skirt fabric, a jacket, a couple of dresses, and a vest. With those requirements in mind and the colors at my fingertips, I chose the yarns most likely to give me what I wanted.

A-line skirt fabric (#1, page 109)

I started with the skirt. The slightly A-line skirt I had in mind would need a firmly woven fabric to hold its shape. I generally hang on to my clothes for a long, long time, and I travel quite a lot, so I wanted a fabric that would stand up to long use and shed wrinkles.

Both those requirements suggested worsted wool. The colors available didn't include the slightly greenish blue I wanted, but I could buy a green-blue and a true blue, bracketing the color I wanted. A mixture of those two would give the effect of greenish blue, so I made a sample warp, one blue on one side and the other on the other. In theory, A crossed with B should look like B crossed with A, but in real life, the subtle shift in warp-to-weft balance means that they will be slightly different.

I wove the sample both ways, made my choice based on what I saw, and wove the piece you see here.

Cotton skirt or dress fabric(#2, page 109)

The second fabric was a cotton fabric suitable for a skirt or a dress. The blue-violet I wanted was unavailable, so I ordered a true blue and as blue a violet as I could find, which was really a tint of red-violet.

Again I made a sample with one color on one side and the other on the other. This time I added very fine, closely spaced stripes of B in A and wider, more widely spaced stripes of A in B. I wove across this warp first with A and then with B. The color I was seeking was not there. I walked around my studio looking for another yarn to try. I had a pale grayed violet, but in the cloth it looked white and was all wrong.

Disappointed, I went for a walk. When I returned, I decided to experiment with weft color rotations. I had no desire to weave several yards for a dress alternating shuttles or using some other rotation, but I knew that I could do it for a small sample, then in the final fabric, use the weft order as the warp order and weave it off with just one shuttle. I "doodled" to the end of the sample warp and hit on the combination that gave just the color I was after. I had experimented with stripes, too, and combined these ideas to make the fabric you see here.

As I wove the final version, I noticed, as I have noticed many times before, that the colors I choose frequently come directly from an object or landscape I have seen. Sometimes they seem just to pop into my head, and only later, as I am weaving them, do I make the connection. This time I saw that I was weaving the color of the penstemons I had seen at the garden center when I went to buy rosemary. I was frugal and came away with a plant of rosemary but the memory of the penstemon. (The next spring I went back for penstemon.)

The little border of stripes was intended to be a border for a skirt or used in another way. When I made the dress of this fabric, I planned those transverse stripes to fall into crosswise tucks at the top of the bodice, literally taking out the pattern pieces and measuring to see where the stripes ought to be placed. I have worn and loved that dress for a long, long time.

Mohair coat fabric (#3, page 110)

This fabric was intended for a coat. I had chosen two gorgeous wool/mohair yarns to use on the surface of the cloth. I wanted to weave them fairly loosely to show them off, but to support them I wanted a firm plain-weave back.

While in appearance it's a plain weave ground with interlacing warp and weft floats, this cloth is actually a true double weave. The surface structure is plain weave and so is the back. There are two warp systems and two weft systems. The bottom layer is firm enough to stand on its own but the upper layer is not. The latter is "stitched" to the lower layer at strategic—and hidden—intervals to keep it from shifting. That problem yielded quickly to drafting and a couple of samples to double check that it was as I wanted it.

As I wove the final version, I was surprised again. Earlier in the year, I had been watching a neighbor's vegetable garden grow as I walked each day after supper. I had loved seeing the mauvy potato blossoms rise out of rosettes of deep blue-green leaves and at the time thought, "I'll have to remember that." Although you'd think that I'd be accustomed to seeing my life, so to speak, develop in front of me at the loom, I was surprised again, but pleased, as I saw the potato blossom colors in this cloth.

Bronson lace worsted dress fabric (#4, page 110)

The next fabric, a soft, buttery worsted, was also intended for a dress. The first two fabrics had plain surfaces (2/2 twill for the skirt and plain weave for the cotton dress) so I designed this one with a textured structure. I used a bluish green fine worsted, about the color of rosemary leaves. Because I have always liked Bronson lace, I threaded a two-block lace using four shafts. This soft, draping fabric developed smoothly, without a lot of sampling. That was a relief; the first two had required quite a lot of effort, and the next two were to be very exacting.

Plain weave striped jacket fabric (#5, page 111)

Next, I wanted to make a fabric for a close-fitting jacket or vest, one that was striped on one side and plain on the other. The first step was to work out the stripe proportions and color sequence in a plain weave fabric. I drew stripes on paper first to establish the proportions and then wrapped a cardboard strip with yarns. When I was satisfied with the arrangement, I made a plain weave warp to check it out. The balance of the plain weave cloth was fine, but the stripes were loud: they looked like clown pajamas. I looked at my sample and decided that the violet was too heavy, so I removed every other end and replaced them with peacock. Now the plum shouted, "Look at me!" so I cut out every other end of those and replaced them with violet. The result was fine: richly colored yet a little subtle, exactly my preference.

This fabric became the four-shaft version you see here. It is plain weave and lighter weight than the double faced fabric which follows, but very satisfactory.

Having established a pleasing stripe sequence in the previous fabric, my next task was to translate that into a heavier cloth with the stripes on one face and a solid color on the other.

My first structural idea was to weave a double faced fabric with a twill on the face and plain weave on the back. I knew the setts would be different for each and planned three twill ends for each pair of plain weave ends. The threading was rather complicated, but if it worked, it would be worth the trouble. It didn't. It was a mess and I couldn't fix it.

I started with another idea. The striped face would be woven in 3/1 twill, and the plain color back would be woven 2/2 twill, all at once, with one weft. I knew how to do that in the other direction, using one warp and two wefts, so I wrote down the sheds and imagined them turned the other way. (Now I know how to turn drafts—a simple matter.) The sett requirements for the two sides were the same, so the threading was simplified enormously—hallelujah! (I try not to design fabrics for HANDWOVEN that are especially difficult to thread or weave, so that was a relief.)

After several false starts, several hours on hands and knees tying and re-tying treadles. I reached the cloth you see here, striped on one side and plain on the other. I went a step farther, actually, reasoning that if I were interested in stripes a broken twill on either side might be better. It wasn't. I chose the previous version.

That evening I went into the back yard to pick raspberries and saw the colors I had worked with during the day. The leaves were deep green and the berries, at various stages of ripeness, were violet to plum color.

Double faced jacket/ vest fabric (#6, page 111)

SWATCH COLLECTION #7

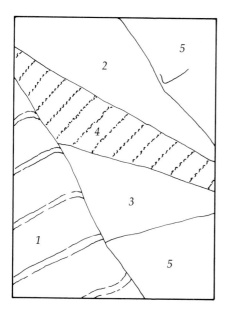

This spring/summer collection appeared in an issue of HANDWOVEN devoted to a theme: the stripe. Of the six fabrics that make up this collection, all but one of them are striped.

This time, instead of choosing a variety of colors, I settled on two, blue and white. I wanted a fresh, crisp, refreshing-looking group of fabrics. Five of the fabrics are all cotton; the sixth is cotton crossed with linen. The cottons range from 8/2 unmercerized cotton through 20/2 mercerized cotton to 100/3 mercerized cotton.

As I designed these fabrics, I considered how the stripe motifs might be integrated into the lines and details of finished garments. For instance, a yoke could be pleated and stitched so as to conceal the stripes—to be released and revealed where the fabric falls free. If your pattern calls for a long sleeve gathered into a cuff or a short sleeve gathered into a band, consider pleating the fabric into a solid color instead of adding the cuff or band. Or position stripes on only part of your web, planning them in such a way that they fall at strategic accent points on a garment.

The structures used in this collection are as simple as possible: plain weave, 2/2 basket, and dornick twill. The textures of the yarns are subtle so that the surfaces are mostly smooth, comforting to hot skin.

Jacket fabric (#1, page 112)

The first fabric is relatively heavy, constructed of 8/2 unmercerized cotton, warp and weft—a suitable weight and firmness for a jacket. Because of the weight of the fabric, I suggest a cardigan jacket, not one with notched lapels. The rule of thumb for notched lapels is this: fold the fabric to make four thicknesses of the cloth. Four thicknesses of cloth is what will show up at the notch in the lapel; if it is too thick to be graceful and trim, cut the garment differently.

The cloth is mostly white with narrow, four-end stripes of blue and wider stripes of a tick pattern, which "changes feet" right in the middle with two white ends.

The fabric is firm enough for a jacket set at 20 e.p.i. but can be adapted for use as a skirt by opening the sett to 16 or 18 e.p.i. If you want to weave a skirt with the same stripe as the jacket, put on enough warp for both plus some to retie after you cut and weave the jacket first. Cut it off and resley for the skirt and finish off the warp.

This unmercerized cotton grows softer and more velvety with each washing. Time only makes it "friendlier".

Dress or skirt fabric (#2, page 112)

The second fabric was intended for a dress or skirt. The yarn here is also cotton, but Egyptian cotton that has been combed, mercerized, and gassed to produce the most refined, silky cotton possible.

The cloth is mostly blue with three fine stripes of white, each two ends wide, separated from each other by two ends of blue. The simplicity of this stripe is what makes it work so well. This cloth requires an even beat; advancing the warp often at short intervals and weaving to music to regulate your

weaving rhythm will help.

This cloth is just a little heavier than oxford cloth. It would make a wonderful shirtwaist dress, a nice shift or chemise, or a cool sundress.

Solid fabric for culottes or walking shorts (#3, page 112)

The next fabric is solid blue, the only unstriped cloth in this collection. Like the jacket, it's woven of soft and velvety 8/2 cotton. This time the structure is 2/2 basket, a softer, more draping structure than plain weave.

The instructions show how to thread the draft on just four shafts in such a way that it's not necessary to go around a floating selvedge with each pass of the shuttle. It is essential to weave 2/2 basket weave with two passes of the shuttle in each shed. Do not be tempted to wind the weft doubled on the bobbin; the result will not be the same.

Dornick twill jacket fabric (#4, page 112)

The fourth fabric is another jacket fabric, and the only structure that deviates from the plain-weave family. The structure is dornick twill, a twill whose diagonals move "uphill" and then "downhill". At the point where the change of direction takes place, a thread is omitted in this four-shaft version. That omission prevents the formation of the three-end (or -pick) floats characteristic of an ordinary reversing twill. This fabric is mostly white with two-end stripes of blue arranged so that they fall on either side of the break in the threading.

The warp is a very slightly slubby, unmercerized 8/2 cotton. The weft is 14/1 bleached linen. The weft is a little smaller, smoother, and much more lustrous than the warp, adding a bit of extra definition to the twill lines and a little more texture **and** firmness to the cloth.

This jacket fabric is lighter weight than the first one and can be used in applications where the first would be too heavy.

Shirt and trim fabric (#5, page 113)

The shirt and trim fabrics are from the same warp. For some time, I had been wanting to pull out all the stops and make a handwoven fabric fine enough for a proper shirt: this is it. It's a bit of an indulgence for me because it is so fine, but so **right** for a shirt. The cotton threads are as refined as those in the dress fabric but finer and more tightly twisted. They resemble a good, strong cotton sewing thread. The resulting fabric is crisp and light and cool—a delight to touch. The stripe is as simple as can be, ten ends of blue and two of white.

As I thought about the shirt I could make, I thought it might be nice to make a contrasting collar and cuffs, or front placket band, depending on the cut of the shirt. I wove several versions, a square, a near square and the rather squatty rectangle you see here. Any of them would have done, but the flattened rectangle seemed the most interesting to me.

A cool, fresh collection of stripes. None of the fabrics is very fancy, but they are just right.

SWATCH COLLECTION #8

This is the "corduroy" collection. I don't know when I've been so excited about a structure as I was about this one. I had been thinking about fall and what kinds of things make their appearance then. I remembered a favorite pair of corduroy slacks whose only fault is that the cotton pile crushes, and then I knew what this collection would contain. What is the most resilient natural fiber? Wool, of course. Why didn't we see wool corduroys in the stores? I dived into the corduroy so deeply that an article about the structure accompanied the collection. (I had to have somewhere to put all the variations I had woven!)

I built this collection around brown and a soft, mellow red.

The first fabric I wove was the plain red cloth for a skirt. It used the same yarn and the same color in warp and weft. I experimented longer than I expected with the sett. I wanted it to be perfectly stable but also soft enough to be softly pleated or slightly shirred at the waist.

Heather skirt fabric (#1, page 113)

I discovered that this heathery tweed is "sticky" enough that three ends per dent caught on one another and introduced skips into the cloth. For that reason I settled on a reed requiring two ends per dent. The yarn has a good, hard twist as well. Though it makes the yarn stronger, it also makes it kink if not watched carefully. Winding the bobbins firmly helped to minimize the kinks; luckily, most occurred near the selvedges, where they are easier to mend. When you find one, lift the loop out of the cloth with a tapestry needle and work the excess to the selvedge where it can be trimmed away.

The yarn is dyed in the fleece and then blended before spinning. Close examination shows burgundy, pink, and gray fibers in the yarn. The fibers are fairly short, hence the high rate of twist, and there is a fair amount of spinning oil in the yarn. The transformation produced by washing the fabric is astounding. It goes into the warm, sudsy water looking like rather nasty, light burgundy window screening and emerges soft and supple. The washing waters—it needed two washes—turn milky pink as the oil leaves.

Do not be tempted to wash the yarns before you weave with them! If you do, the yarns will be softened; the protective oil, which slicks the ends down in the yarn, will be removed; and the warp will abrade easily, cling to itself, and be very difficult to weave.

The next fabric uses the same yarns but is intended for more tailored garments. Its sett, 24 e.p.i. as opposed to the 20 e.p.i. above, is firmer. Four colors are used to make the stripe: a light and dark burgundy and a medium and dark brown. The sequence repeats in 24 ends, making the stripe small and easy to wear.

Striped jacket fabric (#2, page 114)

Designing stripes is not a trivial occupation. I begin with the general proportions, by sketching on graph paper with pencil, crosshatching to show darkest values. When the proportions look right, I turn to the yarn itself and wind strips of cardboard in the proportions I have worked out to see how the colors work. Finally, I go to the loom to test the design. The stripes you see in these collections have been through many modifications before they appear here, and the neat little stripe in this collection is no exception.

Woolen-spun fabrics are more likely to wrinkle than worsted ones, so I suggest that the striped wool be used for a jacket and a skirt or slacks be constructed of the worsted which follows.

Skirt or slacks fabric (#3, page 114)

The worsted fabric is dark brown and plain weave. It is fairly lightweight. I wanted to show how more texture can be introduced into a plain-weave cloth by doubling ends every now and then. In one inch there are at least four additional ends added through doubling.

Warp ends may be doubled in two ways. They may be threaded two per heddle, or each may be given its own heddle. The difference between the two methods is subtle but important. When two threads are carried through the same heddle, they twist and turn around each other as they are woven, sometimes lying side by side and sometimes one over the other, varying the width of the doubled end. When each is given its own heddle, the two ends lie side by side throughout the cloth without the variation seen in the former method. In a yarn as fine as this, that may be considered a fine point, but I think that it is on such fine points that the difference between a satisfactory and an excellent fabric depends.

I envisioned this worsted wool as a softly pleated skirt or a pair of pleated, man-tailored slacks, worn with the striped jacket.

Blouse, shirt, or dress fabric (#4, page 115)

I wanted to weave a blouse, shirt, or dress fabric to include in this collection. My first impulse was to look for silk because it is a good insulator. The only silks I could find that were fine enough were either bright, gleaming white or honey-colored tussah. They looked very jarring beside the rest of the colors used here.

I went around my studio picking up cones of cotton of various colors and found that there were four colors I liked very much with the others: dark brown, wine, navy, and dark green. In a flash, I decided to see what would happen if I used all of them, all at once.

I noticed that two yarns were warm colors (brown and wine) and two were cool (navy and green). I made a plain-weave fabric—plain weave shows off color blending best of all the structures—using a warm and cool in the warp (wine and navy) and the other pair (brown and green) in the weft. The result is one of my all-time favorite fabrics. It is richly colored, asking the eye to look at it twice. Folds in the fabric reveal other colors the way changeable taffeta does when it is turned.

An even beat is essential.

Wool corduroy jacket or vest fabric (#5, page 115)

The last fabric was the corduroy. In the construction of a corduroy, the first pick weaves the ground structure and the second and third form the pile, making progress slower than you might expect. The warp is subjected to quite a lot of beating, and hard beating at that, because the cloth must be woven very firmly to work. I chose a worsted wool for its strength and resistance to abrasion.

The weft, on the other hand, had to be woolen-spun; washed woolen-spun yarns are fluffier and bigger than the same yarns before they are washed; washing also wedges the yarn tightly into the structure.

I chose the same red for the pile that I had used in the first fabric. The heathery effect of the tweed adds a visual softness which further emphasizes the softness of the corduroy.

When the cloth is woven, there is no pile. The pile appears only after the floats are cut. Cutting the floats—they are short—is tedious work. I would weave about 2¹/₂"–3" and then stop to cut the floats. My scissor blades were very slender and sharp so as to cut just the floats and not one thread of the ground cloth structure. After cutting the floats, I handled the cloth very carefully. I pinned an old tea towel across the part of the warp that goes around the breast beam (so as not to abrade the cloth) and moved it as I advanced the warp. After I had washed the cloth, the cut ends were quite secure, but I didn't want to take any chances in the meantime.

Woolen corduroy is wonderful. If it weren't for the tedium of cutting all those floats—don't even **think** of a rotary blade cutter!—I would weave it often. I can imagine an easy chair covered in it. It would be wonderful, but until I find a safe, quick way to slice those floats, I will restrict myself to smaller yardages.

When I decided to weave a wool corduroy, I became curious about the origins of this cloth. First I went to a modern source: Webster's New Collegiate Dictionary tells us that corduroy is "a durable usu. cotton pile fabric with vertical ribs or wales." If we pursue the origins of corduroy via the Shorter Oxford English Dictionary, things become even more interesting: "1787 [prob. f. CORD sb. 6—duroy, deroy (XVII) coarse West-of-England woollen stuff of unkn origin.] 1. A kind of coarse thick-ribbed cotton stuff 1795." It was interesting to me to see that the first corduroy is thought to have been woven of wool: it pleased me to think that I had perhaps completed the circle by planning and weaving a woolen cord.

I wanted to weave a corduroy that looked a lot like the commercial fabric. I had woven loom-controlled pile weaves that looked like vees in cross-section; this time I wanted to produce a cloth with softly rounded wales—that looked like little semi-circles in cross-section. It was clear that in order to obtain those rounded shapes I needed to cut the pile wefts so that they were different lengths. I was not going to sculpt the wales. The cloth structure itself, then, had to make the floats different lengths which meant that I would have to weave at least two pile picks for each ground pick. That was good news because a two to one ratio would be helpful in making the pile thick and full-feeling.

The obvious first choice for the ground structure was plain weave. It is always convenient to plan a threading so that it can be done on a straight draw, so I drew that first. Diagram 1 shows the draft that resulted. You can see that there are two pile picks—denoted by Xs—for each ground pick. The float length is pretty short; with a sett of 24 e.p.i. the pile would be hard to cut and probably look skimpy so the draft was expanded a bit (see Diagram 2).

As I wove it I thought that it ought to be possible to expand the draft more to make wider wales. Diagram 3 shows the same draft made wider.

The corduroy was good and I liked it, particularly after it was washed. If there ever was a cloth that ought to convince handweavers that washing their fabrics is a good idea, this is it. When it is cut but not washed, the corduroy is slightly fragile and hardly recognizable. Washing transforms it into a velvety, stable cloth.

Diagram 1

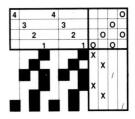

Diagram 2

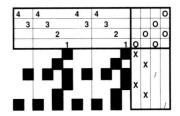

Diagram 3

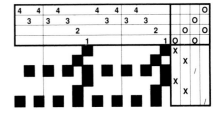

There are other ways to vary corduroy. The first variations that come to mind are ones of color. We are used to seeing corduroys that are all one color. It ought to be possible, by using several closely related colors, to create an ombré effect by changing the color of the weft as the cloth is woven. I have woven a small sample of a striped corduroy shown here. Each stripe is fairly fine, but the structure is only hinted at in the cut, washed fabric; the lines are blurred. The stripe draws the eye from side to side while the wales draw the eye up and down. The over-all effect is rather unsettling. At the least, it is probably the first striped corduroy you have ever seen.

It is not necessary to cut the pile picks everywhere. If the floats are cut according to a pattern, the face of the cloth has a sort of sculptured quality. The cut/uncut pile surface offers the opportunity for a very subtle sort of patterning of the cloth. Be wary of doing this freehand without a sketch, because once the pile is cut it cannot be uncut. The longer the pile the more marked the sculptural effect will be.

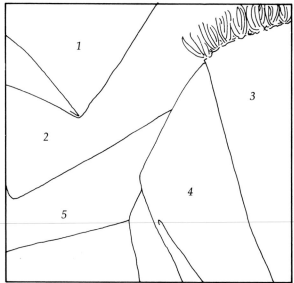

SWATCH COLLECTION #9

This collection of fabrics is the product of a particularly long and dismal winter. It had been gray and cold for so long that I was beginning to think spring would never come. Reflecting on just what I longed for most, I thought of pale yellow sunlight, purple crocuses pushing up out of the frozen ground, and the subtle haze of green that presages the appearance of the leaves themselves. Those are the colors in the yarns you see here. I chose a very pale, clear yellow, gentle violet, delicate celadon (soft, pale, somewhat grayed green), with a little tan thrown in to keep it all from becoming too sweet.

At the end of dark, cold winter it would be warm again, and I knew that during warm days, cool, comfortable cotton would be welcome. All of these yarns are cotton, and all came from the same source, which made shopping easy. I was able to find two versions of the soft, mauvy violet, 20/2 pearl cotton and 8/2 unmercerized, slightly textured cotton, and two versions of the celadon as well.

Striped skirt or dress fabric (#1, page 116)

In the first cloth, I wanted to show off just how textured the 8/2 cotton is. When used by itself, as it usually is, its texture is almost lost. This time I made a warp of 20/2 pearl cotton and inserted the 8/2 cotton ends singly at intervals across the warp. To dramatize the contrast more clearly, I set the celadon 8/2 cotton into the violet 20/2 cotton. The design is subtle, very quiet, even restrained, but interesting. At a distance, the eye picks up the violet, and at closer distances, the green stripe shows up. The violet shifts the green a bit toward the yellow, further emphasizing it. This fabric, like the two that follow, was intended to be used for a skirt or a dress.

The luster of pearl cotton comes from combing the fibers, spinning and plying the yarns with a soft twist, and mercerizing the yarn (which also makes it stronger). The soft twist, however, makes the yarns more vulnerable to abrasion. I found that the pearl cottons in this collection were a little soft for warp yarns.

There are many ways to help preserve tender yarns. The first involves good technique: carefully measuring and beaming the warp will go a long way toward avoiding difficulties. Advancing the warp frequently by small amounts reduces the wear and tear on any particular part of it. Carefully, evenly wound bobbins will release smoothly without hanging up in the shed and stressing the threads at the edges. When all of these precautions are not enough, there are still more things one can do. For cotton, linen, and ramie, misting the warp lightly with water will strengthen the fibers. (But don't advance damp cloth to the cloth beam, where it could mildew!) I've found that beeswax, sold in sewing notions departments for waxing the thread used to sew on buttons, helps to strengthen the selvedge threads of pearl cotton. As I advance the warp, I reach behind the shafts and treat the selvedges before they get to the heddles. While waxing works for pearl cotton, some unmercerized, uncombed cottons tend to get caught in the wax and tear apart, but I had no breakage problems with the unmercerized yarns used here, which were heavier and had more twist.

The next fabrics are two colorways of the same design. The main thread in both warp and weft is the 20/2 pearl cotton, with two ends of 8/2 cotton separated by three ends of pearl cotton in both directions at intervals forming a windowpane check. In each case, the 8/2 cotton is the same color as the ground thread: violet is used on violet and green on green. The larger green thread is very slightly lighter in value than its pearl counterpart. That small difference seems to lift it farther out of the cloth than its size would alone. Both of these fabrics are very quiet.

Windowpane-checked skirt or dress fabrics (#2 and #3, page 116)

The next cloth, a pale yellow, is a variation on plain weave called haircord. Two sizes of yarn are used, 10/2 and 20/2. Two ends of the pale yellow 10/2 cotton are used side by side on the same shaft, but threaded in separate heddles and sleyed in different dents. The smaller, natural 20/2 cotton lies singly between the pairs of the larger yarns. The two heavier yarns act in unison against the single finer yarn. The resulting fabric, with the heavier yarn used as weft, is a mesh that lets air move through freely but is opaque enough for the most modest wearer.

I made the first sample using the pale yellow throughout the fabric. It looked flat and dull to me, so I substituted the natural yarn as described. The change in the fabric was surprising: it looked finer and became a more interesting color. It's a subtle point, but little things like these make all the difference.

Haircord shirt-weight fabric (#4, page 117)

I designed the next fabric to be dainty, and it is. The colors are gentle and delicate and the yarns are all 20/2 pearl cotton, making the cloth fine and light; little squares of Bronson lace further add to the daintiness of the design.

I used four colors in the warp, but only three in the weft. When I wove this fabric as drawn in, the natural thread crossing itself stood out too much in the cloth. When I replaced the natural with pale yellow, everything came together harmoniously, and the cloth warmed up subtly at the same time.

Two repeats of the Bronson lace unit used side by side in the warp and two repeats woven in the cloth are necessary to produce the little windows that are characteristic of the structure and so appealing. Don't be alarmed if as you weave this fabric you cannot see the lace clearly; it develops only after you've taken the cloth from the loom and washed it. The threads in it need to shift from their locations under tension on the loom to the more relaxed but stable configuration of the open lace.

In the green stripes are a few fine, pale yellow stripes. Where the stripes cross in the cloth, a small color-and-weave effect pattern is formed. From a distance, the cloth is light and pretty, but up close, there is a lot to see.

Bronson lace skirt fabric (#5, page 117)

The last fabric in this series is the heaviest and also one of the most interesting structurally. I used 8/2 cotton throughout, after a sample showed that the luster and brightness of the 10/2 pale yellow pearl cotton made it stand out obtrusively.

What I had in mind was a fabric that would resemble one woven of ribbons. Mine would be much more stable—ribbons 4/5" wide would roll and curl—and perhaps easier to weave. I decided to use a two-block twill: the first block is warp-faced (3/1 twill) and the second is weft-faced (1/3 twill). As the color changes in the weft direction, the blocks reverse so that what was warp-faced becomes weft-faced and vice versa. The twill within the blocks is broken so that emphasis is on color rather than structure.

Two-block twill jacket fabric (#6, page 118)

The colors are soft, like the texture of the finished unmercerized cotton fabric. Three colors repeat 1, 2, 3, 1, 2, 3, etc., in both the warp and weft directions. Because the structure repeats in two blocks, the whole design repeats in six color changes in each direction: for example, the first time tan appears, the block is warp-faced; the second time it is weft-faced. Although the structure of the cloth is simple, the addition of three colors makes it look much more complex than it is.

This fabric, sleyed at 20 e.p.i., is intended for a very softly constructed garment. For a more tailored cut, please set the warp at 24 e.p.i. and beat accordingly. In either case, the unmercerized cotton will produce a soft, almost velvety surface as the fabric is used.

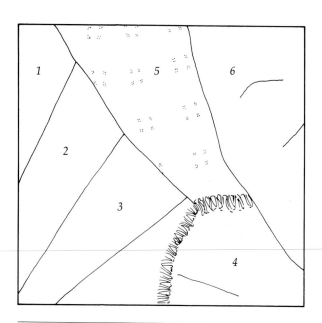

SWATCH COLLECTION #10

This collection of fabrics was to appear in a theme section on ethnic weaving in the September/October 1984 issue. To be honest, I was a bit put off by the theme. I associate ethnicity with funky fabrics, and funk is not my style. The idea of designing something that ran contrary to what felt "right" to me was not appealing at all.

The fabrics I design and weave are products of my life. The places I go, the things I see, fabrics and art exhibits all influence what I do. More and more, as time goes by, I see my life and the experiences of it reflected back at me by the cloth before me on the loom.

Ethnic fabrics. I had to think.

I was given colors which would be part of this section: black, tan, saffron yellow, and brick red. That got the collection started.

Striped skirt fabric (#1, page 119)

Weavers have striped cloth since the beginning of weaving. It's a way of putting a pattern into the fabric fairly painlessly: the spacing is defined by the spacing in the warp and by the reed—no need to keep measuring weft repeats—and only one shuttle is needed. The first fabric is striped as a tribute to all the weavers who have striped fabric over the ages.

I designed the stripes in this worsted fabric by playing with strips of colored paper. I arranged and arranged, rearranged and began again. Finally, I had an arrangement of stripes in which the charcoal/black and brick red stripes were constant. The camel tan stripes peeked out from under the red stripes, first two ends, then four, then six and eight. The sequence began over again after the widest stripe. The brick red stripe from which they emerge is intended to seem nearer the viewer. I threaded and wove it as a broken warp-faced twill, which makes it rise up above the dark ground and the variable stripe.

I had in mind a skirt for this fabric. I could imagine several ways of pleating it, either soft or stitched pleats which would reveal or conceal different aspects of the stripe. If the pleats were stitched and folded so that only the darkest color (charcoal crossed with black) showed, then where the pleats released there would be a flash of color. Other schemes could also be used.

Monk's belt vest fabric (#2, page 119)

The second fabric contains a small, lively overshot pattern called monk's belt—a nod toward Swedish weavers in a very un-Swedish colorway—that repeats over and over again. I envisioned this fabric in a vest; I prefer to see busy patterns like this one used with restraint. It could also be used to weave a border for the yoke of a shirt/jacket or a dress or for the bottom of a skirt (one or the other, please, not both!). Both versions are shown here.

The warp and plain-weave weft for this fabric are worsted wool. Worsted wool not only makes a good, reliable warp, but also produces a fabric which is highly wrinkle-resistant. The pattern yarn is woolen-spun, at 2000 yd/lb. When washed, it fluffs out to fill in the pattern so that it doesn't look skimpy. For the border pattern weft, I used only the brick red color; in the vest fabric, I inserted a few shots of camel now and then to light up the pattern. Experiments with off-white and camel alternating were unsatisfactory. The off-white was too bright and jumped out of the cloth.

The overall weight of the vest fabric is not very heavy. Although the fabric is fairly closely woven (24 e.p.i.), the pattern makes it look coarse. Avoid any vest pattern with exaggerated points or narrow pieces in it.

The third fabric was intended to be used for a jacket. It is about the weight of commercial tweed fabric but a lot softer. The narrow dotted lines running through it make it a simple, bold design. The stripes are as simple as can be: one end of camel, four ends of charcoal.

Warping this sequence is a snap for weavers who thread the reed and heddles before beaming. For the rest of us, it is a good idea to use a warping paddle or a rigid heddle to run five threads at once. The heddle method is simpler for me than using a paddle. I clamp the heddle at about waist height in front of my warping board and thread slot, hole, slot, hole, slot. To make the threading cross, I first push down on all the ends so that the hole ends are up, then lift them all so that the slot ends are up. Very neat. (Thanks, Harry P. Linder!)

The sett on this fabric is about the lower limit for plain weave so that the fabric will be supple. For a very tailored cut, I'd recommend a firmer sett.

The next fabric is the only plain fabric in this collection. It gives the bold patterns something to play against. The plain fabric may be purchased or, as here, woven to echo the background of one of the other fabrics. In general, I advise against weaving what you can buy, but the probability of finding a solid wool of this quality that is exactly the right color is about zero. The plain and striped fabrics could be used together to make a suit or they could be used to trim one another.

Here, as in the pinstriped fabric just above, the warp is charcoal and the weft is black. In all fabrics in which the warp and weft are different colors, it is especially important to strive for an even, consistent beat. The streakiness that an uneven beat causes is always emphasized when two colors are used, even if they're very close.

The Shetland-style yarns used in the above two fabrics crock. That is to say, as you handle the unwashed yarns, color rubs off on your fingers, your warping board, the back beam of your loom, and on you if you lean against the breast beam as you weave. After the cloth has been washed, there is no more crocking, and the crocking that has occurred washes off your hands and wipes off a waxed warping board and back beam; it washed out of my dark blue denim weaving apron, too. (I wore the dark one just in case!) Crocking occurs when there is excess dye on the surface of the fibers. If washing the fabric solves the problem, as it did here, there is no harm done. Otherwise, the problem is terminal: a cloth that keeps crocking or bleeding is no asset because it rubs off onto everything and bleeds into the wash. Sampling is the way to find out. I watch intense colors, especially blacks, reds, and dark blues; I have never seen crocking in medium to light values.

The stripes in the last fabric in this collection emulate jaspé. The technique used to produce real jaspé stripes is lengthy: the warps are measured, tied to resist the dye in some places, and then put into a dyebath and the dye fixed; the warp is then dried and taken to the loom. The stripes in my fabric have not undergone this process!

I approximated the subtle variegations of jaspé stripes by loosely spinning together one end of woolen-spun brick red wool with one fine end of

**Pinstriped jacket fabric
(#3, page 120)**

**Plain skirt fabric
(#4, page 121)**

**Mock jaspé
striped skirt fabric
(#5, page 121)**

saffron yellow worsted. I used a spinning wheel because I have one, but a drop spindle could have been used instead. If you have neither, but have a hand-powered bobbin winder, you can ply the two yarns loosely by spinning off the tip of the spindle that the bobbins fit on. It's important to produce the same number of twists per inch throughout the length of the yarn, so take your time. It isn't difficult: treadle the same number of "beats" for each arm's length of yarns, or turn the crank of your bobbin a given number of times per length. About four twists per inch is optimal for these yarns.

When you have plied your yarn, skein it and set the twist by wetting it in warm water (a drop or two of liquid detergent will help the wetting process). Weight the skein just enough to prevent its kinking and allow it to dry. When it is dry, use it as you would any other yarn.

Each end of the fancy yarn is separated by two ends of worsted wool, and each jaspé stripe is set into a ground of more worsted wool. Separating the fancy yarns from each other allows their texture and color to show to best effect: the idea is to make a stripe such that its colors seem to flicker through the cloth.

This fabric, a one-shuttle weave, is easy and quick to weave. Moreover, it is fun to watch the mock jaspé stripe and see just where the flash of yellow will show up next.

You may have noticed that all the fabrics in this series use a charcoal warp, wholly or in part, and black weft. There are two reasons for this: first, for the livelier color; black crossed by black looks flat and a bit dull. Second, black warps are difficult to thread because they are hard to see. Even the relatively small change from black to charcoal helps. I look for every way I can to make the weaving processes move more smoothly and error-free.

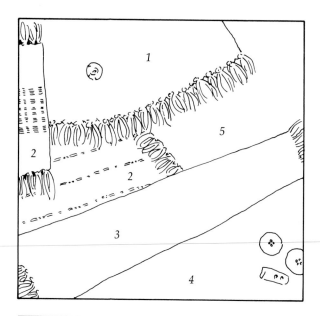

SWATCH COLLECTION #11

This, the largest of all the collections, was part of a theme issue on using one warp to produce many different fabrics or projects. There are ten fabrics: five from one warp, two from another, and three from a third. The fabrics from one warp are easily identified, but small differences in wefts, alterations of the warp, and different structures change the appearance and hand remarkably.

In exploring this idea, I learned that some approaches are more fertile than others. For example, a threading on which a true plain weave can be woven is far more versatile than one on which it cannot. I learned, too, to be more open-minded about setts. Even a two-end-per-inch variation can make a terrific difference, whether the weft is changed or not. To increase my options for experimenting, I used all my shafts; two- and four-shaft weaves can be woven on eight, but the reverse is not true. Finally, I was reminded that nothing I put into a warp has to stay there for all time. I have no compunctions about cutting out warp ends and replacing them with others, cutting them out and leaving a space, or cutting them out and resleying to close the gaps. The fabrics in this collection reflect that philosophy. Particularly in a sampling warp, nothing is engraved in stone; that warp is mine to do with as I will. The results may sometimes look messy at the back of the loom, but who cares? Exploration is the whole idea. One caution, though: if you plan to cut ends out, try to weave the variations in which you need them first. Restoring ends to the warp is not as easy as cutting them out!

As usual, there is a color theme in this collection. I was thinking of the colors of sherbet (raspberry, orange, pineapple, lime) as played against the creamy off-white of vanilla ice cream. Isn't that a refreshing thought for a hot summer's day?

Cotton is the only fiber used in this collection. The ice cream color is natural 20/2 pearl cotton and the sherbet colors, except for a 20/2 bright pink, are slightly textured 8/2 cotton, unmercerized.

20/2 pearl cotton fabrics for tops and dresses (#1–#5, page 122)

The first five fabrics all came from a warp composed primarily of 20/2 natural pearl cotton. The colored stripes, two ends of 8/2 cotton each, are twelve 20/2 ends apart (at 30 e.p.i.). Their color sequence is regular: pink, orange, yellow, pink, orange, green. I noticed as I made yarn wrappings that the yellow and mint green packed a lot of punch and had to be used in moderation.

All the fabrics are relatively lightweight and well suited for blouses or tops without lots of gathers, pleated or lightly gathered skirts, culottes, simple dresses, beach cover-ups, or caftans. They may be used singly or in combination: the plaid, cut in bias strips, could bind the stripe, for example.

The first fabric is very plain. The warp is simple plain weave using just 20/2 pearl cotton. The stripes contrast with the ground cloth because they are made of larger, colored, slightly textured threads. A one-shuttle weave, this cloth moves along well.

The second fabric is like the first except that it is woven as drawn in. The colored yarns are used in the weft in the same order in which they appear in the warp. This plaid must be woven evenly to ensure a good match when sewn. I weave a few inches to establish my beat and then make a template to keep track of my beat.

The third fabric has colored warp stripes like the first. The natural pearl cotton weft alternately weaves plain weave and bands of weft-faced broken twill that look like off-white satin ribbons lying across the warp stripes. I chose broken twill to avoid diagonals that would compete with the primary effect of color stripes that seem to come and go.

For the eight-shaft version of this structure, I had to remove two of every twelve ends of the 20/2 pearl cotton and resley. When I used all twelve ends, there was a distracting long float at the colored warp stripes; without the last two ends, the floats were equal and looked correct. See the drafts given here and thread according to what you want.

Fabric four is the same warp minus all the colored ends. I cut them out and threw them over the back of loom. It was a gay but messy sight! I left the gaps in the warp to produce a skip-dented cloth. If this cloth is the only one you're weaving, omit the colored ends altogether and sley with a slightly larger gap than shown here. The fabric is subtle.

As an accompanying project, I wove this fabric again for a dolman-sleeved top. For that purpose, I sleyed the fabric three per dent in a twelve-dent reed with two empty dents to form the gap. The cloth, after many machine washings, is perfectly stable and much more dramatic than the fabric shown here. You have a choice: for subtlety, leave the small gap; for drama, the larger gap and more crammed warp.

Those gaps were what I wanted for the fifth and final fabric from this warp. I had in mind inlaying short pieces of the colored yarn to form diagonal patterns in the cloth. I used the gaps in the reed to mark the entry and exit points of those supplementary wefts. I merely walked behind my loom and harvested the colors I needed from the warps hanging there. I cut the pieces 1½ inches long and laid them in two at a time with equal amounts of "tail" protruding from the shed. I consider the side without the tails the "right side". When I wove a dolman-sleeved blouse with this inlay just in the center front and back, I used yarn butterflies instead and recommend that to you highly. The cut tails fray away in the wash and create a lot of lint. I think they are secure for many, many washings, but carrying the yarn from site to site is easier and neater. The float on the back formed where the inlay thread is carried from one site to the next does not show on the front of the fabric. Weaving the cloth firmly at 30 p.p.i. also helps keep the inlaid wefts from snagging and pulling out of the cloth.

If you use eight shafts for this fabric, you can thread the areas between the gaps in the reed on 1 through 4 and 5 through 8. Each group, or block, can be lifted by itself, making the inlay very simple. There is no need to count threads because the open places in the reed tell you where to start and stop.

I laid in the colors to form diagonal lines. I experimented with deep V's and even tried a dornick twill inlay (it looked like a mistake). All the stripe colors may be used or just some of them. The diagonals can turn at any point you like and move the other way. There are many possible variations.

The second warp was solid colored but had woven texture. The yarn was 20/2 mercerized cotton in bright, hot pink. I wanted the solid color to use with the patterns in the first five fabrics but I wanted to weave two variations: one with warp stripes and the other with isolated squares in a plain-weave ground.

Textured mercerized cotton fabrics (#6 and #7, page 123)

The structure of these fabrics is mock leno or canvas weave. I chose a threading based on six ends so that a true plain weave would be possible, so that I could weave isolated squares. I adapted a threading from page 68 of *A Handweaver's Pattern Book*, by Marguerite Davison.

Canvas weave is the structure used to make needlepoint canvas. It looks fragile and delicate but is really quite tough. It may be washed repeatedly by machine with no shifting beyond that which takes place initially in the finishing to open up the lacy holes.

I sleyed the sixth fabric two per dent (in a twenty-dent reed) in the plain-weave sections and 3-0, repeat, in the canvas-weave areas. The special denting helps to dramatize the structure and makes the canvas-weave stripes more open than the ground: 30 e.p.i., rather than 40. The fabric is soft and draping and well suited for use as a skirt.

When I wove the seventh fabric, I resleyed the cloth to 40 e.p.i. throughout. I wanted the plain-weave sections between the canvas squares in the warp direction to match the plain-weave areas between the squares in the weft direction. The canvas weave doesn't open up quite as dramatically, making the fabric a little less revealing.

I intended the third and final warp for "bottom weight" cloth: slacks, shorts, culottes, more tailored skirts. The warp is unmercerized 8/2 cotton.

The eighth fabric was made by crossing the 8/2 warp with 8/2 weft. The warp is a very bright pink. I crossed it with the duller pink from the first warp. The result is a richer fabric than either color crossed by itself and a much softer looking fabric than the warp color had led me to expect.

The weft of the ninth fabric is the same weight and texture but orange, a lighter value than the warp. I've been interested in producing iridescent cloth, and while it is relatively easy to do with fine, silky threads, I want to see how far I can push the idea in other yarns. This is about as coarse a fabric as I have made which seems to change color as it is moved and folded. Once again, it is a subtle point, but I like subtlety.

In the tenth and final fabric, the color is about the same in the warp and weft, but the texture varies. Instead of using a single thread of 8/2 cotton as weft, I used 20/2 mercerized cotton doubled on the bobbin. Doubling 20/2 cotton produces a weight about the same as a single thread of 10/2 cotton, which is still smaller than 8/2 cotton. The result is a lighter fabric than the eighth and ninth fabrics, with a subtle luster where the weft shows between the warp yarns.

When you double threads on the bobbin, it is essential to keep the tension on each exactly the same; otherwise, little loops of weft rise to the surface of the cloth. I made this cloth two ways, only the first of which was published. In the first, I was careful to tension the two threads identically and produced a fairly featureless cloth. In the other, I deliberately wound one thread a bit slack so that little loops would be formed in the fabric—an interesting variation.When an act produces an effect you do not want in the cloth, you can either avoid the unusual or "unwanted" effect or step through the looking-glass and do that something decisively for a new twist. Each time I run up against what appears to be a limitation, I try to turn my thinking around and consider what appears to be a limitation, I try to turn my thinking around and consider that it just might be an opportunity, now or in the future, to do something I couldn't do before. It's worth considering.

Unmercerized 8/2 cotton, bottom-weight fabrics (#8–#10, page 124)

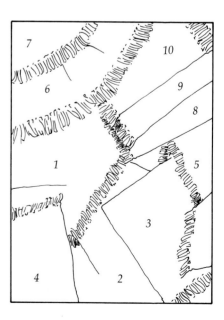

SWATCH COLLECTION #12

I designed this collection with a city in mind. I wanted fabrics appropriate for suit elements: matching and contrasting fabrics for skirts and jackets or vests. I chose dark blue, grays, and bluish reds, a fairly refined and sophisticated palette that would not look out of place in the winter in San Francisco.

Just as the colors are refined, so the textures are relatively smooth. One is a bold tweed, but the others are understated. I wish you could stroke the fabrics themselves! Two of them use extra-fine Merino and are heavenly to touch—soft and buttery smooth. All but one of these fabrics are a variety of twill. The trend that fall and winter (1985) was toward the use of menswear fabrics in women's clothing. Slick, sophisticated, urbane, smooth: those were the words in my mind as I designed this group of fabrics.

Dornick twill suit fabric (#1, page 124)

The first fabric is the boldest graphically. The threading is a dornick twill, a four-shaft twill which reverses direction without producing a three-end float. The warp is light gray with two ends of dark gray, one on either side of the break where the diagonals change direction. A regular treadling—1-2, 2-3, 3-4, 1-4, etc.—produces stripes of reversing diagonals. In this fabric, though, the treadling was treated the same way as the threading; it was reversed with a clean break in it as well. The last pick of the old direction was dark gray, as was the first in the new direction, all others were medium blue. The result is a goose-eye sort of fabric with a built-in check.

The yarns are all heathery tweeds, which soften the contrasts a little and make a lovely visual texture. I could see this fabric made into a suit with a short, boxy jacket and sporty pleated skirt. To keep the checks even, I used a template.

These tweeds were tightly spun, which made them tend to kink in use. To deal with this problem, I measured my warp, beamed it using a raddle, inserted the lease sticks and then cut the ends for the first time and threaded, sleyed, and tied on the front. While weaving the fabric, I took care that my bobbins were wound firmly so that the weft was held under some tension. When I took the shuttle out of the shed, I was careful not to reel out extra yarn; that would tend to introduce kinks toward the edges of the cloth. Boat shuttles encourage that tendency; I recommend using end-feed shuttles, which work nicely with kinky yarns as with others.

If kinks creep by you—and they will—try to spot them in the cloth before you wash it and tease them along with a tapestry needle to form loops at the selvedge, where you can either leave them or cut them and darn them in.

Tweed yarns are woolen-spun. The spinning oil they contain must be removed in the finishing process. The cloth on the loom is handsome enough, but the washed cloth is wonderful both to see and to touch. Washing not only removes the oil but softens the yarn and opens it up so that it fills in the spaces between threads and fills out the cloth. Some days I am convinced that a bath does me almost as much good, but it is never quite as beautifying for me as washing is for tweeds!

The next fabric is plain—but not really. It, too, is a tweed, and the yarn itself, used in both warp and weft, is a mixture of many heathered colors. The same medium-blue color used above was used here so that the fabric would coordinate with the checked dornick twill and with the fabric that follows. It is woven in a standard 2/2 twill. Use an even beat.

"Plain" twill
skirt fabric
(#2, page 125)

The next fabric is another of those variations on a simple structure that has been used so often that it has its own name. This cloth is called granite weave. It is a broken twill using a dark color in one direction and a light one in the other. It can be woven on the same warp as the plain weave above. The threading is a straight draw on four shafts and the treadling is broken: 1-2, 2-3, 1-4, 3-4, repeat. The same effect may be produced by threading a broken twill and using a regular treadling. I almost never weave it that way because the threading is more limiting and it is simpler to thread a straight draw and tie the treadles so that they lie in the proper sequence. In general, I thread to a straight draw whenever possible because it is so much easier to keep track of where I am. (The more I use it, the more automatic it becomes, providing even more reason to do it that way!)

Granite-weave
skirt fabric
(#3, page 125)

The second and third fabrics must be washed with plenty of detergent, just as the first one was. The spinning oil makes the water milky as it comes out of the yarns. I am excited each time I put a tweed fabric into the hot, sudsy water, anticipating the transformation I know is going to happen!

The next two fabrics are woven with very soft, fine worsted wool. One is another dornick twill, using four shafts. The warp threading, as in the first fabric, changes direction without creating three-end floats at the point of change. The last thread in the ascending threading and the first end in the descending threading are both silk; the threads where the directions change again are silk, too. I chose a silk almost the same color as the rich, blue Merino so that the textural difference would show the luster of the silk as it forms a double dotted line down the cloth on either side of the break in the threading. Unlike the first fabric, the weft always remains the same, and the treadling is regular throughout the cloth with no reversals. The stripes thus produced look understated and serene.

Dornick twill
wool/silk suit fabric
(#4, page 125)

The fifth fabric began with the idea of weaving stripes of two colors without having the kind of color mixing that occurs when weft crosses warp in a structure such as plain weave. To accomplish this, I threaded the warp in alternate blocks of warp- and weft-faced twill. The warp is a bluish red and the weft a second, slightly warmer bluish red. In the warp-faced (3/1) stripe, three-fourths of the visible color is that of the warp; conversely, in the weft-faced (1/3) stripe, the weft color is dominant. The result is understated, elegant, and very beautiful.

Striped Merino
suit fabric
(#5, page 125)

I was surprised and delighted by the appearance of the cloth. It was my understanding that Merino wools, because of the fineness of the fibers and the fineness of their crimp, produced a matte surface. In this fabric, though, the stripes alternate with a subtle but distinct luster. (I was careful to press, not iron, so it wasn't an iron-induced shine.)

Where the stripes come together, there are no floats that pass from one stripe to the other. This "clean break" is essential if the stripes are to look neat and tailored. If a weft straddles the break, then the warp threads at the edges

of the stripes drift, making slightly curving lines. (Sometimes that is **exactly** what I want to make, but not this time.)

Plain-weave jacket or coat fabric (#6, page 126)

I designed the final fabric to provide a kicky contrast to the other five. I had in mind making a fabric to be used for a slightly flared jacket or three-quarter-length coat with rounded, padded shoulders. The dominant red is similar to the Merino red with irreverent brighter red and orange flecks to add sparkle. I like it teamed with the elegant blue worsted and with the matching red worsted. The contrast in textures and attitude pleases me.

This yarn is the heaviest in the collection and strong enough visually all by itself that I felt no need to introduce a fancy structure. In fact, a fancy structure would be wasted on such a flamboyant yarn, so I chose a balanced plain weave and then fulled well to remove the spinning oil, soften the yarn, and bring the cloth together.

This yarn has a tendency to kink in the weaving and to track as it is washed. If you like the tracking, manipulate the fabric as soon as you get it wet. If you prefer not to have it—as I did—soak the fabric in hot, sudsy water until the water cools down and then wash again. As you press it, pull it straight and press it flat to obliterate any tracking that may have occurred. All you need now is a couple of silk blouses and your city wardrobe is ready!

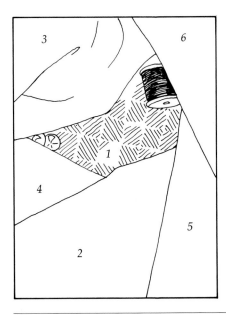

SWATCH COLLECTION #13

This collection began with a chance remark from a participant in a workshop I was leading. The young woman said that the fabrics I design for HANDWOVEN always have a lot of color in them and she prefers to wear neutrals. When I reminded her that the fabrics may be interpreted by the weaver in other colorways, she responded that it would be nice to *see* a collection of neutrals.

When I got home, I set a challenge for myself: design a lively group of fabrics using a neutral palette. I turned to *Color Trends*, then a biannual color forecasting service for craftsmen published by Michele Wipplinger. I looked at the neutrals forecast for spring/summer 1986 and selected a beige that was the color of light tussah silk, a darker beige, and a silvery gray. To add a little punch to that grouping, I added the dark green from the same forecast and, to balance that, a warmer neutral, a rosy beige.

These are warm-weather fabrics and must be lightweight. The best structural choice for light fabrics is our old friend, plain weave. The collection relies heavily on plain weave, which allows the beauty of the threads and their contrasts in texture and color to be the focus of interest.

I thought, as long as I was using a tussah silk color, why not use silk? Silk absorbs moisture well, which makes it comfortable to wear. It is a good insulator, but woven with lots of "air holes"—plain weave is chock full of them—the fabrics would breathe well.

Silk skirt or dress fabric (#1, page 126)

The first fabric is 100 percent silk. I intended it for use as a skirt or simple two-piece dress. The sett is about as open as possible for this yarn, 18 e.p.i., but because the texture of the tussah noils keeps the ends and picks from sliding around on each other, the fabric is quite stable. The drape of the fabric is wonderful: it is neither limp nor stiff, but simply flowing and soft.

Cotton and silk top fabric (#2, page 126)

The next fabric, designed to coordinate with the first—another top for the skirt, perhaps?—has a subtle, private joke woven into it. It consists of cotton and silk used in both the warp and weft. Ordinarily one thinks of silk as being lustrous and cotton as having a matte surface, but in this case the silk is noils (dusty to the touch and not at all light-reflective) and the cotton is pearl cotton (lustrous and smooth), just the opposite of what one would expect. (I said it was a subtle joke! Some of us are easily entertained.)

To highlight the luster of the pearl cotton, I contrived to let it float now and then. I put the floats at the intersections of the four-end cotton stripes, warp and weft. The small, knotlike pattern that occurs at those intersections consists of floats in the cotton only, creating a little glimmer of light reflection where they come together.

I used a template to be sure that the squares I was weaving stayed uniform. As time goes by, unless you are weaving in a time of great stress, it becomes easy to maintain a steady, even beat. I find ballet music is the perfect accompaniment for weaving because the rhythms are very human; I just dance with my hands and arms.

Both of the first two fabrics wash easily and well. I was pleased to find no shrinkage differential between the silk and the cotton. If you use different materials from those specified here, be sure to test a generous woven sample to see whether differential shrinkages will distort the finished cloth. (Not washing is not an option!)

The third fabric is 100 percent linen, the coolest of all natural fibers. Linen conducts heat away from the body, is absorbent and, most important, dries very quickly. It crushes and wrinkles because it is not resilient or elastic. Keeping that characteristic in mind, I decided to use it for a jacket fabric, not a skirt.

I was able to find all three of the neutrals I had chosen in 16/2 linen. Because they are close in both hue and value, the differences are subtle. I experimented with wrappings until I came up with the small stripe you see here. From a distance, the colors blend together but on closer examination—certainly when one is wearing it!—the subtle stripes can be seen and appreciated. All three colors were used in equal amounts in the warp, and the middle value, the tussah color, was used alone for weft.

Linen yarns tend to be rather wiry. This wiriness can be exasperating as you weave. I use plastic bobbins, not wooden bobbins or paper quills, so I'm able to dunk them in lukewarm water and then allow them to drain. If you begin weaving with dampened weft, you must continue because the weft beats in a little differently when wet; however, the advantages will persuade you that it's a good idea in any case. Dampening the weft stops the overspin that makes using linen in boat shuttles such a trial.

It is important to allow the fabric to dry before rolling it onto the cloth beam. Damp linen rolled onto itself will mildew as you work. It is very dry where I live—which, incidentally aggravates the overspinning problems—so the cloth is always dry before it is rolled onto the cloth storage beam. A handheld hair dryer will do the job if the ambient humidity is high where you live.

I used an even, strong beat for this fabric to make it firm and stable. I soaked it well in hot, sudsy water and worked it well to obliterate the reed marks. Always iron linen while it is damp and you will be rewarded by a smooth, lovely surface. Polish the fabric a bit with your iron.

The next two fabrics are based on what I thought of as the "bouncing-ball stripe". The stripes are tussah noils in a fine, 20/2, dark green pearl cotton ground. Two ends of tussah are always used together, but the interval between them varies. It starts out long—20 ends of pearl cotton—and shortens to 4 ends in the final stripe. Think about the sound a ball makes as it is allowed to bounce without being caught: the bounces are widely spaced in time for the first bounces and quite close together for the final ones. That's the idea I was trying to reproduce in cloth.

There were two fabrics from this warp: one is simply crossed with the green cotton to show off the textural contrast between noils and pearl cotton and the rhythm of the tussah stripes. The second is woven to square so that the order in the warp is repeated in the weft, making a very interesting grid pattern. I like the two of these used together, one as blouse, the other as skirt or one as the main fabric of a dress and the other as its trim.

Linen jacket fabric (#3, page 126)

Bouncing-ball striped and checked fabrics (#4, page 127)

Striped fabrics (#5 and #6, pages 127–128)

The fifth and sixth fabrics are both striped. In both cases, the warps are made of 8/2 cotton, heavier than any of the other yarns used so far.

Designing stripes is not a trivial matter. I spent a long time working on these before I was satisfied. The sixth fabric has a fairly complicated stripe sequence. Unlike the bouncing-ball stripe or the one I'll describe next, it is an even stripe: it has a point of symmetry so that what lies to the left of that point is a reflection of what lies to the right. These stripes are easy to sew, although I think uneven stripes are more interesting.

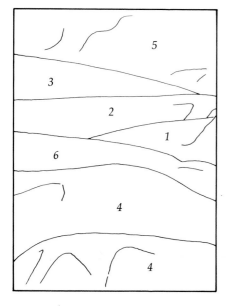

The last stripe was born as an offshoot of the sixth fabric. I began to see a little figure repeating in one of the stripe sequences I explored which pleased me but didn't seem to fit into the complex stripe. I experimented with it and pushed it further and further until I came up with what you see here, one of my all-time favorites. All the stripes are two ends wide. Dark green stripes alternate with the other colors through the cloth like a matrix into which the other colors are set: first the darker beige for three beige stripes, then lighter beige for three beige stripes, and finally silvery gray for three stripes before starting over again. The quietness of this stripe, the way the values of the neutral stripes change stepwise, and the regular rhythm all please me very much.

For both the fifth and sixth fabrics, I used tussah noils as weft. The effect that makes in the hand of the fabrics and their apparent weight is striking. 8/2 cotton crossed by itself would have produced a sturdy, fairly hefty fabric. These flow nicely and would lend themselves to skirts, shorts, culottes, shirt/jackets, any of a number of garments. The addition of the silk weft also seems to make them more wrinkle-resistant.

Sometimes I am surprised how far a seemingly chance remark leads me.

SWATCH COLLECTION #14

This collection began with a long-term desire of mine. I have always thought it would be interesting and fun to gather a study group of weavers, choose one yarn together (it need not be dyed), and order quite a bit of it. Then we'd all carry away our share and working independently, use that yarn, by itself and in combination with others, to see how many interesting and beautiful fabrics we could construct. Because I haven't found anyone willing to play at this idea with me, like the Little Red Hen, I thought I would do it myself.

I turned to *Color Trends* for a hint about the color and chose a singles tweed yarn. It's blue with black and pale red-violet flecks in it—hardly a featureless yarn!

When I am getting acquainted with a yarn, I always begin by using it in both warp and weft and weaving it plain weave. I see how strong it is, what kind of sett suits it, what happens to it when it is washed, and what kind of hand it produces in the cloth.

Plain-weave jacket or skirt fabric (#1, page 128)

The first fabric in this collection, accordingly, is just that: plain weave. It is well suited for use as a jacket: loose-fitting and untailored. It could be made with cut-in-one lapels that simply fall into folds at the front, no buttons or other closures. It is also light enough to use for a skirt; in that case, I would line it.

Merino with floating tweed vest fabric (#2, page 128)

The second fabric was a result of what I call "listening to the yarn". I compared a swatch of the first fabric, finished, with the same fabric under tension on the loom. I thought about the "blooming" that occurs when the spinning oils are washed out of tweeds and considered what I might be able to do with it. I thought that if I first crammed the tweed, then allowed it to float for a distance, and then confined it again, the floating yarns would bloom into an oval on the surface of the cloth. As long as the floats were not too long, the cloth would be sound and functional.

To produce that effect I needed another yarn to act as the ground. I chose a fine Merino wool for the ground, as close to the base color of the tweed as I could find in hue and a little lighter in value so that the tweed would be visible. I threaded the Merino for a firm plain-weave ground and grouped ends of the tweed, cramming them into one dent. In the weave, the tweed threads are alternately caught down in the plain-weave ground and allowed to float. The ground takes just two shafts, so I had two shafts left which I could use for managing the tweed yarns. The ones in one bundle are all carried on the same shaft, so that left me one shaft more. It was perfect: I could float one bundle while its nearest neighbors were weaving plain weave, and vice versa. The resulting half-drop pattern is far more interesting than having the floaters all in a row across the cloth.

Color-and-weave effect tunic-jacket fabric (#3, page 128)

I designed the next fabric from another point of view. I wanted a color-and-weave effect in which the tweed appeared like a magnified plain weave in a matrix of black merino. First I drew out the pattern on graph paper and, working back from that, figured out the color sequence for the threading and treadling as well as the structure.

As it turned out, the design I wanted is woven plain weave, the best structure possible because the pattern is not distorted by floats and subsequent shifts in the cloth. The fabric looks tweedy at a distance but reveals its pattern on close observation. The fabric is lightweight and was intended for a belted, hip-length tunic-jacket with one button holding its asymmetrical closing. It can be worn over a blouse or on its own as a top for a slightly offbeat suit.

Tweed and worsted fabric (#4, page 129)

Using the tweed again, I picked up its main color (blue) and the color of one of its flecks (black) in the same Merino worsted that I had used in the second fabric. I used the three yarns in the same order, over and over: tweed, black worsted (doubled), blue worsted (doubled). I threaded them onto a straight draw on four shafts. Simple inspection will show that the tweed falls on shaft 4 in the first threading repeat; in the next one, the black is on shaft 4, and in the third one, the blue. After three threading repeats, twelve ends, the color-and-threading repeat is completed. That sequence continues throughout the cloth.

As I wove the cloth, the ends on shaft 4 were up for three out of four picks while the remaining ends wove plain weave. That threw the three colors, in sequence, to the face of the fabric, making floats of tweed, black, and blue, repeat. The repeat is small, but the textured effect is interesting. The weft is woven at 20 p.p.i., so that the three-pick floats are only $^3/_{20}$ inch long; the cloth is stable and not inclined to snag.

Mohair coat fabric (#5, page 129)

I wanted to make a cozy, cuddly, showy fabric for a loose-fitting coat, one with raglan sleeves or some other very simple shape. I picked up the colors of the tweed in fancy yarns: two loopy and two brushed mohairs. The structure is a variation on plain weave. Each area weaves plain weave half the time and a large basket half the time.

The color arrangement in the cloth creates a series of large overchecks that seem to lie at different levels in the fabric. This is an uneven plaid, which would require extra care in laying out a pattern for cutting, but the results are interesting and well worth the effort.

The brushed mohair tends to stick to itself when sheds are opened, so you might want to substitute the loop mohair throughout. Woven that way and simply washed and pressed, the loop-on-loop areas become like "poodle cloth".

Did you know that loop mohair is the precursor to brushed mohair? All brushed mohair is spun looped and then brushed to rupture the loops and open up the fibers. When I am faced with a project which might be difficult in brushed mohair, I use loop mohair when it is available and brush the fabric after it is woven, washed, and steamy from its first pressing. Brushing brings up the fuzzy yarn. If you want fuzzy areas and loopy areas, you can combine the yarns as I did here, or take your chances brushing some loops and not others. You might decide to brush one side (inside for insulation or outside for effect) and not the other; the choice is yours.

Isn't that the point of all of this? **As a designer you decide how you want to have the fabric look, feel, and drape and work to achieve that goal.**

Use a template to ensure that the plaid stays even as you weave. I found that beating lightly before and after each shot helped to clear the shed when it stuck. Sticky yarns take more effort to use. Many times (although not here), I tie the loom to a direct tie-up and lift some of the shafts with one foot and the others after that to get a clearer shed.

Overchecked dress fabric (#6, page 130)

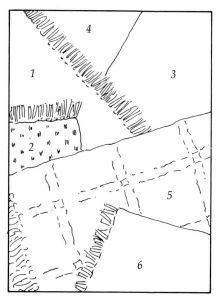

The last fabric is the only one that doesn't use the tweed yarn. Nevertheless, it uses the colors of the tweed yarns, and is another of my all-time favorites. I used 20/2 pearl cotton to make a dress fabric. If the repeat were reduced, it would work nicely for a blouse, too.

The cloth is mostly medium dark blue plain weave with a large overcheck of magenta composed of four threads in each direction. In the middle of the squares thus formed I threaded a mock leno or canvas-weave square. In a way, this is a simplified version of the coat fabric just above. Unlike the coat, only four shafts are required to weave this cloth. Most of the warp is carried on shafts 1 and 2, so be certain that your heddles are distributed accordingly before you begin threading. (It's possible to shift heddles from one bar to another while the threading is in progress—I have done it—but it is easier to do so beforehand.)

You could also weave this fabric of very fine worsted wool. However, the canvas weave is likely to be a little less clear. For maximum structural clarity, do not full the cloth very much.

It is interesting to compare the weights, the moods, the drape, the feel of all the fabrics containing the same tweed. I wove a few more variations than are shown here and you could, too.

If you live in an isolated place—or even if you don't—you, too, can have a do-it-yourself study group just as I did. Set your problem or your goal and go to work!

SWATCH COLLECTION #15

Almost every swatch collection has begun with its colors. I'm not sure why that approach seems to work so well for me, but having discovered that color is a powerful trigger, I do not struggle. I imagine the colors first and go from there.

I was due to begin work on this collection right after I returned from a workshop trip to Dallas. I left Salt Lake City with the goal of deciding on the colors while I was away. I had no idea what lay ahead. In Dallas, I visited the Dallas Museum of Art. There Carol Robbins, Curator of Textiles and Associate in New World Cultures, showed me some of the treasures in the textile collection; it was easily the highlight of the trip and haunts me still, three years later.

Some of the pieces touched me unexpectedly deeply. I recall the tiny shirts spun, dyed, and woven by hand for the *santos* figures used in religious festivals. The tenderness that went into their design and construction—using the same cut as the garments the worshippers themselves wore—was evident and very affecting.

I felt a connection to many of the pieces I saw that afternoon, but one amazed me—a woman's mantle. I marveled at its colors: I have spun brown cotton, but was unaware that cotton grew in the grayed blue colors I was seeing. I loved the way the gray was shifted toward the blue by the warm brown and hoped later to obtain that shift in my woven pieces. And I felt embarrassed to have told anyone, anywhere, at any time, "Yes, I am a spinner."

I was delighted and touched by the painstaking care that went into designing and weaving the seven widths that were seamed together to make this mantle. Everything seemed to have been thought out carefully and woven with close attention. I loved the stripes and the colorful tapestry woven into the corners.

Carol Robbins told me that Ann Rowe (author of *Warp-Patterned Weaves of the Andes,* Washington, D.C.: The Textile Museum, 1977) had suggested that the mantle might have been a woman's garment, perhaps worn horizontally, with the long upper edge flipped over to expose the right side of the wrong-side-up tapestry. In Ann's words, "The fold was designed in."

At times like these, I find myself looking at my own hands and thinking, "This was woven with hands just like these, although perhaps smaller and browner." I wondered about the weaver(s). No one knows whether this piece was the work of one weaver or a collaborative effort, with a specialist weaving the double-cloth representations of animals in profile within squares and perhaps another specialist weaving the complementary warp-weave line of birds (they look like pelicans) in profile moving diagonally across one band.

I am always examining my own life—I don't want to come to the end of it and not have noticed what was happening along the way!—and so I wondered about those weavers. What was their life like? They certainly didn't carpool, have magazine deadlines, outside jobs, or volunteer work. Were their lives quieter, more contemplative? Were they held in high regard by their fellows? Oh, I hope so! Did they feel the same joy I do in weaving a fabric that pleased them? I think so. The work was not done grudgingly or stintingly.

When I realized that I couldn't get the mantle out of my mind, I knew that this collection would grow out of it. I didn't want to copy or reproduce the fabrics I had seen; rather, I wanted to "quote" them as I made fabrics which can be useful in our lives.

Striped cotton skirt fabric (#1, page 130)

Three of the fabrics here were taken from other textiles I saw at the museum. The gray stripes on brown is a nod to an old Guatemalan fabric woven with red stripes on a deep blue ground.

I used a fine brown cotton, as close as I could get to the darker brown natural cotton, in place of the deep blue of the original. The heavier, slightly textured gray cotton takes the place of the red. The original fabric was entirely warp-faced and quite thick and ruggedly serviceable as well as beautiful. This fabric is lighter in weight, a balanced plain weave.

The stripe sequence repeats regularly across the cloth with two ends of gray cotton widely spaced and then more closely spaced. All the planning and measuring goes into the warp so that it is a breeze to weave.

Sure enough, the gray seems blue in the vicinity of the warm brown yarn. It was just what I had hoped for!

Checked dress fabric (#2, page 130)

The checked fabric is a liberal interpretation of another Guatemalan fabric. A medium gray 20/2 cotton makes up the ground, with stripes in both warp and weft composed of one thread of slightly textured brown 8/2 cotton, four threads 20/2 pearl cotton in the same brown, followed by one more 8/2. The result is a very simple fabric but another of my favorites. The little ridge at the edge of the brown overcheck is just right: it defines the edge and gives it an extra punch but lets the quietness of the design speak for itself. The weight is appropriate for a shirtwaist dress—I'd like to see the skirt cut on the bias.

Twill striped skirt fabric (#3, page 131)

The third fabric is based on the Peruvian mantle. It has a natural-colored cotton plain-weave ground with raised stripes (warp-faced, 3/1 twill). The latter are warm brown bordered with two ends of the cool gray and paler brown similarly bordered.

The stripes I have quoted here were warp-faced plain weave in the original. Here, only the twill stripes are warp-faced. This fabric is much lighter and more supple and would serve well as a skirt.

Six shafts are needed to weave the cloth: two for the creamy white plain-weave ground and four for the warp-faced twill stripes. If you have only four shafts, you can turn the threading and weave this fabric the other way around. For a four-shaft structure, thread the warp in creamy white natural cotton to a straight draw on four shafts. Weave with the white yarn to create the plain weave, then change to the gray shuttle for two picks, weaving a 1/3 twill, then use the brown shuttle for the remainder of the stripe, ending with two shots of gray before returning to the plain weave.

If you weave the cloth this way, it will take longer because you are changing shuttles frequently, and you will need to use a template to keep things even, but you *can* produce it on a four-shaft loom.

Vest fabric (#4, page 131)

The fourth fabric also takes its cue from the mantle. It is visually very strong and ought, therefore, to be used in relatively small doses. I see it as a vest. I wanted to produce a raised surface in the cloth that would echo the little checkered border to the fancy pick-up stripes in the mantle. I wove those borders several times before they pleased me. I wanted the two grays to interchange so that the cloth would be reversible: light gray on the top to dark gray on the back and vice versa. I knew that if I raised those threads and just ran weft between them for long distances, they would become flaccid. I wanted, therefore, to weave in a supporting structure entirely hidden on the inside of the cloth. The most support comes from plain weave, and that doesn't require adding a lot of shafts: the complete structure is woven on four shafts.

The floating ends are really supplementary warps because they decorate and do not provide the structural integrity of the cloth. These ends must be crammed in the reed. I had no trouble with that but suggest that you use a ten-dent reed, as I did. The ground cloth is set at three per dent for the natural 20/2 cotton, two per dent for the brown 8/2 cotton stripes; in the supplemental areas, there are four ends of gray 8/2 cotton (two light, two dark) and two ends of natural 20/2 per dent.

Brocade blouse fabric (#5, page 132)

The fifth and last fabric in this collection is loosely based on one of the textures I saw in an elaborately brocaded Guatemalan huipil made for a saint figure. These figures are carried in processions on the saints' days in the Roman Catholic calendar. Similar processions (although the figures did not wear handspun, handwoven clothing) took place some Sunday mornings where I grew up in California.

My cloth is loom-controlled with supplementary weft picks that zig and zag across the cloth in a spider weave. I chose creamy natural 20/2 cotton for the base and pale gray 8/2 cotton for the supplementary wefts. In the original, the brocaded areas did not extend selvedge to selvedge as this does, but were woven in as the brocades are in huipils seen in that area today.

Because of the floats, this cloth ought to be used in applications where it will not be subjected to abrasion or snags. It would be lovely in a yoke framing the face—just like the huipils—but not over an elbow or in a cuff, where a lot of wear is expected.

The draft permits the weaving of plain weave or near plain weave, so the fabric for a complete blouse or smock-style dress could be woven on one warp. The yoke could be either woven in or cut and sewn in. The pearl cotton has a lustrous surface, which contrasts with the matte finish of the 8/2 yarns.

As you weave this fabric, it is important to use a wide arc when putting the 8/2 cotton into the shed. The extra slack is necessary so that the decorative thread can move in the cloth as it is finished. Do not be disappointed in the appearance of the cloth on the loom: the pattern will develop fully when you wash it.

I walked into the Dallas Museum full of hope but no particular expectations; I walked out with so much more. A textile collection is a wonderful place to visit for inspiration. I find that a collection of paintings, whether of textiles or not (many portraits say a lot about the textiles of the era), also spark ideas for fabrics. The important thing is to pay attention, and then your own thoughts move freely and make connections between colors and textures which you may not have seen before; synthesize the things you see into something new, something new with a borrowed history that is now part of *your* history.

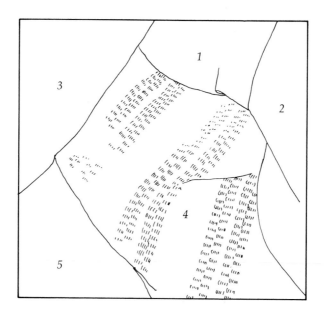

SWATCH COLLECTION #16

I designed this collection around a rich but softened red taken from *Color Trends'* fall/winter 1987–1988 palette. Instructions are given in that publication for dyeing that color, but as usual in my work for publication, I needed to find it in stock yarns, already dyed.

It is at times like this when the virtue of keeping an up-to-date yarn sample file pays off. I sorted through my samples collection and found just the red I was looking for plus a variation in one yarn supplier's catalog, and a lively tweed variation in another's.

I wanted to use another color with the red but rejected some of the most obvious—but really satisfactory—combinations: red and cream, red and blue, red and black, or red and gray. As I looked at the various combinations, I was struck by the gentleness and sophistication of the red with a cool, pale beige. I used three: a subtle, heathery beige blend, a slightly pinkish beige, and another that tends toward gray. I added a darker taupe for the authority it lent to the color chord I was building, sat back, and gave a sigh of relief. (Choosing colors is a pleasurable but intense business!)

Although the collections always begin with their colors, I spend a lot of time thinking about the structures, too. I like to find a balance between a simple structure, a fancy structure, and something that I invent. This time the plaid with the loop yarn and the 3/1 twill stripe, and the combination twill and basket weaves were relatively simple. The double-weave fabric requires more complex equipment (eight shafts, although a four-shaft Bedford cord that gives a similar effect is also described), and the dress fabric with little squares of red using a supplementary warp was my invention.

I work to make as much of each collection as possible accessible to weavers limited to four shafts, and when I design a fabric that requires more, I try to figure out a way to get a similar, if not identical, effect on four. I always weave that alternate fabric to double check, even if it is not shown in the magazine.

As I design a collection, I pay attention to how the yarns are behaving in the cloth and how they change in the finishing, because they suggest variations on my original plans. I'm often rewarded for watching and paying attention as I go. Each path to a new fabric is an adventure, and I like that.

Loop mohair coat fabric (#1, page 132)

The first fabric is a jacket or coat fabric, spongy and cuddly with loops on its surface. I wove it rather softly for an untailored cut; if you plan something more tailored, increase the sett from 12 e.p.i. to 15. The interesting texture that the loop mohair adds to the fabric will be a little more subdued, perhaps more appropriate for a tailored look, and the repeat will be about 20 percent smaller.

The yarns in the warp are used six ends at a time: a stout rosy two-ply, a camel wool/mohair loop, and a singles wool tweed containing both the rosy and camel colors. The same order repeats in the weft. I used a template to keep the repeats even, simplifying laying out the fabric for cutting.

The loop yarn is a little finer than the others and tends to beat in more easily. Tailor your beat—or nudge?—to suit. Use restraint.

When I washed the fabric, the loops became more apparent in the cloth, and the tweed brightened a little as the spinning oil was washed out of it. As I pressed the fabric, I fluffed the loops with my fingertips while the cloth was hot and steamy.

Double-cloth vest or jacket fabric (#2, page 133)

I intended the second fabric for use as a close-fitting vest or short jacket. I imagine a vest with the vertical stripes placed from the shoulder down and the little checkerboard as a border at the waist. You might prefer to make a jacket with checked bodice and striped sleeves, or vice versa. Both stripes and checkerboards may be easily woven on the same warp, or you may choose to weave and use only one or the other.

As shown here, the fabric is double cloth, plain weave, two layers throughout. That structure requires eight shafts. I wove a four-shaft version that looks quite similar—on the face. Bedford cord on four shafts produces vertical stripes of solid red crossing red, taupe crossing taupe. This structure needs only four shafts, but requires a sticky yarn to keep it from shifting. The back of the fabric consists of long floats that limit the way the fabric can be used: it must be lined or used in an application where the back is not exposed. Cut from the loom and washed, Bedford cord draws up in the weft direction because the long floats on the back shrink more than the warp ends do. The weft woven into the face of the fabric cannot shrink far because the warp ends hold it firmly. This differential shrinkage creates curves in the cords which may be pressed out or emphasized by needle-weaving in fat, soft wadding ends to support them.

It's not possible to weave the checkerboard effect in Bedford cord. The instructions for the four-shaft structure are given on page 133.

Dress or suit fabric (#3, page 133)

I intended the third fabric to be used for a dress or light suit. I wanted to put squares of the singles tweed into the cloth to ornament the surface. These ends are actually warp brocade; they are not essential to the structural integrity of the cloth but merely supplement it. The cool beige Merino is buttery soft to the touch.

I knew that a simple float on the surface of the Merino might catch if I made it big enough to show very much. I experimented with several structures for the squares and finally settled on a 1/3 interlacement.

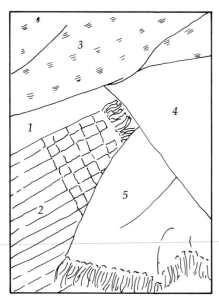

I experimented to see what I could do about the long supplemental warp floats on the back of the fabric. I was concerned lest the wearer snag them with fingers or jewelry as the garment was slipped on. I knew that the woolen-spun yarn would full if I cut the floats before washing. When I tried this, the floats fulled and were secure against pulling out of the cloth, but they also made little "puffs" on the back of the fabric so that smoothed over my lap, the cloth seemed to have smallpox! Ultimately, I found that the least obtrusive solution was simply to leave the long floats intact and line the fabric with a very light lining. The floats lie very flat and do not distort the surface.

The tweed yarns tend to cling to one another in other threadings, but here they are spaced out enough that they behave nicely. Their tendency to kink is controlled by warp tension.

This fabric taught me something new about tracking. In experiments with tracking in the washing of fabrics, I've found that plain weave tracks more than twill, open setts more than tighter ones (there is nowhere to go in a

tight sett), and tightly spun yarns more than less tightly spun ones. Overspinning a yarn produces wonderful collapses in the fabric—super-tracking—and highly elastic cloth, but that is a possibility for experimentation another time.

When I washed the first sample, I manipulated it in the hot, sudsy water right away. As I was about to wash the second, I was called away right after I put it into the sink. By the time I returned, the water was cold so I let it out and started over. To my surprise, this sample tracked very little. Thinking that I might have discovered something important, I tried different soaks and discovered that I can reduce tracking in all kinds of yarns by allowing the fabric to steep and cool off in the water. When I want to avoid tracking, I use that technique routinely now. It is important to pay attention!

Striped jacket, coat, or suit fabric (#4, page 134)

I intended the fourth fabric in this collection for a jacket, light coat, or suit. I combined the cool beige with the sparkling tweed singles. This is a four-shaft structure with stripes of 2/2 twill and 2/2 basket. The structure is determined by the threading and woven with a regular 2/2 twill treadling. The take-up for 2/2 basket weave and 2/2 twill is the same and so is the sett, making these structures compatible in the same cloth. The design is bold and clean. Because the values of the colors are close together, the resulting fabric is quite wearable. The same structure woven in black across white would be very strong visually, best worn in a swashbuckling mood.

Twill skirt fabric (#5, page 134)

The fifth and final fabric in this series combines in one warp several of the yarns used in the other fabrics. I designed it with a softly pleated or slightly flared skirt in mind. The yarns appear in a regular rotation, the heaviest one turning up only once every seven ends.

The warp was very handsome; I wanted to show it off. A warp-faced twill (3/1 twill) was a fairly lightweight way to weave this cloth to exploit the color and texture mixture in the warp. I tried two different yarns as weft and show here the lighter one, 20/2 worsted. The other experiment used the Merino as weft with the same structure and produced a heavier, firmer fabric, perfect for another suit but not soft enough for the skirt I had in mind.

When cut from the loom, this warp-faced fabric, like many warp-faced fabrics, tended to curl a little toward the weft-faced side. Washing and pressing it well persuaded it away from that curvature. On the other hand, if the warp-faced side is used on the outside, the curl can work to soften the pleats in the skirt or enhance the shape cut into the cloth.

Remember that you can weave two fabrics on one warp simply by using a different weft for each or by changing the tie-up or treadling. Many interesting companion fabrics may be woven this way. I like the look of a jacket and skirt which do not match exactly but are related to each other visually and texturally through sharing the same warp.

The most interesting discovery I made designing this collection was the insight into tracking. I think that allowing the fabric to soak **with no agitation whatsoever** allows the unresolved spin in the yarns to relax without distorting the fabric. This technique, which works even with 8/2 cottons, has become one of my "bag of tricks". When I want more tracking, I agitate the cloth a lot in the washing right away, but I can also minimize it with undisturbed soaking. I like being able to choose the effect I want.

SWATCH COLLECTION #17

This is one of my favorite collections for several reasons: all the structures in it are inventive, I love the colors, and I liked a discovery that I made—again—during its creation.

I began, as usual, with the colors. I had designed and woven a luxurious silk scarf previously which used blue-violet and a coral color, as well as some others. (It appeared in the January 1988 issue of HAND-WOVEN.) The places where the blue-violet and coral played off one another gave me that "aaahhhh" feeling when I looked at it, and I wanted to see what else I could do with these colors.

Just before, or perhaps in the early stages of, the creation of this collection, I drove into southern Utah to visit Capitol Reef National Park. The weather in Salt Lake City had been gray and snowy, but the sun in southern Utah was bright, the air heady, and the sky so clear and intensely blue that I thought, "It makes my throat hurt to look at it." (Do you know the feeling? Something is so lovely that it brings tears to my eyes and my throat constricts.)

I watched eagles flying for the sheer pleasure of maneuvering in that sky, lay on rocks to feel the sun on my face, walked in the silence of that extraordinary place, found the tracks and scat of my fellow creatures, and speculated about who they were. At night the sky was a blaze of stars, so bright I felt I could fall into it—and be glad.

Back home, I dived into my yarns and drafts with renewed vigor and turned out this swatch collection. I wrote the instructions and shipped it off and was reporting that fact with a sigh of relief to a friend when it dawned on me just where those colors had come from: I had woven the colors of the land. There they were, spread out on my table: the peach, rose, and corals of Wingate sandstone and Moenkopi shale formations, the intense blue, bordering on violet, of the sky. I rewrote the article that afternoon.

Each time I think that an idea has come out of "nowhere" (I always welcome them gratefully!), the source usually turns out to be the natural world. I look back at some of the earlier collections and see my own and neighbors' gardens; fallen leaves, twigs, and rose hips against the snow. I am always delighted to "recognize" something on the loom. Sometimes, to be sure, I set out deliberately to incorporate the colors of the land or a little vignette into a cloth, but often it seems to happen almost unconsciously. When one is visually oriented, it is very easy to be entertained; even the "commonplace" has subtle beauty. I find myself always thinking about how to incorporate a beautiful thing I see into a fabric design.

The structures in this collection are built around squares and stripes. The first fabric plays dull, slightly irregular cotton stripes off against a lustrous, fine cotton. The stripes seem now thinner, now thicker as they run through the cloth. They alternate between rose and peach on an intense blue ground.

Striped cotton skirt or dress fabric (#1, page 135)

I wanted to make the cloth reversible, and I wanted the variation in stripe width to be strong enough to be visible at 6 to 8 feet. First I made a rough sketch of how I wanted the fabric to appear; then I set out to make that happen.

I could narrow the stripes, I knew, by treating the two ends that make them as one. They rose and fell together and were tightly bound by the weft passing over and under them. The two threads making each stripe were carried on different shafts—the ground is plain weave and may be woven on two shafts, if necessary—so they could weave in a true plain weave. I tried weaving them plain weave and found that that made the stripe wider, as I expected, but not wide enough to be visible at a distance. Because the ends in the stripes were carried on different shafts from the ground, I could weave them in a half basket: one over two wefts that cover the second and the second over the next two wefts that cover the first. That produced just enough width to work. If it hadn't, I'd have tried over three and under three, but I wanted to use the minimum float which would still produce the effect I wanted.

With six shafts, two rhythms in the stripes are possible at once: one stripe can be weaving half basket while the stripes on either side are behaving as if they were made of one end, and vice versa. This alternation across the cloth keeps the emphasis on a vertical stripe. If the broad places in the stripes are always woven at the same time, they form a horizontal line which competes for attention—a fine point, I admit, but important. With eight shafts, the ground can be spread out to four shafts. If only four shafts are available, the stripes may vary in width, but all do the same thing at the same time in the cloth.

Vest or jacket fabric (#2, page 135)

I intended the second fabric for use as a vest or a jacket. I was interested in the luster on the cones of pearl cotton. I knew that breaking up the surface of the cloth prevents any coherent reflection and produces a matte surface; plain weave does that best. If I could play floats against plain weave, then I could show off that soft luster.

I threaded the warp on four shafts, four ends and four ends: 1, 2, 1, 2, and 3, 4, 3, 4. This threading produces plain weave readily enough and also gave me the option of lifting 1 and 2 and passing over 3 and 4 with my shuttle, or the reverse. I was interested in two colorways: orange floats against a blue-violet ground, and blue-violet floats against an orange ground. To achieve both of these effects in one fabric, I decided to alternate colors in the warp, 3-inch bands of orange and blue-violet (the number of ends to be evenly divisible by four). With the blue-violet shuttle, I wove a plain weave shot, making solid blue-violet in the blue-violet warp stripe and blue-violet/orange in the orange stripe. When I threw the orange weft, I wove the pattern shed, creating orange vertical stripes against blue-violet and against the combined colors. I threw these two shuttles alternately. When I changed pattern sheds, I also changed the shuttle assignments, making vertical lines of blue-violet in the solid orange areas and the mixed orange/blue-violet areas. This way none of the vertical lines ever matched the plain-weave ground, which would have made them disappear. This way I got to see both colorways in one cloth.

I'd like to sew this fabric sometime so that instead of matching the weft stripes at the seam, I deliberately offset them in a half drop. Or instead of matching the stripes so that the color continues across the seam, I'd make the color change at the seam by lining up the blue plain-weave weft areas with the orange plain-weave weft areas. It would be interesting, too, to choose three weft repeat sizes, bearing some relationship to each other, for example ¾ inch, 1½ inches, and 2¼ inches, and change the weft colors at those intervals, mixing them up, and then not worry at all about matching at the seams—even cutting narrow strips and sewing them together to make a strip garment like African kente cloth, in which the discontinuities are an important part of the design.

Of course, the colorways could be woven separately, or the pattern sheds could be arranged to make little squares of floats. This method weaves more quickly because most of the time only the shuttle for plain weave is used. This design is full of potential variations.

Log cabin skirt fabric (#3, page 136)

The third fabric in this collection uses all three colors: blue-violet, rose, and peach. The structure is very simple, but interesting things happen in it.

The cloth is plain weave. What could be simpler? But there is a twist: this variation on log cabin is threaded by alternating a very fine, firmly spun, 30/2 blue-violet mercerized cotton with a softer, larger, light peach 8/2 unmercerized cotton. The sequence is peach, blue-violet for 32 ends, then blue-violet, peach for 32 ends.

In the weft direction, the same sequence applies, except (and this is the twist) instead of peach 8/2 cotton, rose 8/2 cotton is used. The result is a log cabin with alternating squares of peach and rose in a matrix of blue-violet. The fineness of the 30/2 cotton puts "hinges" into the 8/2 cloth, making it far more supple than a straight 8/2 cotton cloth. I have gone on to experiment with other fibers, yarn styles, and colors using this idea and have yet to be disappointed. The important features are the contrast in yarn styles and sizes and the substitution in the weft of a different hue of similar value for the larger yarn of the warp.

Blue dress fabric with orange floats (#4, page 136)

The fourth fabric was sandstone against the sky: orange squares against a blue-violet ground. The blue cotton is very fine, 30/2, and the orange is less fine, 20/2. The luster of this exceptional cotton is shown to great advantage by this structure. The orange floats create squares of color in the cloth. I used just four shafts, but offset the squares by the way I threaded and treadled the cloth so that they don't line up horizontally in the cloth, but move around a bit.

As you weave this cloth, the supplemental warps (orange) may not present a smooth change—and therefore a straight edge to the squares—when they first surface. Keep an eye out for straggling warps; if they appear, slip a tapestry needle under the floats and pop them into place. The crisp rhythm of the squares is important.

This fabric is reversible, with equal floats on both sides. This is not the cloth to wear when you pick raspberries because, although the floats are fairly short—just over ⅛ inch—they could snag if subjected to abrasion, claws, or thorns.

I iron all fabrics with floating ends or picks in the direction of the float, never perpendicular to it or at an angle. The idea is to smooth and polish the floats and take advantage of the effects they produce.

SWATCH COLLECTION #18

This collection of fabrics has an autumnal air, like rusty, oak-covered hillsides in twilight when the shadows tend toward the violet. The colors are rich and slightly mysterious, like the colors and scents of autumn.

I was interested in producing very sensuous textures. They are all silky, soft, light, and warm; the waffle weave is like a warm hug.

Striped Merino wool skirt fabric (#1, page 136)

The first fabric is a soft Merino wool. It has stripes of tick weave (alternating colors in warp and one color in weft) in a plain-colored ground. The ground, when woven, seems hardly plain at all. It is iridescent where the coppery color is crossed by violet. Although the yarns are not extremely fine, 18/2, the cloth is as light as a feather. It moves beautifully, further showing off its iridescence. I had in mind a soft skirt, either softly pleated (not stitched or pressed pleats) or softly shirred in a slightly A-line cut to take advantage of its suppleness and fluidity.

It is always important to strive for an even beat but especially important when one color is woven across another. Any variations in beat dramatically affect the resulting color blend. This fabric uses a single shuttle, so weaving progresses at a good rate.

I wove a variation of this fabric by following the warp order in the weft, substituting copper for violet and vice versa to form a plaid. The iridescence is present in the unfigured part of the cloth, and there are interesting color-and-weave-effect squares where the tick-weave stripes cross one another. This fabric would coordinate beautifully with the striped fabric described above. I'd like to see this one woven as a trim and cut on the bias.

Overchecked jacket fabric (#2, page 136)

I intended the second fabric for use as a jacket. Again, the weight of the cloth was kept to a minimum to allow more tailored details without the danger of creating clumsy seams. I had in mind the sorts of jacket Giorgio Armani does so well: not closely fitted but soft-looking and very clean-lined, cropped or below waist length.

The yarns used here are all wool. The ground is 18/2 superfine Merino worsted, soft, light, and warm. The overcheck is a singles tweed. The ruggedness of the latter contrasts nicely with the refinement of the Merino and adds considerable color interest.

The structure is basically plain weave with the overcheck in two twill structures: the warp stripes are warp-faced (3/1 twill) and the weft stripes are weft-faced (1/3 twill). The structure causes the tweed stripes to lie up above the plain-weave ground so that they are brought into relief, making a twill grid superimposed on the soft, light, plain-weave ground. They are treadled and threaded straight so that the diagonals run the same way in both warp and weft.

In weaving a cloth like this, you must decide whether you want squares or rectangles. Squares must be exactly square—I use a cardboard strip as a template—or your eye will see that they are off. If you decide to weave rectangles, they should clearly be rectangles, not "nearly squares", which will look like an error. Depending on how you want to draw the eye and whether you want to make use of bias in your garment (in which a square is quite handsome), you may treadle the sequence given here to weave the figure either way.

The woolen-spun tweed yarn fulls a little more than the worsted-spun Merino when the fabric is washed. Full the cloth only enough to fluff the tweed but not enough to full the Merino. The fulling makes the overcheck more highly textured.

Wool and silk skirt fabric (#3, page 137)

The third fabric is made of Merino wool and silk. The warp is a coppery blend of silk and Merino. The weft is 100 percent silk. The structure is mostly plain weave with a little knotlike figure composed of warp floats alternating with weft floats to form squares. The floats in adjacent quadrants run in different directions. The silk, a more lustrous yarn—also slightly stronger, so you may wish to use it for warp instead—adds a bit of sparkle to the ground-cloth areas and a lovely textural contrast in the knots.

Where the knots appear in the cloth there is less friction, encouraging a tendency to beat the cloth more closely. I took care not to overbeat those places. If you keep the plain-weave areas constant, everything will be all right.

Waffle-weave sweater fabric (#4, page 137)

The fourth and final fabric in this collection was intended to be used for a sweater. I visualized the body and sleeves—dolman sleeves perhaps, all cut in one—woven of this highly elastic fabric, with knitted cuffs and waistband.

I chose a six-shaft waffle weave. Four-shaft waffle lacks drama and an eight-shaft waffle has, perhaps, too much, at least for most garments. Simple waffle weaves have long floats: double the number of shafts and subtract 3 to find out how long the floats will be. Thus, a four-shaft floats over 5 ([2 x 4] – 3), a six-shaft float, over 9, and an eight-shaft float, over 13. Unless the yarns are fine and closely set, waffle-weave structures soon get out of hand and produce long floats that tend to snag on everything.

I used several yarns in the warp and weft. I chose the tweed for the face of the fabric because it fulls the most, stabilizing the longest floats. The next yarn into the cell is worsted. At the center of the cells is a little surprise, a single thread of intense violet. At a glance from a distance it is more or less hidden, but closer inspection reveals a bright little dot winking up from the deepest part of the cell.

These yarns in themselves are a little elastic, but the structure adds enormously to the stretchiness of the cloth. I like a sweater with some give; it is the elasticity of knitting that makes knitted sweaters so comfortable. When I decided to weave a sweater fabric, I chose an elastic structure to produce the same comfort. This fabric is very cuddly, besides being elastic. I can barely touch it without wanting to bury my fingers in it, squeeze it, and watch it rebound when I open my hand. I'd love to wear it.

When I completed this set of four fabrics and looked at them again, I realized that I had chosen colors bearing the same relationship to each other as those in the collection just before it. These colors are forested hills in smoky, autumn light. They are also the colors of southern Utah as the winter sun goes down, saddening the orange and peach to copper and casting violet shadows which repeat the violet gray of the fading sky.

I wish you could touch them. When I show them in a seminar or workshop, I find myself stroking them as I speak and handling them more than is actually needed. Magnetic cloth . . . a whole new concept. . . .

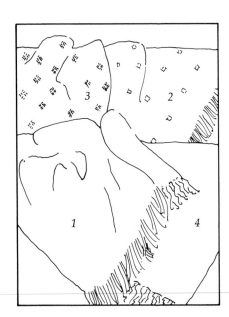

SWATCH COLLECTION #19

This collection appeared in the March/April 1989 issue of HAND-WOVEN, an issue almost entirely devoted to linen: where it comes from, how to use it, and practical tips for success in weaving it. When the theme was announced, I thought that this was the time to make an entire spring/summer collection from pure linen. Of all the fibers readily available to us, linen is the coolest: it conducts heat well. It is also absorbent, and dries so quickly that it wicks the moisture away from your skin and surrenders it to the air.

I thought about the other things that commend linen, particularly the lovely crispness of freshly ironed linen. I wanted to suggest the crispness visually as well, so that the eye would send the message "crisp" before the hand touched the cloth. I thought, too, about the kinds of structures that are most beautiful in linen. To suggest crispness, I contrasted a deep blue with half-bleached white. Because that looked slightly austere, I added natural linen to soften the contrast and provide a slightly sophisticated color pairing with the blue.

I have used a lot of linen and have grown to love it. I especially like what happens to it as it is laundered repeatedly. I think linen, like cheeses and fine wines, grows better and better as the years pass.

I have learned that linen is rather like my favorite English teacher in high school. Miss Thompson was demanding; nothing less than best work would do. And by demanding a lot she taught me to love doing more than I knew I could do. Linen is like that: you must use good weaving technique as you handle it because it is not elastic and forgiving like wool. The rewards of the extra effort and attention are correspondingly great.

Take extra care as you measure and beam your warp. If you introduce tension inequalities, they will persist throughout the warp. Linen is not elastic, so if you design a fabric with two different rates of take-up, either alternate the structures in the cloth so that the different blocks "catch up" with each other or beam them separately.

Linen is stronger damp than dry. Although it has wonderful tensile strength, it is subject to abrasion. The mere action of the reed on a very fine singles yarn can cause it to seem to evaporate before your eyes. If you find your selvedge threads starting to fray away, dampen the warp with a plant mister to strengthen it. That is usually all that is required. In more extreme cases, a warp sizing might be the best plan, but it was not necessary for the yarns used here. Be certain that the cloth is dry before it is wound onto the cloth storage beam to avoid mildew!

I routinely tame snarly bobbins by dunking them briefly in warm water just before I use them and draining them before putting them into the shuttle. Sometimes I just use the plant mister on the bobbins if I don't want to dunk them (plastic bobbins only: water makes paper quills too limp and is not good for wooden bobbins).

Remember that linen wrinkles easily and simply let that happen. You may consider the wrinkles the hallmark of a linen fabric. The only way to avoid them in an all-linen fabric is to apply resinous surface finishes, a process not available to the handweaver and one, incidentally, which robs linen of most of its absorbency and wicking properties.

Reed marks tend to stay in linen fabrics longer than in any other. Thorough manipulation of the fabric as it is washed will help erase them. That manipulation is also required to develop the full beauty of lacy structures woven in linen. Thoughtful selection of a reed is a good place to start: two ends per dent is preferable to three, and an even denting is preferred over an irregular one (such as 2/1/2/1).

The first fabric is woven entirely of half-bleached linen. Linen threads stay crisp and a little formal in the cloth, exactly the right thing for a lace weave because the lace is crisply defined.

I chose a very simple structure, Bronson lace in two blocks. I concentrated throughout this collection on squares; they appear in all four fabrics. The lace blocks alternate in a checkerboard, which produced the squares I wanted and evened up the take-up of the warp.

Washed, the lace develops fully and makes a light, cool, summery fabric. I had in mind a very simply cut, loose-fitting top, one cut like an over-sized T-shirt with cap, rather than set-in, sleeves.

Bronson lace top (#1, page 138)

The second fabric is jacket weight. It combines plain weave and 2/2 basket weave in a checkerboard pattern. The warp is natural linen and the weft deep blue, which further highlights the structure because there are little dots of blue and natural in the plain weave and dots four times the size of the little ones in basket weave.

Eight shafts are required to weave this structure. If you have four shafts, you may weave something similar by threading alternating blocks to plain weave and 2/2 basket. You may weave those structures in warpwise stripes but not create the checkerboard. You may alternately thread to a straight draw and weave stripes in the weft direction if you prefer. The former way permits you to set the basket areas a little more closely but requires beaming the two areas separately because the rates of take-up are different. The latter does not allow for changes in the thread count, except in the weft direction.

Checkerboard jacket fabric (#2, page 138)

The third fabric is just the right weight for a shirt/jacket or a long skirt with soft pleats. The check combines half-bleached and dark blue in the warp and natural and dark blue in the weft. It is woven like a classic gingham but is more interesting, I think, because of the interplay of the half-bleached and unbleached yarns. The structure is classically simple: good, reliable plain weave. It feels wonderful.

Checked shirt/jacket or skirt fabric (#3, page 139)

The fourth and final fabric in this series is also jacket weight and uses the square motif again. This time the squares do not show up in a checkerboard but are isolated. I wanted to create a more dramatic fabric calling attention to the square and allowing it to stand on its own.

A first attempt just didn't work well in linen. I created squares made up of little squares of warp-faced and weft-faced twill. They alternated five across

Color-and-weave-effect jacket fabric (#4, page 139)

and five up and down. It was an interesting idea, but the structure would have required fulling to hold its integrity—not an option with linen.

Disappointed in that structure, I decided to create one which was as firm as could be. What I wanted to do was make a very graphic-looking cloth with squares on a ground. I decided to stripe the squares and the ground, but make the stripes run one way in the squares and the other way in the ground.

What I needed was a color-and-weave effect cloth. I drew out a color-and-weave effect-diagram that showed how I wanted the cloth to look and worked backward from that to come up with the threading, the warp and weft color sequences, and the treadling. In no time, the cloth was coming off the loom just as I had envisioned it. The structure is basically plain weave, the most stable structure of all; there were no distortions or sleazy places in this cloth!

There they were: four 100 percent linen fabrics, all patterned with squares, either standing alone or in a checkerboard array. They looked crisp, cool, and very linen-y.

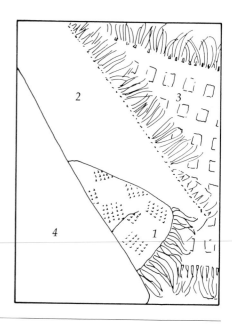

SWATCH COLLECTION #20

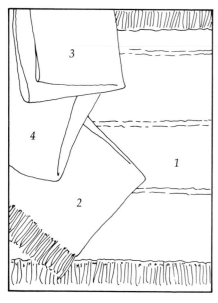

The fabrics in a collection are always linked by their colors; this one is no exception. In addition, these fabrics are linked structurally: all have some kind of twill structure. Twill is a good choice for winter fabrics because the thread count (number of ends and picks per inch) is always higher in a twill than in a plain weave and twill provides a pleasant drape in the cloth.

Brown was my first color choice. I wanted to create a sense of elegance and warmth in these fabrics so I played the brown off against warm gray and then warmed the fabrics further by introducing a strong bluish red.

Three of the fabrics are wool, one cotton. Of the wools, one is worsted and two, woolen-spun. The worsted yarn produces a sophisticated fabric with a clear, smooth surface while woolen yarns create earthier fabrics that full for greater warmth and wind resistance and look less formal.

Twill suit fabric (#1, page 140)

The first fabric in this collection is a Katharine Hepburn sort of fabric: tailored, elegant, understated, and very "finished" looking. It is a simple 2/2 twill, woven firmly yet fairly lightweight, suited for use in making slacks, a tailored jacket, or a suit.

The colors in this fabric are also understated. The warp is mostly dark brown with four-end gray stripes. The weft is primarily gray with fine stripes of dark brown. The result is a fabric made up mostly of a blend of gray and dark brown with vertical stripes of gray and horizontal stripes of dark brown.

The hand of the finished fabric is wonderfully crisp. Crumple it in your hand, squeeze it very hard, and then release it; it comes back practically wrinkle-free. That quality makes it a good choice for slacks or a skirt. (Lining the garment also helps to make it wrinkle-resistant.)

Undulating twill jacket fabric (#2, page 140)

The second fabric is an eight-shaft undulating twill. Undulating twills may be constructed in several ways: by cramming and skipping dents to vary the sett of the cloth (not the most dramatic) or via the threading or the treadling—or both!

An undulating twill created on a straight draw by skipping sheds and throwing more than one shot in some sheds works very well, but when more than one shot is introduced into the same shed, some technical problems arise. The second pass of the shuttle through the same shed pulls the first shot out—unproductive, to say the least. To avoid that, the weft must be caught somehow at the edge. A floating selvedge is the most practical solution. The treadling of an undulating twill is more complicated than that for a straight twill; if matching the fabric at seams is not a consideration, it can be changed freely as the weaving progresses so that it doesn't repeat in an even and obvious way.

The twill shown here was treadled very simply but threaded in a complex way. By putting the undulations into the threading, the repeats may be even as they are here and easily matched at seams (or uneven if you prefer). The weaving goes swiftly because, for an eight-shaft twill, there are eight trea-

dles used one after the other in a straight treadling. (Be sure to arrange them so that you can alternate feet in a walking motion.) It is necessary to pay attention as you thread so that errors are not introduced.

I like undulating twills for lots of reasons. I like their curvaceous lines; there are only a few ways to distort dramatically the grid that is such an integral part of weaving weft across warp. I like the drape of the cloth and the weight of it.

Undulating twills have some qualities characteristic of their structure. They tend to be spongy at best and mushy at worst where more than one thread is on the same shaft (or more than one shot is in the same shed). I get around that problem by sleying the warp everywhere about 10 to 15 percent more closely than I would for the same yarn in that twill if it were not undulating. Don't be tempted to sley it irregularly (by using a different warp density at different places in the cloth), because the variable sett will reduce the undulations. The threading—or treadling, or both—is relatively complicated. There is no way to avoid that complication: it is the basis of the structure. The floats in the fabric may be quite long. I always make a sample first to see whether the float length is acceptable. A woolen-spun fabric can support a longer float than one that is worsted-spun because the fulling process helps hold the threads in place, but too vigorous fulling can blur the structure significantly.

Striped cotton dress fabric (#3, page 140)

The third fabric, the only cotton cloth in this collection, has contrasting stripes on a plain-weave ground. It is made of a lustrous pearl cotton. I wanted to highlight the stripes by raising them up above the surface of the cloth. There are fine, two-end gray stripes separated by two ends of dark brown and heavier, eight-end red stripes.

I knew that I could lift the stripes up onto the surface of the cloth by weaving them in a warp-faced twill interlacement, but I didn't want the four-end stripes which a full repeat would require. I couldn't see why I needed to thread a full repeat for each stripe and sampled to see how the fabric would look with smaller stripes; two-end stripes were the narrowest ones which would make a smooth, unbroken line.

The scale of the cloth shown here is right for a shirtwaist dress, either cut straight or with a waistline and a pleated skirt. If the fabric were used for a blouse or shirt, the large expanse of brown might be reduced by one-third and half the gray stripes (and the brown stripes between them) eliminated to make a smaller repeat.

Striped coat fabric (#4, page 141)

I designed the fourth fabric in this collection for an eye-catching coat. I wanted strong vertical stripes crossed by an occasional strong horizontal stripe of a contrasting color. Because I intended to use the fabric for a coat, I wanted a woolen-spun fabric which could be fulled to be more windproof.

I could have made the vertical stripes using double weave, but I didn't want the fabric to be double-layered. I decided to use two-block twill, treadled so the same block was always warp-faced, except where the contrasting stripe streaked across. Each twill block requires four shafts, so this would be an eight-shaft structure. The warp is warm gray and the primary weft is dark brown. The red horizontal stripe is weft-faced twill (1/3) all the way across. Eight treadles are required: four for the two-block (vertically striped) sections and four for the horizontal weft-faced stripes. Any time you have more than one twill block, they may be woven as if they were just one block by making the same structure appear in all blocks.

I would like to weave this fabric in a bolder colorway as well: a white warp and black weft would make black-and-white vertical stripes which I could cross at intervals in narrow horizontal stripes with the three primary colors, bright red, yellow, and blue, one at a time. It wouldn't fit into this collection and wouldn't be suited to the shy, but I think it would be very handsome.

Each of these fabrics incorporates twill structure but each one feels different. The cotton is lightest, mostly by virtue of its plain-weave ground and the fineness of the 20/2 pearl cotton. The worsted fabric is next, with its allover 2/2 twill making a supple twill in this crisp worsted. The two-block twill is the next heaviest fabric, with 1/3 and 3/1 twill interlacement in considerably bulkier yarns; and the undulating twill, in the same yarns, is thickest of all because of the places where the undulations occur. I'm always pleased when I can take one structure and create several very different fabrics based on it.

GENERAL INSTRUCTIONS

Please read the instructions thoroughly before beginning a project. The instructions assume that you have basic weaving knowledge, can warp a loom, and can understand drafts.

WARP & WEFT: The size, fiber, and type of each yarn is listed along with the yardage per pound. If a specific brand has been used, it is listed with color names and numbers. Amounts needed are calculated in yards, making yarn substitutions easier.

REED SUBSTITUTIONS: Maintaining the number of ends per inch is very important to obtain the same weight and hand of a fabric. Most fabrics are sleyed one or two ends per dent, but a particular dent reed or denting is used for a certain effect or to accommodate large or textured yarns.

DRAFTS: Threading drafts read from right to left and treadling drafts read from top to bottom. *Threading repeats* are shown by brackets. Sometimes double brackets

are used to show a small repeat within a larger one. *Tie-ups* are shown for rising-shed or jack looms. The small circle in the tie-up indicates that the shaft referred to *rises* when the treadle is pressed. To convert the tie-up for sinking-shed or counterbalanced looms, tie the treadles according to the *blank* squares. Countermarch looms use all the squares; the upper lamms are tied to the blank squares and the lower lamms are tied to the squares with circles.

MAKING CHANGES: We encourage you to create, adapt, and change the swatches featured here. Although following the directions with no deviations will produce a copy of the fabric shown, use the directions as a starting point for your own design. Just remember, as designers do, to allow yourself plenty of leeway for any changes you make. Extra yarn and a

longer warp are a wise investment when you anticipate *any* changes from the printed directions. Our publication *Yarn* will help when making substitutions, and weaving a sample of your intended design will provide you with needed information.

WEAVING WITH TABBY: Sometimes weavers use the terms tabby and plain weave interchangeably. In the directions we differentiate plain weave as the weave structure and tabby as the binder or background weft in pattern weaves such as overshot. In weave structures which use tabby, the plain-weave treadles are noted separately, and only pattern rows are written in the treadling with a note saying "Use Tabby". "Use Tabby" means to alternate a row of pattern with a row of plain weave. The plain-weave treadles alternate also. Two shuttles are needed, one for the pattern yarn and the other for the tabby yarn. The shuttles alternate row by row for the length of the pattern.

FLOATING SELVEDGES: Some weave structures don't make good selvedges; the weft doesn't catch the edge warps as often or as consistently as you would like for a good-looking and structurally sound selvedge. When this problem occurs, float-

---

YARN CHART. To help identify yarns and make creative substitutions in your weaving, use this yarn chart along with *Yarn, a Resource Guide for Handweavers* by Celia Quinn, available from Interweave Press.

Wools

24/2 worsted at 6400 yd/lb (12,880 m/kg)

20/2 worsted at 5600 yd/lb (11,280 m/kg)

18/2 worsted at 5040 yd/lb (10,150 m/kg)

2-ply worsted at 4900 yd/lb (9870 m/kg)

18-cut single-ply woolen at 3600 yd/lb (7250 m/kg)

12/2 worsted at 3200 yd/lb (6440 m/kg)

12/3 worsted at 2240 yd/lb (4510 m/kg)

2-ply Shetland-style at 2000 yd/lb (4030 m/kg)

Singles at 2000 yd/lb (4030 m/kg)

Singles tweed at 2000 yd/lb (4030 m/kg)

Singles tweed at 1700 yd/lb (3420 m/kg)

2-ply at 1470 yd/lb (2970 m/kg)

Bouclé at 300 yd/lb (600 m/kg)

Silks

30/2 at 7250–7850 yd/lb (14,600 m/kg)

Singles noil at 4400 yd/lb (8860 m/kg)

12/2 at 2970–3300 yd/lb (5980 m/kg)

YARN CHART. To help identify yarns and make creative substitutions in your weaving, use this yarn chart along with *Yarn, a Resource Guide for Handweavers* by Celia Quinn, available from Interweave Press.

Cottons

00/3 mercerized at 14,000 yd/lb (28,210 m/kg)

30/2 mercerized at 12,600 yd/lb (25,390 m/kg)

20/2 mercerized at 8400 yd/lb (16,920 m/kg)

16/2 mercerized at 6700 yd/lb (13,500 m/kg)

10/2 mercerized at 4200 yd/lb (8460 m/kg)

8/2 at 3600 yd/lb (7250 m/kg)

5/2 mercerized at 2100 yd/lb (4230 m/kg)

3/2 mercerized at 1260 yd/lb (2530 m/kg)

Slub ratiné novelty at 1000 yd/lb (2010 m/kg)

Linens

16/1 at 5450–5500 yd/lb (10,980 m/kg)

14/1 at 4200 yd/lb (8460 m/kg)

10/1 at 3000 yd/lb (6040 m/kg)

16/2 at 2420–2720 yd/lb (4870 m/kg)

16/2 dry-spun at 2400 yd/lb (4830 m/kg)

Cottolin

22/2 (50% cotton/50% linen) at 3170 yd/lb (6400 m/kg)

Ratiné (80% cotton/20% linen) at 720 yd/lb (1450 m/kg)

Other

18/2 wool/silk (50% wool/50% silk) at 5040 yd/lb (10,150 m/kg)

Loop (58% wool/30% mohair/12% nylon) at 1350 yd/lb (2720 m/kg)

2-ply linen/rayon (50% linen/50% rayon) at 1200 yd/lb (2420 m/kg)

Brushed (70% mohair/25% wool/5% nylon) at 1170 yd/lb (2350 m/kg)

ing selvedges are often recommended. Floating selvedges are the first and last warp yarns sleyed in the reed but omitted from the heddles. Instead of rising and falling with the treadling, they float slightly above the bottom of the shed and are woven by hand. As the shuttle enters the shed it goes on top of the floating selvedge. As the shuttle exits the shed it goes under the floating selvedge. The thumb of the hand that receives the shuttle can assist by holding the floating selvedge up. In every row, the sequence is the same: over, then under. It's alphabetical. By the way, if you're treadling plain weave you don't need floating selvedges because the weave structure will give you over, then under.

PRODUCT INFORMATION. Your local yarn shop will carry many of the yarns featured in this issue. If they don't have a particular yarn in stock, check with them about substituting similar yarns or ordering yarns for you.

If you don't have a local yarn shop, you can write to these suppliers about locating the dealers nearest you. Wholesale suppliers have been noted with an *.

Borgs, Glimåkra Looms 'n Yarns, 1304 Scott St., Petaluma, CA 94952.

Cotton Clouds, Rt. 2, Desert Hills, #16, Safford, AZ 85546.

Frederick J. Fawcett, Inc., 1304 Scott St., Petaluma, CA 94954.

Fort Crailo Yarns, PO Box 6, Newburgh, NY 12550.

Halcyon Yarn, 12 School St., Bath, ME 04530.

*Harrisville Desgins, Harrisville, NH 03450.

*Henry's Attic, 5 Mercury Ave., Monroe, NY 10950.

JaggerSpun, Water Street, PO Box 188, Springvale, ME 04083.

*Oregon Worsted, PO Box 02098, Portland, OR 97202.

Robison-Anton, PO Box 159, Fairview, NJ 07022.

*Scotts Woolen Mill, 528 Jefferson Ave., Bristol, PA 19007.

Silk Tree, Box 78, Whonnock, British Columbia, Canada V0M 1S0.

Weaver's Way, PO Box 70, Columbus, NC 28722.

#1: Skirt Fabric

PROJECT NOTES: When choosing colors for this cloth, it is a good idea to pick ground colors that are nearly the same, for uniform intermixing, but they should contrast in value with the twill stripes. With brilliant colors, use clear white or a clear dark color for the twill stripes. Off-white works nicely with subdued colors.

FABRIC DESCRIPTION: Skirt: plain weave with warp-faced twill stripes and weft-faced twill bands. Pants: 2/2 twill with same stripes and bands. 4-shaft versions: plain weave and 2/2 twill.

WARP & WEFT: 20/2 mercerized cotton at 8400 yd/lb: light green, light blue, and natural off-white.

E.P.I.: Skirt: 36 of colors and 54 of natural (that is, in an 18-dent reed, sley the colors 2 per dent and the off-white 3 per dent). Pants: 48 of colors and 72 of natural (that is, in a 12-dent reed, sley the colors 4 per dent and the off-white 6 per dent). 4-shaft versions: 48 e.p.i.

TAKE-UP & SHRINKAGE: 8% in width and 11% in length.

WEAVING: Follow the warp color order in the weft, treadling each fabric to square the warp sequence.

FINISHING: Hemstitch both ends of fabric while on the loom. Machine wash on regular cycle; hang to dry. Press while slightly damp.

WARP COLOR ORDER FOR FABRIC #1: For the 4-shaft versions, use only 8 ends of natural (instead of 12) in each stripe.

		X			
light green			36	36	= 72 per repeat
light blue	36	36			= 72 per repeat
natural		12	12	12	12	= 48 per repeat

DRAFT FOR FABRIC #1:

C = color   N = natural

4-Shaft Version:

plain weave (skirt)

twill (pants)

#2: Caftan Fabric

PROJECT NOTES: This fabric takes advantage of the differences in elasticity and shrinkage of cotton and wool to create seersucker.

FABRIC DESCRIPTION: Plain weave.

WARP: 20/2 mercerized cotton at 8400 yd/lb: yellow, light green, and light blue.
20/2 wool worsted at 5600 yd/lb: white.

WEFT: 20/2 mercerized cotton at 8400 yd/lb: white.

E.P.I.: 24 of wool, 40 of cotton (that is, in a 12-dent reed, sley the wool 2 per dent and the cotton 3, 3, 4 in 3 dents).

WARP COLOR ORDER:

			X		
yellow cotton				10	= 10 per repeat
lt. green cotton		10			= 10 per repeat
lt. blue cotton	10		10		= 20 per repeat
white wool	6	6	6	6	= 24 per repeat

DRAFT:

TAKE-UP & SHRINKAGE: 9% in width.

WEAVING: Beam this warp firmly, allowing the wool to stretch as it is beamed so that wool and cotton parts are the same length. Weave with the cotton weft.

FINISHING: Hemstitch both ends of fabric while on the loom. The way this fabric is washed is crucial. Hand wash it in warm water, rinsing well. Hang the fabric and shake and straighten it by hand. The wool sections pucker by themselves. Do not press this fabric. If pressing is unavoidable (as in construction of the garment), dip the fabric/garment in warm water and permit it to dry again. To hand wash a finished garment, use lukewarm water and mild detergent. Rinse thoroughly and hang to dry—a truly drip-dry fabric. Expect to weave 37" to get one yard, washed.

#3: Blouse Fabric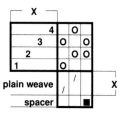

PROJECT NOTES: Spaced warp and weft create little windows in a plain-weave cloth for this airy blouse fabric.

FABRIC DESCRIPTION: Spaced plain weave.

WARP & WEFT: 20/2 mercerized cotton at 8400 yd/lb: natural off-white.

E.P.I.: About 27 (2, 2, 2, 2, 2, 2, 0, 0, 0 in a 20-dent reed).

DRAFT:

P.P.I.: Same as e.p.i.

TAKE-UP & SHRINKAGE: 10% in width and length.

plain weave

spacer

WEAVING:
Weave 12 picks of plain weave. Lift shafts 2-3 and insert the first spacer (see below). Weave another 12 picks of plain weave. Lift shafts 2-3 and insert the second spacer. Repeat this sequence, removing the first spacer and reinserting it, then removing and reinserting the second

spacer. The warp and weft spaces should be exactly balanced.

Spacer: The spacer needs to be very smooth and slick. A wooden dowel probably won't work. An acrylic rod 1/16" in diameter (look in the Yellow Pages under "Plastics") is perfect. A very good substitute is 2mm rat-tail satin cord. The spacer needs to be at least 8" longer than the width of the warp so that it sticks out far enough at one selvedge to be grasped and pulled out of the cloth.

FINISHING: Hemstitch both ends of fabric while on the loom. Machine wash in hot water on regular cycle. Air dry; iron. (This structure is stable under normal home laundry conditions.)

ALTERNATIVES: The spaces in the cloth must be balanced exactly, warp and weft. If larger spaces are wanted, the cloth may be set 4, 4, 4, 0, 0 in a 10-dent reed. This sett requires a ⅛"-diameter rod or 3mm cord as a weft spacer to balance the warp spaces.

If you wish to experiment, you will find that the shed through which the spacer is inserted is critical for the size of the weft space left. A tabby shed produces a larger hole and a one-over-three shed makes a smaller hole. It is essential to launder the cloth before judging the balance of the spaces.

#4: Dress Fabric ❽

PROJECT NOTES: Any color can be used for this fabric, but lighter colors show the texture best. Size 10/2 cotton can be substituted for the doubled 20/2 warp and weft; the resulting cloth will not be as supple.

FABRIC DESCRIPTION: Twill variation.

WARP & WEFT: 20/2 mercerized cotton at 8400 yd/lb, used doubled: light blue.

E.P.I.: 20 doubled ends.

DRAFT: (at right). Note that the third and fifth and the fourth and sixth treadles are tied up alike.

P.P.I.: 20 doubled picks.

TAKE-UP & SHRINKAGE: 2% in width and 10% in length.

WEAVING: Use the weft doubled on the bobbin. Follow the treadling draft, striving for an even beat and squared pattern.

FINISHING: Hemstitch both ends of fabric while on the loom. Machine wash in warm water on regular cycle. Air dry until slightly damp; press on both sides until dry.

#5: Jacket Fabric ❹

PROJECT NOTES: This jacket cloth is a weft-faced twill with tabby ground. It is a surface-interest fabric with strongly textured face and smooth, comfortable backing.

FABRIC DESCRIPTION: 1/3 twill and plain weave.

WARP: 20/2 mercerized cotton at 8400 yd/lb, used doubled: natural off-white.

WEFT: Tabby—20/2 same as warp, used doubled: natural off-white.

Twill—cotton/linen ratiné at 720 yd/lb: natural off-white/tan.

YARN SOURCES & COLORS: This twill weft is Irish Lace (80% cotton/20% linen) from Henry's Attic.

E.P.I.: 18 doubled ends.

DRAFT: Note: The understated diagonal line in the fabric can be broken by changing the ratiné treadling sequence to 1, 3, 2, 4; do not change the tabby sequence.

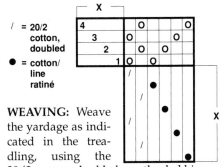

/ = 20/2 cotton, doubled

● = cotton/line ratiné

WEAVING: Weave the yardage as indicated in the treadling, using the 20/2 cotton doubled on the bobbin as tabby alternately with the ratiné pattern.

FINISHING: Hemstitch both ends of fabric while on the loom. Machine wash in hot water on regular cycle; air dry. When nearly dry, press from the wrong side to preserve the surface texture.

DRAFT FOR FABRIC #4:

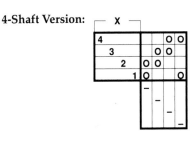

SWATCH COLLECTION #2

pages 26–28

#1: Coat Fabric ❹ ❻

PROJECT NOTES: This twill jacket fabric features an overcheck of bulky wool novelty yarn. If the heddle eyes of your loom are too small, you may need to tie large-eyed string heddles for the novelty warp ends.

FABRIC DESCRIPTION: 2/2 twill with 1/3 overcheck.

WARP: Twill—wool singles at 2000 yd/lb: white, gray-tan, and beige.

Overcheck—wool bouclé at 300 yd/lb: natural off-white.

WEFT: Twill—wool singles at 2000 yd/lb: beige, gray-brown, and gray-tan.

Overcheck—same as warp.

YARN SOURCES & COLORS: This wool singles is Harrisville Singles: White, Suede (gray-tan), Oatmeal (beige), and Hickory (gray-brown). The bouclé is Toros II from Henry's Attic.

E.P.I.: 18 for singles and 6 for bouclé (that is, in a 6-dent reed, sley the singles 3 per dent, with 2 in the last dent of the stripe, and sley the bouclé 1 per dent).

WARP COLOR ORDER: (on next page).

DRAFT: *Six-shaft version*: Follow Warp Color Order in the threading. In the treadling, use 20 gray-tan (Suede), 2 bouclé, 20 gray-brown (Hickory), 2 bouclé, 20 gray-tan (Suede), 2 bouclé, 20 beige (Oatmeal), and 2 bouclé. *Four-shaft version*: Follow the same Warp Color Order and treadling color order as the 6-shaft version. The cloth will be similar, although lacking some of the contrast in texture.

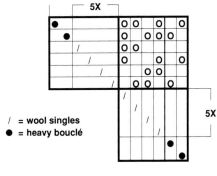

/ = wool singles
● = heavy bouclé

4-Shaft Version:

WARP COLOR ORDER FOR FABRIC #1:

	X				
white (White)	20				= 20 per repeat
gray-tan (Suede)		20			= 20 per repeat
beige (Oatmeal)			20	20	= 40 per repeat
bouclé	2	2	2	2	= 8 per repeat

P.P.I.: 18 for singles and 6 for bouclé.

WEAVING: Follow the weft color order given with the draft. Beat to square, and avoid crushing the bulky bouclé weft into a tight shed.

FINISHING: Hemstitch on the loom at both ends to prevent raveling. Wash by hand in very warm water (about 100° F) and mild liquid detergent. Allow the fabric to soak, then squeeze in large handfuls. Rinse at the same temperature. Hang to dry. Steam press on the wrong side with a folded terry towel under it to pad the textured surface.

#2: Skirt Fabric ❹

PROJECT NOTES: Cloth like this with one color of warp and another of weft will show clearly any unevenness of beat. If that is likely to be a problem, you should choose warp and weft colors that are close in value or identical.

FABRIC DESCRIPTION: 2/2 twill.

WARP: Wool singles at 2000 yd/lb: gray-brown.

WEFT: Same as warp: gray-tan.

YARN SOURCES & COLORS: These are Harrisville Singles. The warp is Hickory and the weft is Suede.

E.P.I.: 20.

DRAFT:

P.P.I.: 20

WEAVING: Strive for an even beat and a 45° twill angle.

FINISHING: Hemstitch ends to prevent raveling. Hand wash in mild liquid detergent solution at about 100° F and rinse three times. Hang to air dry and steam press.

#3: Dress Fabric ❷ ❹

FABRIC DESCRIPTION: Plain weave.

WARP: Single-ply wool at 3600 yd/lb: tan.

WEFT: Same as warp: pale gray.

YARN SOURCES & COLORS: The yarn originally used is no longer available. You could substitute a comparable wool singles such as Halcyon's Coventry Heather.

E.P.I.: 24.

DRAFT:

P.P.I.: 20 (which will finish to 23).

FINISHING: Hemstitch ends of fabric. Steam press on both sides before washing to help control tracking. Wash gently, following yarn supplier's instructions. Spin briefly in a washing machine to remove excess water, and hang or lay flat until nearly dry. Steam press until smooth and dry. A professional press will give a crisper finish if desired.

#4: Blouse and Dress Fabrics ❷ ❹

FABRIC DESCRIPTION: Plain weave.

WARP & WEFT: 16/2 mercerized cotton at 6700 yd/lb: earthy red.

10/2 mercerized cotton at 4200 yd/lb: brown.

YARN SOURCES & COLORS: The 16/2 that was used is no longer available. You could substitute Carolina Cotton Perle 16/2 from Weaver's Way.

E.P.I.: 30.

WARP COLOR ORDER:

	X	
red 16/2	30	
brown 10/2		2

for large check, or . . .

	X
	15
	1

for small check.

DRAFT:

P.P.I.: 30.

WEAVING: Weave plain weave, following the same color order in the weft as in the warp. Strive for an even beat that will square each check.

FINISHING: Hemstitch ends on the loom or machine stitch to prevent raveling. Machine wash, regular cycle. May be partially machine dried. Iron the fabric before it is completely dry.

#5: Coat/Sport Jacket Fabric ❹

PROJECT NOTES: This fabric combines stripes of dornick (broken point twill) with stripes of 2/2 basket weave. For a man's sport jacket, you might prefer a slightly more conservative weave attained by narrowing the basket weave to 8 or 12 ends. The basket-weave stripe must be threaded in multiples of 4 ends or the edges of the stripe will merge with the herringbone and look messy and flawed.

FABRIC DESCRIPTION: 2/2 dornick twill and 2/2 basket.

WARP: Single-ply wool at 3600 yd/lb: pale gray.

WEFT: Same as warp: dark gray.

YARN SOURCES & COLORS: The yarn originally used is no longer available. You could substitute a comparable wool singles such as Halcyon's Coventry Heather.

E.P.I.: 30.

DRAFT:

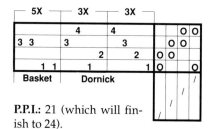

P.P.I.: 21 (which will finish to 24).

WEAVING: Strive for an even beat to avoid streaks in the finished cloth. This one-shuttle weave moves along nicely.

FINISHING: Hemstitch the ends to prevent raveling. Steam press on both sides to help prevent tracking. Hand wash following manufacturer's instructions. Spin briefly in the washing machine to remove excess water and hang or lay flat until nearly dry. Steam press until smooth.

SWATCH COLLECTION #3

pages 29–31

#1: Blouse Fabric ❹

PROJECT NOTES: The floats in this fabric can be woven with a contrasting color—the stronger the contrast, the more dramatic the fabric. If the floats are not cut, they will fluff up for an interesting effect when the fabric is washed.

FABRIC DESCRIPTION: Plain weave with loom-controlled brocading.

WARP & WEFT: 16/2 mercerized cotton at 6700 yd/lb: yellow.

YARN SOURCES & COLORS: The yarn originally used is no longer available. You could substitute Carolina Cotton Perle 16/2 from Weaver's Way.

E.P.I.: 30.

DRAFT: on next page.

P.P.I.: 30.

TAKE-UP & SHRINKAGE: 5% in width and 10% in length.

DRAFT FOR FABRIC #1:

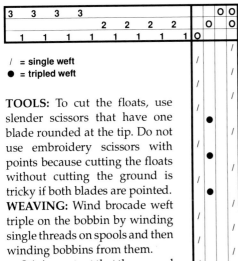

/ = single weft
● = tripled weft

TOOLS: To cut the floats, use slender scissors that have one blade rounded at the tip. Do not use embroidery scissors with points because cutting the floats without cutting the ground is tricky if both blades are pointed.

WEAVING: Wind brocade weft triple on the bobbin by winding single threads on spools and then winding bobbins from them.

It is important that the ground cloth be woven square so that the floats, when cut, will be secure to washing. Every two or three inches, cut the floats while the fabric is still on the loom. Insert the rounded blade of the scissors under the float and cut it in the middle. Be careful not to cut the ground.

FINISHING: Hemstitch on the loom. Machine wash warm, gentle cycle, and line dry. Steam press from the wrong side; fluff the right side with the fingers while still warm and steamy. The cut ends become velvety.

#2: Dress Fabric   ❷ ❹

PROJECT NOTES: This fabric combines three weights of mercerized cotton for a subtly checked texture. The effect could be accentuated by using three very closely related colors instead of all one color.

FABRIC DESCRIPTION: Plain weave.

WARP & WEFT: 3/2 mercerized cotton at 1260 yd/lb: UKI color #111, Dark Gold.

5/2 mercerized cotton at 2100 yd/lb: UKI color #111, Dark Gold.

10/2 mercerized cotton at 4200 yd/lb: UKI color #111, Dark Gold.

E.P.I.: In an 8-dent reed, sley the 3/2 1 per dent, the 5/2 2 per dent, and the 10/2 3 per dent.

WARP ORDER:

		X		
3/2	2			= 2 per repeat
5/2		4	4	= 8 per repeat
10/2			6	= 6 per repeat

DRAFT:

P.P.I.: Same as e.p.i.

WEAVING: Weave in the same order to square. Allow a couple of inches of warp to get the hang of it. The heavier yarns need a lighter beat.

FINISHING: Hemstitch on the loom. Machine wash warm to hot, gentle cycle. Line dry until barely damp and steam press. If allowed to dry without pressing, the fabric has a bubbly surface which is regular and very interesting. Do not overpress; the three-dimensionality (thick threads vs. thin ones) is the interesting thing about this fabric.

#3: Shawl Fabric   ❷ ❹

PROJECT NOTES: The loose, open fabric is about the weight of a sweater and is intended to be used that way. It is best in minimally constructed garments. A shawl (which requires no cutting and sewing except hemming), the Shannon sweater shown on page 52 of *Fashions from the Loom* by Betty J. Beard (Interweave Press, 1980), or the granny shrug on page 90 of the same book are suggested.

I think of this kind of fabric as "weaver's delight" because it uses up odds and ends of yarns and gives a rich-looking fabric that is seldom found in fabric shops. Almost any variety of yarns can be used this way. As long as they are used consecutively, the differences in the way yarns shrink will not be a problem; the shrinkage will only add to the texture. It is a good idea, however, to be sure that none of the yarns used in a mixed warp like this will bleed and discolor the cloth in a way that will be unacceptable.

FABRIC DESCRIPTION: Plain weave.

WARP: 16/2 mercerized cotton at 6700 yd/lb, used tripled: yellow.

2-ply linen/rayon at 1200 yd/lb: dark orange and dark yellow.

10/2 mercerized cotton at 4200 yd/lb: orange.

WEFT: Cotton slub ratiné novelty at 1000 yd/lb: natural off-white.

YARN SOURCES & COLORS: The linen/rayon warp is Scott's Linnay (50% linen/50% rayon): #21 Burnt Orange and #9 Straw. The novelty weft is Twirly from Henry's Attic. (Note: Some of the Linnay used in the original project was a single-ply version, no longer available.)

E.P.I.: 12.

WARP COLOR ORDER: below.

DRAFT:

P.P.I.: 8 or 9.

TAKE-UP & SHRINKAGE: 12% in width and 10% in length.

		X		
dk. orange linen/rayon	1	1		= 2 per repeat
16/2 yellow (used triple)		1		= 1 per repeat
10/2 orange			1	= 1 per repeat
dk. yellow linen/rayon			1	= 1 per repeat

WEAVING: While on the loom, this fabric looks quite open. To avoid beating it too closely, you may want to close the shed before beating (nudging, really) the weft into place.

FINISHING: Hemstitch on the loom. If the fabric is to be used as a shawl, it will be a good idea to finish the warp with a twisted fringe or hem as the Linnay yarns become flaky when washed much. Hand wash in very warm water.

#4: Skirt Fabric   ❷ ❹

PROJECT NOTES: The single-ply fine linen/rayon yarn used in the original version of this skirt fabric is no longer available. You might substitute one of the other yarns from the other swatches in this collection or design your own coordinating fabric.

FABRIC DESCRIPTION: Plain weave.

WARP: Single-ply linen/rayon at 2400 yd/lb: dark yellow and dark orange.

WEFT: Same as warp: dark orange.

YARN SOURCES & COLORS: No longer available (see Project Notes above).

E.P.I.: 15 or 16, depending on the reed available.

WARP COLOR ORDER: Alternate ends of the two colors.

DRAFT:

P.P.I.: Same as e.p.i.

TAKE-UP & SHRINKAGE: 9-10% in width and length.

WEAVING: Beat to square.

FINISHING: Hemstitch on the loom. Machine wash warm, gentle cycle. Shake out, smooth by hand, and hang to dry. Steam press while still slightly damp. Fabric will shed lint in this initial washing. Fabric hand improves with washing!

#5: Jacket Fabric ❷ ❹

PROJECT NOTES: This fabric is rather bulky and is best made in a style without a collar. It would also work nicely for a long vest without lapels.

FABRIC DESCRIPTION: Plain weave.

WARP & WEFT: 2-ply linen/rayon at 1200 yd/lb: dark orange.

YARN SOURCES & COLORS: This is Scott's Linnay (50% linen/50% rayon): #21 Burnt Orange.

E.P.I.: 12.

DRAFT:

P.P.I.: 12.

TAKE-UP & SHRINK-AGE: 10% in warp and weft.

WEAVING: Beat to square.

FINISHING: Same as for Fabric #4.

SWATCH COLLECTION #4

pages 32–35

Note: Several of the yarns used in this collection are no longer available. For the yarns mentioned in the text, the following substitutions have been made in the instructions: For the Shetland from Glass House Fiber Imports, substitute Harrisville Shetland Style in Garnet, Plum, and Aster. For the singles English wool from Glass House, substitute Harrisville Singles Tweed in Lavender (which has light brown flecks instead of the red-violet flecks of the original). The Zephyr worsted from Fort Crailo and the 20/2 worsted from Fawcett (Oregon Worsted's Willamette in #29 Wine) remain the same. For the 20/2 cotton from Robin & Russ, substitute UKI color #70, Orchid.

#1: Skirt Fabric ❷ ❹

PROJECT NOTES: The yarn originally used for this fabric was stretchy, so you may need to allow as much as 10% extra warp length in addition to take-up and loom waste allowances.

Use the fabric for an A-line or slightly flared skirt. When choosing a pattern, look for one that calls for "lightweight woolens", "lightweight flannel", or "Shetland".

FABRIC DESCRIPTION: Plain weave.

WARP & WEFT: 2-ply Shetland-style wool at 2000 yd/lb: dark red.

YARN SOURCES & COLORS: This was an import that is no longer available. You could use Harrisville Shetland Style: Garnet.

E.P.I.: 15.

DRAFT:

P.P.I.: 15.

WEAVING: Avoid beating too firmly—that will produce a stiff, boardlike fabric. Instead, use a light touch and strive for 15 p.p.i., which will produce a light, supple fabric.

FINISHING: Hemstitch on the loom. Hand wash in lukewarm water. Spin in a washing machine briefly to extract most of the water. Hang and smooth by hand. Steam press on both sides when nearly dry to the touch.

#2: Tweed Skirt Fabric ❷ ❹

PROJECT NOTES: Like fabric #1, this fabric would be suitable for an A-line or slightly flared skirt. Look for the description "medium-weight woolens" or "lightweight tweeds".

FABRIC DESCRIPTION: Plain weave.

WARP & WEFT: Wool singles tweed at 2000 yd/lb: light violet tweed.

YARN SOURCES & COLORS: This was an import that is no longer available. You could use Harrisville Singles Tweed: Lavender (which has light brown flecks instead of the red-violet flecks of the original).

E.P.I.: 15.

DRAFT:

P.P.I.: 15.

WEAVING: Beat gently to square (14–15 p.p.i.).

FINISHING: Hemstitch on the loom. Tweed yarns like this one often contain quite a lot of spinning oil. Wash this fabric in water that feels hot (105° F). If the washing water looks quite dirty (actually, it looks "milky", not dark), you may need to wash a second time. Rinse very well (at least twice at the same temperature). A little fabric softener in the last rinse (disperse it well before adding the fabric) will increase the softness of this tweed. Spin briefly in a washing machine to extract most of the water. Shake the fabric and smooth wrinkles by hand be-

fore letting it dry just a bit. It is absolutely necessary to press this fabric while it is wet. Take this fact into account when you start the finishing process—if you haven't enough time to take it all the way, do it another time.

#3: Jacket Fabric ❹

PROJECT NOTES: Choose a jacket or coat style with uncluttered lines. A pattern that suggests Shetland wool fabrics would be suitable. Be sure that the pattern you select does not rule out plaids. This plaid has stronger vertical lines than horizontal ones, which makes it more flattering for most of us.

FABRIC DESCRIPTION: 2/2 twill.

WARP & WEFT: 2-ply Shetland-style wool at 2000 yd/lb: dark red for main color, and red-violet and light red heather for lines.

YARN SOURCES & COLORS: These were an import that is no longer available. You could use Harrisville Shetland Style: Garnet, Plum, and Aster.

E.P.I.: 20.

WARP COLOR ORDER:

		X		
dk. red (Garnet)	24	24	24	= 48/repeat
red-violet (Plum)		2		= 2/repeat
lt. red heather (Aster)			2	= 2/repeat

DRAFT:

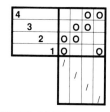

WEFT COLOR ORDER:

		5X	
dk. red (Garnet)	26	26	28
red-violet (Plum)		2	
lt. red heather (Aster)			2

WEAVING: To avoid the free warp end that often arises in weaving twills, start the shuttle on the side of the warp where the edge thread is carried by shaft 1. Lift shafts 2 and 3 for the first shot and continue as shown above. The edge thread will be caught unless a treadling error is made. This is a convenient way to keep a check on yourself.

FINISHING: Hemstitch while on the loom. Hand wash in lukewarm water. Spin briefly in washing machine to extract most of the water. Smooth by hand and hang to dry. Steam press on both sides when nearly dry to the touch.

#4: Blouse Fabric ❹

PROJECT NOTES: For the style of this blouse, take your cue from the pattern you are using for the skirt or jacket and choose a blouse pattern similar to the one shown there. Any pattern which suggests "oxford cloth" is probably suitable. Because the woven cloth is figured, keep the cut simple.

FABRIC DESCRIPTION: Plain weave with warp floats.

WARP & WEFT: 20/2 mercerized cotton at 8400 yd/lb: pale lavender-gray.

YARN SOURCES & COLORS: The Egyptian cotton that was originally used is no longer available. You could substitute UKI color #70 Orchid.

E.P.I.: 36 (3 per dent in a 12-dent reed).

DRAFT:

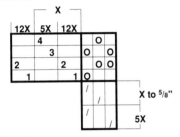

P.P.I.: 36.

TAKE-UP & SHRINKAGE: 9% in width and 11% in length.

WEAVING: This one-shuttle weave proceeds rapidly. Use a light beat on the float block to keep the ground weave uniform. It is necessary to measure as you go to be sure that the areas of plain weave are always the same size. A 6" ruler works nicely for this job, but a little template (a piece of lightweight cardboard cut exactly the size of the space you wish to weave) is more convenient.

FINISHING: Hemstitch the fabric on the loom. Machine wash in warm water, hang to dry partially, and then iron the cloth well on both sides.

#5: Dress Fabric ❷ ❹

PROJECT NOTES: This lightweight worsted cloth was designed to be used for a classic shirtwaist dress with straight lines. Look for patterns that suggest "oxford cloth", "lightweight woolens", or "lightweight tweeds". This soft, supple worsted is a little heavier than oxford cloth and is

about the equivalent of lightweight woolens, although it is a worsted fabric.

FABRIC DESCRIPTION: Plain weave.

WARP & WEFT: 2-ply wool worsted at 4900 yd/lb: dark red.

20/2 wool worsted at 5600 yd/lb: burgundy.

YARN SOURCES & COLORS: The first yarn is Fort Crailo's Zephyr Worsted: Wine. The second yarn is Oregon Worsted's Willamette 20/2: #29 Wine.

E.P.I.: 24 for dark red and 48 for burgundy.

WARP COLOR ORDER:

	X	
dk. red (Wine) 2-ply	24	24
burgundy (Wine) 20/2	8	

DRAFT: Note that the burgundy weft is used quadrupled—see text.

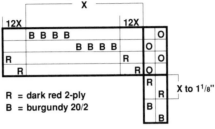

R = dark red 2-ply
B = burgundy 20/2

P.P.I.: 24.

TAKE-UP & SHRINKAGE: 9-10% in width and length.

WEAVING: Make a template (see instructions for blouse) to measure the plain area woven with dark red 2-ply.

The 20/2 burgundy weft is used four ends as one. It is easier to wind a yarn quadrupled if four tubes are used (or some of the yarn can be wound into center-pull balls). Use your fingers to make a tension box: separate the four strands by putting them between the fingers of your nondominant hand (one between thumb and forefinger, one between forefinger and middle finger, etc.). This little trick helps prevent tangling or having one thread slack while the other three are perfectly well-behaved. It is easy to do and pays off.

FINISHING: Hemstitch while on the loom. Wash by hand in lukewarm water. There is no spinning oil to remove. The washing serves to bring the cloth together, not to full it. Spin out excess water, shake the fabric, and drape it smoothly across a clothesline to dry it partially. Steam press when nearly dry.

SWATCH COLLECTION #5

pages 36–39

#1: Tunic Fabric

❻ *(4-shaft alternative)*

PROJECT NOTES: This yarn comes in many colors—more than 100—so you can suit yourself. Be sure to use a plain yarn, though; this is not the place to use novelty yarns.

You may weave part of the garment you have in mind as waffle weave and part as plain weave. Bear in mind that the place where the two interlacements meet will ripple, rather like soft gathering. The plain weave will not narrow as much as the waffle weave does. Use these differences in width and texture in a creative way!

This fabric would be satisfactory for shawls, a quechquemitl, or a tunic and the tabard shown in *Fashions from the Loom*. This fabric has a little stretch built right in, but I would never use it for slacks or shorts because the bulk of the fabric would not be flattering.

The 4-shaft version of this waffle weave will be similar but will lack some of the depth you see here.

FABRIC DESCRIPTION: 6-shaft waffle weave.

WARP & WEFT: 10/2 mercerized cotton at 4200 yd/lb: natural off-white.

E.P.I.: 24.

DRAFT:

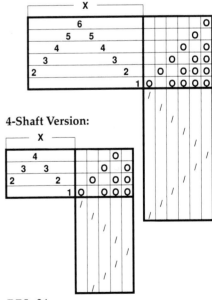

4-Shaft Version:

P.P.I.: 24.

TAKE-UP & SHRINKAGE: 9–10% in width.

WEAVING: This one-shuttle weave moves along quickly. Advance the warp frequently so that there will be less wear on the edge threads because this interlacement draws in quite a bit.

FINISHING: Hemstitch on the loom. Machine wash, warm; shake out wrinkles; and smooth with your hands as you hang the fabric to air dry. If you don't enjoy ironing, this is the fabric for you: a thorough ironing flattens the cells in the waffle weave. If you like the finished look that ironing gives to your clothes, press this fabric briefly when it comes from the washing machine, then give a good shake to restore depth to the waffle weave, and hang it to finish drying.

When this fabric is washed the first time, it becomes lighter in color. Subsequent washings do not seem to change the color further. Undyed and unbleached cotton and linen both lighten with washing.

#2: Jacket Fabric ❹

PROJECT NOTES: This singles linen yarn must be protected from abrasion when used as warp. The use of a 10-dent reed rather than a 20-dent reed minimizes abrasion in the reed. Frequent advancement of the warp will also reduce wear. If you weave this fabric in a very dry place, a light misting of water will reduce breakage of warp ends. Be sure that you do not roll up a damp cloth onto your cloth beam and leave it there to mildew!

You will find that a lot of lint is shed as this warp is woven. The little flax fibers may float through the air as well. Use a strong lamp to see if the air is full of them as you are weaving. If you see them, it is a good idea to wear a dust mask—painting supply stores sell them quite inexpensively. ANY time that you are weaving and you see lots of fibers flying around, do wear one of these masks. There is no reason to inhale any kind of fiber ever while you are weaving.

You can avoid most of the shedding and the warp breakage by using 20/2 linen yarn instead of 10/1. The 20/2 linen, from the same source, has the same yardage, of course, but it is not available as natural gray. It is possible to buy natural—a very, very pale tan—or bleached, which is very white. You might consider buying a dyed 20/2 linen, either nickel gray or charcoal. If you decide to buy the dyed yarns, the cottolin color #0263 would be a better choice for weft than natural. The fabric that results will not look quite the same, but it will have a similar structure and will coordinate with

the other fabrics shown here. The 20/2 yarn has a more uniform diameter; the slight variation in the diameter of the singles linen is one of the attractive features of this fabric.

You might choose to use the cottolin as the warp and use the 10/1 linen as weft instead. Some loose fibers will fly, but not nearly as many.

FABRIC DESCRIPTION: Broken point twill (dornick twill).

WARP: 10/1 linen at 3000 yd/lb: natural gray.

WEFT: 22/2 cottolin at 3170 yd/lb: natural off-white.

YARN SOURCES & COLORS: This warp is Square Sale 10/1 from Frederick J. Fawcett: Grey (unbleached). The weft is Borgs' Bomullin Nel 22/2: #0293 Ecrü or #0000 Oblekt.

E.P.I.: 20 (2 per dent in a 10-dent reed).

DRAFT:

	X							
4		4		4		4		O O
3		3		3		3		O O
	2		2		2		2	O O
	1		1		1		1	O O

P.P.I.: 20.

TAKE-UP & SHRINKAGE: 20% in width (cottolin) and 11% in length (linen).

WEAVING: Wear a dust mask as you weave. Beat evenly. Mist the warp with water if the warp ends begin to break.

FINISHING: Hemstitch on the loom. Machine wash, warm; shake out wrinkles; and smooth with your hands as you hang the fabric to dry until it is just damp. Iron at cotton setting.

#3: Dress Fabric ❹

PROJECT NOTES: It is not necessary to weave this fabric so that it is figured everywhere. The spot-weave pattern could be used as a border on the skirt of a dress, or for the yoke or sleeves of a plain-weave blouse. The cloth is about the weight of oxford cloth, so a garment pattern that suggests that fabric will be satisfactory.

Note that every other warp end is on shaft 1; count your heddles and move them if necessary before you begin to thread.

FABRIC DESCRIPTION: Bronson lace woven as spot weave.

WARP & WEFT: 20/2 mercerized cotton at 8400 yd/lb: coral.

E.P.I.: 40.

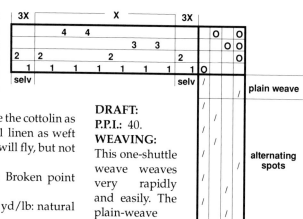

DRAFT:

P.P.I.: 40.

WEAVING: This one-shuttle weave weaves very rapidly and easily. The plain-weave edges produce trouble-free selvedges.

FINISHING: Hemstitch on the loom. Machine wash, warm; shake out wrinkles and smooth with your hands as you hang the fabric to air dry until it is just damp. Iron until dry.

#4: Jacket or Slacks Fabric ❷ ❹

PROJECT NOTES: This striped fabric is designed to coordinate with the other plain skirt fabric and the blouse. If you choose to use other colors for those fabrics, pick matching colors for this cloth. Be sure the garment pattern you choose does not rule out the use of stripes.

FABRIC DESCRIPTION: Plain weave.

WARP: 22/2 cottolin (50% cotton/50% linen) at 3170 yd/lb: natural, dark gray, light gray, and coral.

WEFT: Same as warp: natural.

YARN SOURCES & COLORS: This is Borgs' Bomullin Nel 22/2. Some of the colors originally used are no longer available. You could use #0293 Ecrü (off-white), #0300 (light beige), or #0000 Oblekt (tan) for the natural, as well as #0265 (dark gray), #0263 (light gray), and #0251 (coral).

E.P.I.: 20.

WARP COLOR ORDER: on next page.

DRAFT:

P.P.I.: 20.

WEAVING: This one-shuttle weave moves along well. Maintain an even beat.

FINISHING: Hemstitch on the loom. Machine wash, warm; shake out wrinkles; and smooth with your hands as you hang the fabric to air dry until it is just damp. Iron at cotton setting.

				X				
natural	8	2	2	2	8		8	= 30/repeat
dark gray	2	2	2			2	2 6	= 16/repeat
light gray					6			= 6/repeat
coral				2				= 2/repeat

#5: Skirt Fabric ❷ ❹

PROJECT NOTES: This fabric could be used to make a slightly gathered, simple skirt or a divided skirt. For a more fitted skirt or culottes, increase the sett to 18 e.p.i. and weave at 18 p.p.i. A straight skirt or slacks requires an even firmer fabric—set and weave at 20 per inch.
FABRIC DESCRIPTION: Plain weave.
WARP: 22/2 cottolin (50% cotton/50% linen) at 3170 yd/lb: light gray.
WEFT: Same as warp: natural.
YARN SOURCES & COLORS: This is Borgs' Bomullin Nel 22/2. The warp is #0263. The natural originally used as weft is no longer available; you could substitute #0293 Ecrü (off-white), #0300 (light beige), #0000 Oblekt (tan), or the same light gray as the warp.
E.P.I.: 16.
DRAFT:
P.P.I.: 16.
WEAVING: Strive for an even beat and squared fabric.
FINISHING: Hemstitch on the loom. Machine wash, warm; shake out wrinkles; and smooth with your hands as you hang the fabric to air dry until it is just damp. Iron at cotton setting. The color of the fabric will change slightly when it is washed: the natural weft will be paler, but the dyed warp color will be unchanged.

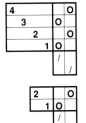

SWATCH COLLECTION #6

pages 40–43

#1: Skirt Fabric ❹

PROJECT NOTES: This fabric was designed to be used for an A-line skirt with a pleat. Its firmness is appropriate for use in a tailored skirt. If you want to make a skirt that is gathered, then you'll need to reduce the number of ends per inch and the number of picks per inch to make the fabric softer. For a gathered skirt, a plain-weave fabric might be more suitable.

This yarn comes in a variety of colors. If the color you need is not available, consider mixing two colors as I did here. If you use other colors, make a sample first that uses one of the colors for half the warp—3"–4"—and the other color for the second half of the warp. Weave across this sample warp with one color for 4"–5" and then with the other one. You may be surprised to find that the part of your sample in which A crosses B is slightly different from the place where B crosses A. Try it and see.
FABRIC DESCRIPTION: 2/2 twill.
WARP: 20/2 wool worsted at 5600 yd/lb: blue-green.
WEFT: Same as warp: dark teal.
YARN SOURCES & COLORS: The yarn originally used in these samples was Oregon Worsted's Willamette in colors no longer available. You could substitute Willamette or JaggerSpun's Heather 2/20 in colors of your choice.
E.P.I.: 32.
WARP LENGTH: This yarn is rather stretchy, so allow about 4" extra for each yard of warp you calculate you will need to put on your loom.
DRAFT:
P.P.I.: 32.
WEAVING: Use dark teal as weft. This one-shuttle weave moves along very swiftly. It is especially important to strive for a very even beat when weaving cloth in which the warp is one color and the weft is another. Uneven beating shows up as colored streaks in the cloth. It isn't as difficult as one might suppose to achieve an even beat with this fabric. The weaving rhythm is relatively unbroken because only one shuttle is used. You will find that advancing the warp frequently—by small amounts—will aid you very much. Tiny differences in beat will even up somewhat as the fabric is washed: wool forgives a lot.

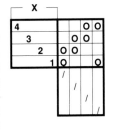

FINISHING: Hemstitch on the loom. Inspect the fabric for flaws and correct them. Wash by hand in warm water. The fabric will bleed color a little, but that is no problem and, if anything, serves to marry the colors a little more. Rinse well, at the same temperature, until the rinse water is no longer colored. Spin out the excess water in a washer and then hang the fabric to dry, smoothing it with your hands as you hang it. Steam press when the fabric is almost dry to the touch. Be careful not to put a shine on it.

#2: Skirt or Dress Fabric ❷ ❹

PROJECT NOTES: This fabric is a one-shuttle weave (using blue) most of its length and so progresses rapidly. If you find that the warp ends at the selvedges break or show wear, advance the warp frequently in small amounts and apply beeswax to the edge warps.

If you choose to weave the border shown here, study the layout of your garment first to see how many borders you will need. (You will probably need to weave the borders only twice: once for the skirt front and once for the skirt back.) It is easiest to weave the border at the beginning of the warp—after weaving some of the blue for the depth of the hem—and then at the other end of the warp. If you make a dress, all of the pattern pieces will be laid out on the fabric so that they fall between the borders with skirt front and back laid out at either end.

This fabric can be used for a simple, very slightly gathered or softly pleated skirt. The pleats can be arranged so that they use the warp stripes to advantage if you like, by arranging them so that the heavy blue stripe lies at the edge of the pleat. This pleating arrangement will accent the fabric design.

If you choose a pattern—skirt or dress—that has some flare to the skirt, omit the borders because they will not be parallel to the hemline in a flared or A-line skirt.

A simple dress may be made using this fabric. The border may be used in a yoke of the dress or at the hem if the skirt is straight. (Please do not use a border in both places because the dress will look too busy.)

This fabric is about the weight of oxford cloth or broadcloth. Look for these fabric names in the list of fabric suggestions on your pattern envelope.
FABRIC DESCRIPTION: Plain weave.
WARP & WEFT: 20/2 mercerized cotton at 8400 yd/lb: gray-blue and violet.
YARN SOURCES & COLORS: These were 20/2 Egyptian Cotton from Robison-Anton: Chicory and Violet. You can use any two colors that are close in hue (color) and value (lightness or darkness).
E.P.I.: 30.

WARP COLOR ORDER:

		X					
	12X		12X		12X		
gray-blue	1	2	1	2	1	4	=44/repeat
violet	1		1		1		=36/repeat

DRAFT:
P.P.I.: 30.

WEFT COLOR ORDER FOR BORDER:

begin						end
	5X		5X		5X	
gray-blue	4	4	4	4	4	
violet	2		2		2	

WEAVING: Use the gray-blue as weft, except as indicated in the border weft color order. Strive for an even beat.

FINISHING: Hemstitch on the loom. Correct any flaws. Machine wash warm, gentle cycle. Shake out the wrinkles, smooth with your hands, and iron while damp.

#3: Mohair Coat Fabric ❻

PROJECT NOTES: If you are weaving more than two yards of this fabric, I suggest that you use two warp beams (one for the worsted ground and the other for the mohair-blend layer). If you don't have two beams, you may need to use sticks to take up the slack in the overlay warps at the back beam as you weave.

This fabric can be used for a tailored coat, a simple suit, or perhaps a Chanel-style jacket to wear with the dress in this collection. Remember that this fabric is very showy and requires a simply cut garment pattern.

FABRIC DESCRIPTION: Stitched double cloth.

WARP & WEFT: Ground—12/3 wool worsted at 2240 yd/lb: dark green.

Overlay—2-ply mohair/wool blend at 980 yd/lb: teal and blue-lavender.

YARN SOURCES & COLORS: This worsted ground is Oregon Worsted's Nehalem: #37 Myrtle Green. The overlay yarn is Beau Monde (55% mohair/45% wool) from Elite Yarns: #846 Teal and #808 Sea Mist. If this is unavailable, you could substitute a similar diameter of brushed yarn, such as Chanteleine's Tiana (formerly Sissi), which is 80% acrylic/10% wool/10% mohair at 1500 yd/lb.

E.P.I.: Ground—12 (in a 6-dent reed; see draft for denting).

WARP COLOR ORDER:

			X			
dk. green worsted	4	4	4	4		=16/repeat
teal mohair				1	1	= 2/repeat
lavender mohair	1	1				= 2/repeat

DRAFT:

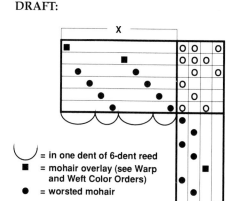

◡ = in one dent of 6-dent reed
■ = mohair overlay (see Warp and Weft Color Orders)
● = worsted mohair

WEFT COLOR ORDER:

		X		
dk. green worsted	4	2	4	2
teal mohair			1	1
lavender mohair	1	1		

P.P.I.: 16.

WEAVING: This fabric is a three-shuttle weave, and so it goes a little slowly at first. Try to weave so that the cloth is square; it will require a light touch. Do not be concerned that the shots of mohair appear to be closer together in the cloth than the warp ends are. When the fabric is washed, the heavy ends in the warp shift so that they lie just as close together as those in the weft.

To help maintain an even beat, you may want to make a little template. Cut a piece of lightweight cardboard (about the weight of cereal-box stock) into a bookmark shape (about 1" x 5"). Draw on this template with crayons or colored pens or pencils the stripe sequence so that it is properly spaced. Compare the fabric you weave with this template as you go; this measurement will help to ensure an even fabric.

FINISHING: Hemstitch on the loom. Find and correct any flaws in the fabric. Hand wash in warm water, rinsing well. There is a little color bleeding the first time the fabric is washed. Hang the fabric to dry, and then press from the back side. Brush the fabric lightly *with the warp* to raise a little nap on the threads that lie on the surface of the cloth.

#4: Dress Fabric ❹

PROJECT NOTES: This fabric is very soft and will lend itself well to moderately flowing styles. For example, a deeply cut sleeve—even a dolman sleeve—would be preferable to a tailored, set-in sleeve; the former requires a soft fabric, and the latter is nicer made in a crisp fabric. Likewise, a slightly gathered or eased skirt would be a better choice than a tailored skirt.

This fabric is shown with the lace as an allover pattern. It would be quite all right to weave the lace as a border or just for sleeves. Look at your pattern and think about some ways to use the lace to best effect.

This yarn is available in several colors; choose one that suits you and your wardrobe. It is also the softest worsted I have found: it feels very good next to the skin. If you choose the same weight worsted from another source, be sure to make a good-sized sample and "try it on" to see that it is soft enough to wear the way you want to wear it.

This yarn is very stretchy. Add at least 6" for each yard of warp that you calculate you will need to put on your loom. For example, if you decide that you need to make a warp 5 yards long (which includes waste and take-up), add 30" to that measurement because when you take your warp off the warping board, you will find that as it relaxes it loses 30" in length.

FABRIC DESCRIPTION: Bronson lace.

WARP & WEFT: 2-ply wool worsted at 4900 yd/lb: dark green.

YARN SOURCES & COLORS: This is Fort Crailo's Zephyr: Dark Green. You could also use a 20/2 worsted at 5600 yd/lb (see Project Notes).

E.P.I.: 20.

DRAFT: on next page.

P.P.I.: 20.

WEAVING: Weave to square. Keep your eye on the plain-weave parts of the cloth as it is being woven and strive to keep it balanced. This fabric is intended to be soft and draping and could certainly be beaten harder to produce a fabric which neither drapes well nor is soft. If necessary, stop from time to time and, using a ruler, count the number of picks in 1" and the number of ends in the same 1" of plain weave: they ought to be the same.

FINISHING: Hemstitch on the loom. Correct any flaws, then hand wash in warm water. This yarn is quite clean and so does not need to be cleaned so much as just relaxed by the washing process. You will see that the appearance of the lace is

DRAFT FOR FABRIC #4:

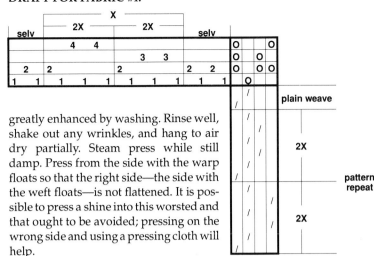

greatly enhanced by washing. Rinse well, shake out any wrinkles, and hang to air dry partially. Steam press while still damp. Press from the side with the warp floats so that the right side—the side with the weft floats—is not flattened. It is possible to press a shine into this worsted and that ought to be avoided; pressing on the wrong side and using a pressing cloth will help.

#5: Plain Weave Jacket Fabric ❷ ❹

FABRIC DESCRIPTION: Plain weave.
WARP: Wool singles at 2000 yd/lb: light blue-green, blue, purple, and red-violet.
WEFT: Same as warp: light blue-green.
YARN SOURCES & COLORS: Same as fabric #5 above.
E.P.I.: 16 (2 per dent in an 8-dent reed recommended).

WARP COLOR ORDER:

	6X	2X	4X	
lt. blue-green (Peacock)		1		= 2/repeat
blue (Azure)	1	8	1	= 16/repeat
purple (Violet)	1		1	= 10/repeat
red-violet (Plum)			1	= 4/repeat

DRAFT:

P.P.I.: 16.
WEAVING: Weave plain weave with the light blue-treen (Peacock) weft.
FINISHING: Hand wash in warm water. The colors bleed a little, but that is no problem with this fabric. Work the fabric with your hands so that it softens and fulls a little. Stop work now and then to see how far the fulling process has gone. When the threads are a little fuzzy—you can tell even when they are wet—then stop and rinse well. Add a little liquid fabric softener to the last rinse if you like. Smooth out the fabric as you hang it to dry. When it is nearly dry to the touch, steam the fabric and brush it lightly to raise a minimal nap, which will blur the threads and blend the colors better.

#6: Double-Faced Jacket Fabric ❽

PROJECT NOTES: This heavy fabric appears to be a double-woven cloth, but it is not. It uses two warps and just one weft. A true double cloth would use two wefts as well as the doubled warp and would use more yarn and be heavier as a result. A cloth with two warps and one weft hangs a little better than one woven with two wefts on a single warp system. A true double cloth would take more time to weave because two wefts would require twice as many picks per inch and possibly two shuttles as well.

Because this fabric is very heavy, its use must be limited to simple vests, unlined jackets with no collars or facings, or capes. The contrasting fabric on the plain-colored side of the fabric serves as a self-lining.
FABRIC DESCRIPTION: Double-faced twill. One side is striped warp-dominant twill; the other is plain 2/2 twill.
WARP: Wool singles at 2000 yd/lb: light blue-green, blue, purple, and red-violet.
WEFT: Same as warp: light blue-green.
YARN SOURCES & COLORS: This is Harrisville Singles: Peacock, Azure, Violet, and Plum. The weft is Peacock.
E.P.I.: 32 (4 per dent in an 8-dent reed recommended).

WARP COLOR ORDER:

	6X	8X	2X	4X			
lt. blue-green (Peacock)	1	1	1	3	1	1	= 34/repeat
blue (Azure)	1		1	1			= 16/repeat
purple (Violet)	1				1		= 10/repeat
red-violet (Plum)				1			= 4/repeat

DRAFT:

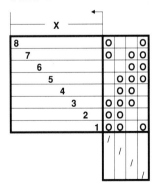

P.P.I.: 16.
WEAVING: Follow the treadling, using the light blue-green (Peacock) weft.
FINISHING: Finish as for the previous jacket fabric.

#1: Jacket Fabric ❷ ❹

PROJECT NOTES: This striped cotton fabric is intended for use as a simple, un-lined cardigan jacket. While fairly heavy, the fabric is firm enough to use in a mod-erately tailored style—no gathers, no tucks. If you want to use this stripe se-quence for a skirt, use a more open sett: 16-18 e.p.i. If you weave a skirt fabric to use with the jacket, put on a warp long enough for both yardages (including loom waste, take-up, shrinkage) plus 10" so that the first length may be cut off and the second length resleyed and retied. The stripes in this fabric, as in many in this striped collection, may be used to good advantage in tucks or pleats (at the more open sett) by arranging the pleats so that the solid blue—or the solid white if you prefer—lies at the folded edge of the pleat.

FABRIC DESCRIPTION: Plain weave with warp stripes.

WARP: 8/2 cotton at 3600 yd/lb: periwin-kle blue and bleached white.

WEFT: Same as warp: white.

YARN SOURCES & COLORS: The 8/2 cottons are UKI colors #47 Copen Blue and Bleach.

E.P.I.: 20.

WARP COLOR ORDER: Note: Two white ends lie side by side in the center of the stripe.

		X			
		4X	4X		
blue	4	1		1	= 12/repeat
white	8	1	1	8	= 24/repeat

DRAFT:
P.P.I.: 20.

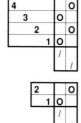

WEAVING: Beat well so that the fabric will be firm enough to tailor if you are making fabric for a jacket. Because just one shuttle is used, the weaving progresses quite rapidly. Because the stripes are all in the warp direction, it is not necessary to stop to measure as it would be if this fabric had weft stripes.

FINISHING: Hemstitch the fabric on the loom. Examine it for flaws and correct any that you find. Machine wash, regular cycle, using warm to hot water. Iron while still damp until the fabric is smooth and dry. The more this fabric is washed, the softer and more velvety its surface will become.

#2: Dress or Skirt Fabric ❹

PROJECT NOTES: This silky, all-cotton fabric is a little heavier than oxford cloth, so choose a pattern accordingly. It would make a wonderfully cool-looking loose summer shift, pleated dirndl skirt, or a light shirt-jacket. Consider taking advan-tage of the stripes by using tucks or pleats to highlight them. You can make tucks or stitched-down pleats so that the white stripes are concealed until the place where the tucks or pleats are released, or the reverse so that the white stripes show to the exclusion of the blue stripes; either way would be effective.

FABRIC DESCRIPTION: Plain weave with warp stripes.

WARP: 20/2 mercerized cotton at 8400 yd/lb: blue and white.

WEFT: Same as warp: blue.

YARN SOURCES & COLORS: The 20/2 cottons are UKI colors #105 Paradise and Bleach.

E.P.I.: 30.

WARP COLOR ORDER:

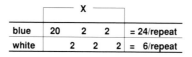

		X		
blue	20	2	2	= 24/repeat
white		2	2	= 6/repeat

DRAFT:
P.P.I.: 30.

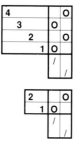

WEAVING: This fabric is easy to weave. Be careful not to draw it in at the edges. If the edge ends begin to wear, strengthen them by rub-bing them with a cake of beeswax and advance the warp frequently.

FINISHING: Hemstitch the fabric on the loom. After it has been cut from the loom, examine it for flaws and correct any that you find. Machine wash, warm, regular cycle. Iron while the fabric is still damp.

#3: Skirt or Shorts Fabric ❷ ❹

PROJECT NOTES: This fabric is fairly heavy, so choose a pattern that is only slightly eased rather than gathered, or a fairly straight or moderately A-line style. If you decided to use the striped cotton fabric for a skirt, at the more open sett given, this fabric could be used to make a shirt-style jacket. It would make a wonderful robe or beach cover-up because the weave structure here is open enough to make the fabric feel very velvety.

FABRIC DESCRIPTION: 2/2 basket weave.

WARP & WEFT: 8/2 cotton at 3600 yd/lb: periwinkle blue.

YARN SOURCES & COLORS: This 8/2 cotton is UKI color #47 Copen Blue.

E.P.I.: 20.

DRAFT:

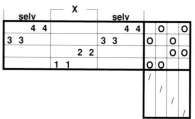

P.P.I.: 20.

WEAVING: Notice that the draft calls for a selvedge threading. This selvedge will make it possible for you to weave this cloth without having to take the shuttle around a floating selvedge. If you have more than four shafts, you will have good results by substituting shafts 5 and 6 for 3 and 4 and threading the main part of the cloth 1, 2, 3, 4, etc.

On a 2-shaft loom, you can achieve the same results by using two shuttles as you weave this cloth. DO NOT use one shuttle with the weft doubled on the bobbin. If you do, you will find that the wefts twist around each other so that the resulting cloth does not look like a basket weave.

Use a moderate beat; aim for as many picks per inch as there are ends per inch. Measure and count to see how you are doing until you get the "feel" of weaving this cloth.

FINISHING: Hemstitch the cloth while it is on the loom. Examine it for flaws and correct them after it has been cut from the loom. Machine wash, warm to hot, and iron while the cloth is still damp.

#4: Jacket Fabric ❹

PROJECT NOTES: This jacket fabric is intended for a cardigan-type jacket with a V neck. It is firm and crisp and will not lend itself to tucks or gathers. The use of linen as the weft makes the fabric very easy to warp and to weave. The linen also adds a textural interest: the cotton is vel-vety and has a dull finish; the linen is smooth and slightly shiny so that the twill lines are subtly emphasized.

FABRIC DESCRIPTION: Dornick twill with warp stripes.

WARP: 8/2 cotton at 3600 yd/lb: bleached white and periwinkle blue.

WEFT: 14/1 linen at 4200 yd/lb: bleached

DRAFT FOR FABRIC #4: In warp, circled ends = blue, remainder = white.

```
                              |—————————— X ——————————|
 4     4     4    (4)    4     4     4     4     4     4    (4)          O O
    3     3     3     3     3     3    (3)    3     3     3              O O
 2     2     2    (2)    2     2     2     2     2     2    (2)        O O
    1     1     1     1     1     1    (1)    1     1     1     1      O         O
                                                                       /
                                                                          /
                                                                       /
                                                                          /
```

white.

YARN SOURCES & COLORS: The 8/2 cottons are UKI colors #47 Copen Blue and Bleach. The linen weft is Square Sale 14/1 from Frederick J. Fawcett: Bleached.

E.P.I.: 20.

WARP COLOR ORDER: Alternate 12 white with 2 blue (see draft).

P.P.I.: 24.

WEAVING: This cloth is very easy to weave. Avoid pulling in the edge threads because the cotton is softly twisted and thus is subject to abrasion. It helps to advance the warp frequently by small amounts. I had no breakage; it was a pleasant surprise.

FINISHING: Hemstitch the cloth on the loom. After it has been cut from the loom, examine it for flaws, correct them, and then machine wash the fabric, hot, regular cycle. Iron with a hot iron while still damp.

#5: Shirt and Trim Fabrics ❷ ❹

PROJECT NOTES: This is the finest yarn that I have used in a swatch collection, and in a way it is an indulgence for me. The yarn is very smooth and very tightly spun, a delight to use. It will take longer to make and to weave off this warp, but the results are certainly worth it. This fabric is the weight of oxford cloth or slightly lighter-weight and ought to be pure pleasure to wear this summer!

The contrasting fabric shown was woven on this warp as trim for the striped fabric. If you use this fabric for a shirt or shirt jacket, you can use the trim fabric to make the collar and cuffs or the front plackets.

I like the idea of using two stripes in one outfit when the stripes are as close in appearance to each other as this fabric and the 20/2 cotton fabric. The colors are exactly the same; only the size and sequence of the stripes and the weight of the cloths are different. If several stripes are combined in one outfit, use restraint; it might be a good idea to skip the trim fabric in that case or use the finer striped fabric to trim the slightly heavier one.

The stripes can be made in the color combination that suits you best.

FABRIC DESCRIPTION: Plain weave

with warp stripes. The trimming fabric is crossed to make small, squat rectangles.

WARP & WEFT: 00/3 cotton at 14,000 yd/lb: blue and white.

YARN SOURCES & COLORS: This is 00/3 from Robison-Anton: Chicory and Bleached White. Chicory is now unavailable; substitute cotton sewing thread in blue and white.

E.P.I.: 40.

WARP COLOR ORDER: Alternate 10 blue with 2 white.

DRAFT:

P.P.I.: 40.

WEFT COLOR ORDER FOR CHECKED TRIM ONLY: Alternate 4 blue with 2 white.

WEAVING: For the main fabric, use the blue weft. Strive for an even beat.

FINISHING: Hemstitch the fabric on the loom. After the cloth has been cut from the loom, examine it carefully for flaws—this examination will take time because the fabric is fine—and correct them. Machine wash, warm, regular cycle, and iron while damp.

SWATCH COLLECTION #8

pages 47–49

#1: Skirt Fabric ❷ ❹

PROJECT NOTES: This heathery, light burgundy wool fabric is designed to do two things. It is soft so that it will drape and can be very lightly gathered. The heathered color gives the illusion of texture—as you will see, a recurring theme in this collection—because of the depth of its color. Heathered yarns are made by blending several colors—dyed in the fleece—into one yarn; if you look closely at the yarn, you will see a dark wine color, white, a little pink, and a little gray in it; When a heathered yarn is woven into a cloth, the color is a lot more interesting, softer and richer.

This cloth is woven at about the lower limit for sett for this yarn. The drape pro-

duced by the cloth set at 20 e.p.i. is soft. If you decide to weave this fabric for a very tailored skirt or for a tailored jacket, as opposed to a shirt jacket, it would be a good idea to set it at 24 e.p.i.

I tried weaving this cloth with different dentages. The cloth shown here was woven at two per dent in a 10-dent reed. I experimented with different setts, one of which required three ends in one dent. I discovered that the warp is sticky enough to hang up on itself when sleyed three per dent, causing errors in the cloth that have to be mended later. It is always wise to avoid making errors that need mending! Using only two ends per dent avoids that problem.

This fabric was designed to be used as a soft skirt, perhaps a modified A-line with slight shirring at the waist. Look for a pattern that calls for a lightweight woolen or tweed cloth.

FABRIC DESCRIPTION: Plain weave.

WARP & WEFT: 18-cut single-ply woolen yarn at 3600 yd/lb: light wine.

YARN SOURCES & COLORS: This is Halcyon Yarn's Coventry Heather: #9 Light Burgundy.

E.P.I.: 20.

DRAFT:

P.P.I.: 20.

WEAVING: Use an even, moderate beat to achieve the same number of picks per inch as ends per inch. This fabric weaves up rapidly and easily. Broken ends

were not a problem, but because they sometimes occur with a singles, woolen-spun yarn, here are some tips to minimize them. Advance the warp frequently to avoid undue wear and tear on the edge threads. Time spent winding your bobbins carefully will pay off in fewer broken ends. Some weavers double thread and sley the two edge threads at either side. I do about as well without doing that, but if you have problems, give that a try.

This yarn has a hard twist—that is good, too, because it makes it stronger—

so it sometimes kinks as it leaves the shuttle. Keep your eye on the fell as you weave so that you can see these kinks as they happen—mine came mostly at the edges where, luckily, they are easier to correct. If kinks become a problem, you can control them somewhat by winding your bobbins firmly and then putting some sort of drag on them as they turn in the shuttle. You can brake them by gluing a tiny piece of sheepskin or a scrap of synthetic fur to the inside of the shuttle where it will brush the bobbin as it turns, slowing it a little and preventing overspinning. If you use end-delivery shuttles, set the tension a little higher than normal to control the kinks.

If you find, after the cloth has been cut from the loom or after you have woven ahead several inches, that you have missed a kink in the fabric, simply pull up the loop that the kink makes, work it out to the selvedge with a tapestry needle, and trim off the excess there. You may also cut the loop in the middle of the fabric and mend the ends back into it, but the former practice is neater.

FINISHING: Hemstitch the fabric at both ends while it is still on the loom. Examine it for flaws and correct before washing.

You would be surprised if you could see the "before" version of this fabric. When it was taken from the loom, it was scratchy and coarse feeling; it looked a lot like heathered burgundy window screening. Not a pretty sight! The washing and fulling processes are absolutely necessary to produce the cloth that you see here. The cloth was washed in moderately hot water with plenty of neutral liquid cleanser. The first washing produced a milky, dark pink wash water; the second produced a much less colored water. The fabric was washed by hand, rinsed three times at the same temperature, and then hung to drip. While still damp, it was ironed, not merely pressed, to smooth it.

Do not be alarmed when tweeds like this one color the wash water or turn it milky. These yarns are oiled when they are spun, and it is this spinning oil that must be washed out to produce the cloth you see here. Wash them until the color stops appearing in the washing water; clearly, you will have to use more cleanser for a large piece than for a smaller one because there will be more oil in it.

#2: Jacket Fabric ❷ ❹

PROJECT NOTES: This fabric is made with the same yarn—size and style but not colors—as the preceding one. There are two differences: most obvious is the different color, less obvious the drape of the fabric. The stripes are designed against a light burgundy ground so that the cloth is tied by its color and texture to the skirt fabric above. The weft is light burgundy, which acts further to blend the colors. Because this striped fabric is firmer by 20% than the plain fabric above, it can be used for more tailored garments. If you prefer, you can weave the plain fabric more firmly and this fabric so that it has the softer drape.

The 24-e.p.i. sett used here was achieved by using a 12-dent reed and sleying it two ends per dent. Do not be tempted to use an 8-dent reed sleyed three per dent: the warp ends will cling to each other and give you a raggedy shed and—in spite of your best efforts—skips. I know.

This fabric was designed for a notch-collared or cardigan jacket and/or a straight skirt. Like other woolen fabrics, it will wrinkle somewhat—although a lot less than cotton—so you may want to consider making a skirt of the worsted fabric that follows.

FABRIC DESCRIPTION: Plain weave.
WARP: 18-cut single-ply woolen yarn at 3600 yd/lb: burgundy, light wine, brown, and dark brown.
WEFT: Same as warp: light wine.
YARN SOURCES & COLORS: These are Halcyon Yarn's Coventry Heathers: #8 Burgundy, #9 Light Burgundy, #6 Brown, and #7 Dark Brown.
E.P.I.: 24.
WARP COLOR ORDER:

	X				
burgundy	4				= 4/repeat
lt. wine	6	6			= 12/repeat
brown			2	2	= 4/repeat
dk. brown			1	2	1 = 4/repeat

DRAFT:
P.P.I.: 24.
WEAVING: The stripes are all in the warp so only one color is used for weft, the light burgundy. This fabric may be woven pretty rapidly; use a firm beat to produce a balanced cloth. This yarn is highly

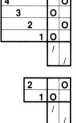

twisted and produces kinks as it is used. See instructions for the skirt fabric for tips on dealing with a kinky yarn.
FINISHING: Hemstitch the ends while the fabric is on the loom. Examine for flaws and correct them, then wash according to instructions for the skirt fabric above.

#3: Skirt/Slacks Fabric ❹

PROJECT NOTES: This worsted fabric was designed for use as a skirt or a pair of moderately loose fitting pants. (If you want more closely fitted pants, set the fabric at 24 working e.p.i.) It can also be used to make a shirt jacket because although fairly crisp, it is lightweight enough to gather into cuffs or onto a yoke.

This fabric is made with very plain yarns, plain in yarn design—two-ply and smooth—and plain in color—not heathered like other yarns used in this collection. The fabric woven with a plain yarn can be a plain one, but it can also be textured because of the way that it is woven. This fabric is woven in a plain weave, but instead of having the weft go over one, under one, the warp ends are doubled sometimes. The texture that such a doubling adds is a subtle one, particularly when woven in a dark color like this one. There are several ways to double warp ends: you may carry two warp ends through one heddle, or you may use two heddles, one for each end. I used the latter method because the ends twist around each other when they are carried by the same heddle, producing a small ridge in the cloth that changes—sometimes it is wider, sometimes narrower as the ends lie on top of each other. When two heddles are used, the ends lie side by side everywhere so that the heavier lines are uniform in thickness.

Warp ends may be doubled in a repeating pattern or in a nonrepeating one. I chose a nonrepeating pattern. In the space of 1" there are 20 working ends; that is, 20 ends that act as though they were single entities. In the space of 1" there are actually 24 threads; some of them are used two at a time. When you thread a cloth like this one, you simply thread a pair of heddles on the same shaft once in a while. I avoided threading two pairs side by side because I tried it and did not like the way it looked. Sometimes the pairs were separated by a single end, sometimes by as many as seven ends. Strive for a random appearance; it isn't hard to do.

FABRIC DESCRIPTION: Plain weave with random doubled ends.

WARP & WEFT: 20/2 wool worsted at 5600 yd/lb: dark brown.

YARN SOURCES & COLORS: This is Oregon Worsted's Willamette: #341 Tobacco.

E.P.I.: 20 working ends (24 actual ends).

DRAFT: Straight draw on four shafts, treadled plain weave. Where doubled ends fall, use two heddles, one for each thread.

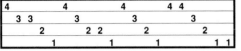

This is only an example of how the doubled ends could fall.

P.P.I.: 20.

WEAVING: This cloth is easy to weave. The warp is pretty strong, and so there was very little breakage. It is still a good practice to wind your bobbins carefully and advance the warp frequently; good technique helps make a warp trouble free.

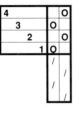

FINISHING: Hemstitch the fabric while it is still on the loom. After it has been cut from the loom, examine it for flaws and correct them.

Wash the fabric in very warm water with a neutral liquid cleanser. Rinse it well at the same temperature, hang to dry, and press when just damp to the touch for a smooth finish.

#4: Blouse, Shirt, or Dress Fabric ❷ ❹

PROJECT NOTES: My first impulse when I was thinking about a blouse or dress fabric for this collection was to use a light-colored fine cotton or silk. The more I looked at it and thought about it, the more jarring an off-white fabric seemed to be. I got out cones of cotton and tried them with the samples I had made and found that there were four colors that were pretty good: dark brown, wine, navy, and dark green. In one of those flashes that all of us hope for, I decided to try using them all—at once.

This fabric, then, is woven in a plain weave so that the color play that takes place in it will show well. The warp is composed of two of the colors: one warm—wine—and one cool—navy. The weft uses the other two: one warm—brown—and one cool—dark green. The result is a fabric that compels the eye to look twice and that changes as it is folded the way changeable taffeta does.

This fabric is set at about the most open sett that is appropriate for this yarn. The result is a soft fabric that ought to be satisfactory for a shirtwaist dress or for a shirt. Look for "oxford cloth" in the fabric suggestions on your pattern; even though this fabric is slightly heavier than true oxford cloth, it ought to work with most patterns that suggest oxford cloth.

The plaid must be evenly woven if it is to be matched as it is sewn. I made a little template—a piece of lightweight cardboard about 6" long—and marked it with a pencil to show where the narrow green weft stripes ought to fall. I used this template all the time as I wove to be sure that the plaid would be woven evenly.

FABRIC DESCRIPTION: Plain weave.

WARP: 16/2 mercerized cotton at 6700 yd/lb: wine and navy.

WEFT: Same as warp: brown and dark green.

YARN SOURCES & COLORS: These yarns were from Robison-Anton: #1671 Wine, #1684 Navy, #1651 Seal, and #1621 Forest. A similar yarn is available from Weaver's Way.

E.P.I.: 24.

WARP COLOR ORDER: 14 wine, 4 navy.

DRAFT:

P.P.I.: 24.

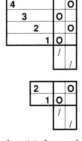

WEAVING: Make a template based on the spacing in the warp. I found that the warp direction shrank a little more than the weft direction did, so I elongated the stripe sequence just a little. I found that 16 shots of Seal followed by 4 shots of Forest was right.

Use a moderate beat. It is possible to beat this fabric so that it will be weft faced, but avoid this if you want the same color play and the same hand that the fabric shown here has.

It takes longer to weave a fabric using two shuttles, particularly when you need to stop to measure to be sure that the plaid will be uniformly woven. If you feel hurried, either weave this fabric using just the brown weft so that it is a warp stripe or make the warp using just Wine and weave across it with Seal for an interesting plain fabric.

FINISHING: Hemstitch the fabric while it is still on the loom. Examine it for flaws and correct them after it has been cut from the loom. Machine wash, hot, gentle cycle. (You may wish to use warm water later, but shrink it the first time you wash it—before you cut into it.) Iron while still damp.

#5: Jacket or Vest Fabric ❻

PROJECT NOTES: This is the most highly textured fabric in this collection. Many of us have woven corduroy for rugs or woven loom-controlled pile fabrics on an overshot threading, but I wanted to make a corduroy that was just like the commercial fabric except that it was made of wool. I decided to use wool because, of all the natural fibers, wool has the most resilience and corduroys are subject to crushing in use. The most successful corduroy is one in which the individual threads fluff out—bloom, weavers say—so that the pile surface is soft and velvety; that suggested a woolen-spun yarn for weft.

The color of the weft yarn is the same as the light burgundy cloth in fabric #1. The velvety texture of this cloth makes its color seem even richer.

It seemed likely that the warp would undergo a lot of stress if the weft were packed in tightly enough to make the cloth good and strong, so I chose a worsted wool for the warp.

This fabric is woven with fine threads so that the cloth looks like a commercial corduroy, but it could also be woven with heavier yarns such as 1/3 worsted and a tweed at 2000 yd/lb. The result, of course, would be a corduroy that looks magnified, an ultrawide-wale cloth.

Just as you must break eggs to make an omelet, you must cut threads to make a corduroy. The cloth is woven so that there are two weft picks for the pile to each ground pick, the picks that hold the cloth together. Cut the pile picks while the cloth is still on the loom to control the scissors more easily and avoid cutting the ground picks. After every few inches of weaving, set the shuttle aside and cut the weft floats that make the pile. I found that it was best to weave about 2½"-3" and then cut. There is no denying that cutting the floats is tedious when there are as many of them as there are here. Perhaps you might like to weave just enough for a vest, instead of making a whole suit of this material. You can make trim or facing fabric to match by weaving the cloth as a 1/2 twill; the color will match and be quite handsome.

Choose a simple pattern, one with few seams.

Approach the weaving of this fabric with a sense of adventure; it would be helpful if you could actually touch the corduroy you see here to feel how luxurious it is. Take my word for it: it is worth the effort.

FABRIC DESCRIPTION: 6-shaft corduroy.

WARP: 20/2 wool worsted at 5600 yd/lb: dark red.

WEFT: 18-cut single-ply woolen yarn at 3600 yd/lb: light wine.

YARN SOURCES & COLORS: This warp is Oregon Worsted's Willamette: #29 Wine. The weft is Halcyon Yarn's Coventry Heather: #9 Light Burgundy.

E.P.I.: 24.

DRAFT:

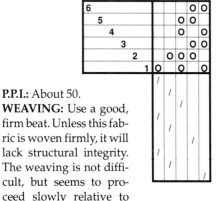

P.P.I.: About 50.

WEAVING: Use a good, firm beat. Unless this fabric is woven firmly, it will lack structural integrity. The weaving is not difficult, but seems to proceed slowly relative to the rest of the fabrics in this collection for two reasons: there are many picks per inch, and the weaver must stop periodically and cut the floats. Use a pair of embroidery scissors to cut the floats. I have a pair of Fiskars that worked beautifully. The blades of the scissors must be slim, pointed, and very sharp. Take small cuts, about ¼" at a time, so that you do not pull the weft floats out of position. After you have cut the floats, do not handle the fabric any more than you must. I covered mine with a piece of fabric so that it would not rub against the apron I wear when I weave. I am not absolutely sure that the cut ends would be dislodged, but I didn't want to take any chances. After the fabric has been washed, the cut ends fluff out so that they are held in place very nicely. The cloth is vulnerable only after it has been cut and before it has been washed.

FINISHING: Hemstitch the fabric while it is still on the loom. Examine it for flaws and correct them after it has been cut from the loom.

Hand wash this fabric in moderately hot water using a neutral liquid cleanser. You will probably need to wash it more than once to get rid of all of the spinning oil (see fabric #1). Rinse three times at the same temperature. Squeeze in your hands, but do not wring. Shake the fabric and hang it to drip dry. When it feels dry to the touch, you will see that the selvedges have curled to the back side, away from the pile. Put the fabric face down on a padded ironing board—a heavy terry towel works well—and lightly steam the edges to straighten them. You may wish to pin the edges, steam them, allow them to cool and dry a little, and then move on.

When you sew with this fabric, bind the edges with a very lightweight binding like Seams Great® or Seam Saver®.

SWATCH COLLECTION #9

pages 52–54

#1: Skirt or Dress Fabric ❷ ❹

PROJECT NOTES: I designed this fabric to include two of the four colors that make up this collection. This cloth is made up mostly of a pale violet thread, shiny and smooth. A textured, dull-surfaced, light green thread makes warp stripes. The stripes run in the warp direction for two very practical reasons: the warp direction is usually used up and down on the figure so warp stripes are flattering, and after the spacing of warp stripes has been established, it does not vary, eliminating constant measurement as the fabric is woven to ensure that the stripes can be matched.

FABRIC DESCRIPTION: Plain weave.

WARP & WEFT: 20/2 mercerized cotton at 8400 yd/lb: pale lavender-gray.

WARP STRIPE: 8/2 unmercerized cotton at 3600 yd/lb: light gray-green.

YARN SOURCES & COLORS: The 20/2 cotton is UKI color #69 Mauve. The 8/2 is UKI color #6 Mill Green.

E.P.I.: 30 for 20/2 cotton; 8/2 cotton is sleyed with 1 end 20/2, then with 2 ends of 20/2 alternately in a 10-dent reed.

WARP COLOR ORDER:

	X	
pale lavender-gray 20/2 (Mauve)	30	30
light gray-green 8/2 (Mill Green)	1	

DRAFT:
P.P.I.: 30.
WEAVING: The soft twist that makes pearl cotton so lustrous and silky to the touch also makes it subject to wear by abrasion at the sel-

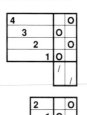

vedges. A simple preventive measure will save those selvedge threads, not to mention the equanimity of the weaver: use a little beeswax, the kind you buy to strengthen thread used for sewing on buttons, to dress the selvedge threads. Rub the wax along the threads and repeat each time the warp is advanced. It is always a good idea to advance the warp often by small amounts as you weave; this is particularly good practice when the warp is fragile or subject to wear. If you use the wax and advance the warp often, you will find that this cloth weaves up very quickly. Use an even beat.

FINISHING: Hemstitch both the ends while the cloth is still on the loom. After it has been cut from the loom, examine it for errors and correct them. Machine wash the fabric, warm water, gentle cycle, and iron it while it is damp.

#2 and #3: Skirt or Dress Fabrics ❷ ❹

PROJECT NOTES: I designed this fabric in two colorways: the first is mauve, the second, celadon. It has the same smooth-shiny/textured-dull contrast that fabric #1 has except that mauve is used with mauve and green with green. The mauve 20/2 pearl cotton and the 8/2 cotton are dyed exactly the same color; the green yarns differ in value just a little; the 8/2 cotton is slightly lighter.

I am interested in the way that the play of light on the smooth, lustrous surface broken by the heavier, textured 8/2 cotton affects the colors in the cloth. Because the 8/2 cotton is bigger than the pearl cotton, it casts shadows beside itself in the fabric. At the same time, it catches the light and so seems to be lighter than it is. In the case of the green cloth, this effect is heightened because the yarn really is a lighter color.

The textured threads are arranged in the cloth so that a windowpane check with doubled lines is formed. I have found that textured threads used in a plain-weave ground of plain threads show off their texture best when used singly. The most effective spacing I tried was three plain threads between the textured ones.

FABRIC DESCRIPTION: Plain weave with heavier overcheck.

WARP & WEFT: Ground—20/2 mercerized cotton at 8400 yd/lb: pale lavender-gray for fabric #2, or gray-green for fabric #3.

Overcheck—8/2 unmercerized cotton

at 3600 yd/lb: lavender for fabric #2 or light gray-green for fabric #3.

YARN SOURCES & COLORS: The lavender and green 20/2 cottons are UKI colors #69 Mauve and #53 Scarab. The lavender and green 8/2 cottons are UKI colors #38 Lavender and #6 Mill Green.

E.P.I.: 30 for 20/2; 8/2 is sleyed alternately with 1 end 20/2, then 2 ends 20/2 in a 10-dent reed.

WARP COLOR ORDER:

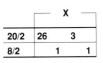

	X			
20/2	27	3	30	= 30/repeat
8/2	1	1		= 2/repeat

DRAFT:
P.P.I.: 30 ground.
WEFT COLOR ORDER:

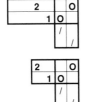

	X		
20/2	26	3	
8/2	1	1	

WEAVING: The same advice about using beeswax on selvedge threads and advancing the warp frequently by small amounts applies to these two fabrics (see Weaving, fabric #1).

The overcheck is woven so that it squares. I found that 26 picks of 20/2 cotton were needed to square the pattern. I made a template that showed three weft repeats and used that to keep the squares even.

FINISHING: Finish as directed for fabric #1.

#4: Shirt Fabric ❹

PROJECT NOTES: I designed this fabric so that it would have a textured surface even though it was woven of plain threads. I tried using all the same color—the very pale yellow—as warp and weft, but I found that the fabric looked dull. When I used a fine, off-white cotton in the warp along with yellow, the result was far more interesting. It is a subtle difference but an important one. The whole cloth became brighter and, surprisingly, finer looking without changing the weights of the threads used.

FABRIC DESCRIPTION: Haircord, a plain-weave variation.

WARP & WEFT: 20/2 mercerized cotton at 8400 yd/lb: natural off-white (used in warp only).

10/2 mercerized cotton at 4200 yd/lb: pale brass.

YARN SOURCES & COLORS: The 20/2 cotton is UKI color #79 Natural, and the 10/2 is UKI color #91 Flaxon.

E.P.I.: 30; use a 10-dent reed, sleying 2 ends 10/2 and 1 end 20/2 per dent. It is important to place the adjacent threads that are carried by the same shaft in different dents; see the draft.

WARP COLOR ORDER:

	X	
Natural	1 (circled in the draft)	
Flaxon	2	

DRAFT:

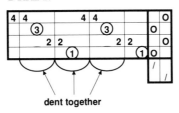

dent together

P.P.I.: 18.

WEAVING: This fabric is very easy to weave. Wax the selvedge threads as advised previously to prevent wear and breakage.

FINISHING: Finish as directed for fabric #1.

#5: Skirt Fabric ❹

PROJECT NOTES: I designed this plaid with the idea in mind that it would be dainty. The colors in it—mauve, off-white, pale yellow, and celadon—suggest that quality. I made the repeat of the plaid small, and to reinforce the daintiness, added lace blocks in the plaid itself.

Although four colors are used in the warp, three colors are used in the weft. When the colors of the warp were repeated in the weft, the off-white was too strong: it called too much attention to itself. Using the pale yellow in place of off-white in the weft softened and warmed the fabric at the same time.

The plaid is not an even one. Because most of the other fabrics in this collection are very symmetrical, I decided to design the plaid so that the lace blocks lie in the corner of the green/yellow overcheck instead of being right in the middle. It is a simple matter to change that if you prefer symmetry.

FABRIC DESCRIPTION: Plain weave and Bronson lace.

WARP & WEFT: 20/2 mercerized cotton at 8400 yd/lb: pale lavender-gray, natural off-white, pale brass, and gray-green.

YARN SOURCES & COLORS: The 20/2 cottons are UKI colors #69 Mauve, #79 Natural, #91 Flaxon, and #53 Scarab.

E.P.I.: 30.

WARP COLOR ORDER: on next page.

DRAFT: on next page.

WEFT COLOR ORDER: on next page.

TOTAL WARP ENDS: 66 per repeat.

P.P.I.: 30.

WEAVING: I like to weave plaids because it is fun to see the color sequence come alive as I work. Plaid requires an even beat and the faithful use of a template. Make your warp 12" longer than you think you will need—taking into account that you must allow extra yardage to match the plaids—and use the first 12" to settle down to an even beat. To make a template, mark a lightweight piece of cardboard with the repeat, taking the measure from the warp (using colored pencils to mark your template will make it easier to follow), and use it as you weave. Using a template marked against the warp will make the plaid square. When you come to the white part of the repeat, use the lace treadling and the yellow weft, as mentioned above.

It takes more care to weave plaids—you do have to pay attention—but the results are worth the effort. Again, refer to fabric #1 for instructions for protecting selvedge threads. Keep in mind that the

WARP COLOR ORDER FOR FABRIC #5:

							X								
lavender (Mauve)	8	8						4	8	8	= 20/repeat
off-white (Natural)		4						12	12		= 28/repeat
pale brass (Flaxon)	2		1	1	1	1			2		= 6/repeat
green (Scarab)			4	1	2	1	4				= 12/repeat

WEFT COLOR ORDER FOR FABRIC #5: *Treadle the 12 picks of Flaxon in lace weave, remainder in plain weave.

lavender (Mauve)	8	8					4	
pale brass (Flaxon)	2	4	1	1	1	1	12*	12*
green (Scarab)			4	1	2	1	4	

DRAFT FOR FABRIC #5:

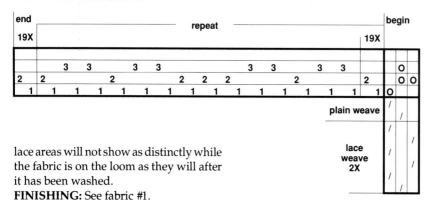

lace areas will not show as distinctly while the fabric is on the loom as they will after it has been washed.

FINISHING: See fabric #1.

DRAFT FOR FABRIC #6:

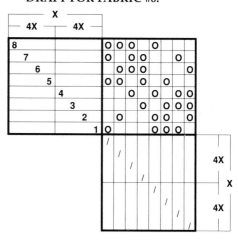

#6: Jacket Fabric ➀

PROJECT NOTES: I designed this fabric so that it would have a lot more texture than any of the others in the collection. The textural difference between it and the other fabrics is a pleasant one. It combines violet, green, and a cool tan. Because all of the colors are about the same value, the fabric has a fairly uniform appearance instead of seeming blotchy.

I wanted to give the appearance of more complexity in the fabric than is actually there. The structure is a two-block broken twill in which the colors repeat regularly: tan, violet, green, tan, violet, green, etc. In a two-block twill, the blocks alternate warp emphasis and weft emphasis. That emphasis is reversed when the treadling sequence is changed. The result is a sort of checkerboard in which the warp color of the first block all but obscures the weft color, and the weft color in the second block all but obscures the warp color in that block. When the treadling is changed, as it is in this cloth after 16 shots, the warp/weft emphasis is reversed. The result is that the color sequence seems to repeat after six color

changes instead of after three. Using a broken twill makes the color more important, visually, than the structure.

If you plan to make a very tailored garment, you may produce a firmer fabric by setting the warp at 24 e.p.i. rather than the 20 used here. The fabric shown will make a nice cardigan-style jacket—no lapels or collar, no buttonholes. It will be a handy garment to wear in air-conditioned buildings in the summer. When you lay out your pattern, treat this fabric as if it had nap. Because the weft color sequence is not symmetrical, all pattern pieces must be placed running the same direction.

FABRIC DESCRIPTION: Two-block broken twill.

WARP & WEFT: 8/2 unmercerized cotton at 3600 yd/lb: beige, light gray-green, and lavender.

YARN SOURCES & COLORS: The 8/2 cottons are UKI colors #16 Polo Tan, #6 Mill Green, and #38 Lavender.

E.P.I.: 20 (see Project Notes above).

WARP & WEFT COLOR ORDER: 16 beige, 16 lavender, 16 green.

P.P.I.: 18.

WEAVING: I found this fabric easy and fast to weave. It was fun to see how the colors appeared and disappeared each time the weft was changed.

I did not wax the selvedges—it is harder with very softly spun or textured threads—and did not have a single end break. I did advance the warp often, a habit I am encouraging myself to make automatic.

Use a moderate beat so that the fabric will be balanced, that is, it will have the same number of warps as wefts per inch. Otherwise, the color play will be lost. Again, make a template and use it. You will want to be able to match the fabric at the seams when you make your jacket.

The fabric shrinks a little more than the others in this collection, fully 10%.

FINISHING: See fabric #1.

SWATCH COLLECTION #10

pages 56–59

#1: Skirt Fabric ❻ ❽

PROJECT NOTES: I worked out the design for this fabric using strips of colored paper to get the proportions right. The gray ground stripes are the same width throughout the cloth. The rust stripes are also uniform in width and are raised so that the color is less broken in the woven cloth. The little camel stripes vary in width in a regular way: they start two ends wide and progress, adding two ends each time, to eight ends wide.

FABRIC DESCRIPTION: Broken twill and plain-weave warp stripes.

WARP: 20/2 wool worsted at 5600 yd/lb: gray, rust, and beige.

WEFT: Same as warp: black.

YARN SOURCES & COLORS: The gray and rust warps are Oregon Worsted's Willamette: #1625 Charcoal and #42 Rust Brown. The beige warp is Fort Crailo's Zephyr Worsted: Camel. The weft is Willamette: #515 Black.

E.P.I.: 24 for the beige and gray, 30 for the rust. (I used a 12-dent reed with 2 per dent and 2/3/2/3 for rust.)

WARP COLOR ORDER: below.

TOTAL WARP ENDS: 148 per repeat.

DRAFTS: below.

P.P.I.: 24.

WEAVING: This fabric is very easy to weave. Maintain an even beat as you weave.

FINISHING: I hemstitched the cloth at both ends while it was on the loom. I examined it for flaws and corrected them after it was cut from the loom. I washed it in very warm water using a mild liquid detergent (Joy) and rinsed it well. While it was still slightly damp I pressed it from the wrong side (it is important to avoid crushing the twill stripe) until it was dry to the touch. There is a little tracking in the plain-weave parts, but I think that it adds to the appearance of the cloth in this case.

#2: Vest Fabric ❹

PROJECT NOTES: I designed this fabric so that it has a small allover pattern. Because it is so busy, it ought to be used in small quantities; I had a vest in mind. I have also woven a little of the ground fabric with the monk's-belt pattern as a border to show that it makes a wonderful border for a skirt. It may also be used in the yoke of a shirt/jacket or a dress. Please do not use it in the skirt *and* the yoke of a dress because it is a strong design and quickly takes over; restraint is necessary!

Although the fabric is relatively lightweight, visually it is as coarse as the overshot on its surface. The vest, therefore, ought to be very simply cut; choose one that does not button, has few or no darts, without fancy points or princess seaming.

Allow an extra 12" or so when you calculate the warp length. Use that extra length to weave the small repeat a few times so that you can establish a standard beat for yourself. Mark a cardboard template using that first bit of weaving: you can weave the balance of the cloth evenly once you have that template, and it will be possible to match seams. This first little bit of patterned cloth can be your souvenir!

FABRIC DESCRIPTION: Plain weave and monk's-belt overshot.

WARP: 20/2 wool worsted at 5600 yd/lb: gray.

WEFT: Ground—same as warp: black.

Pattern—wool singles at 2000 yd/lb: rust and camel.

YARN SOURCES & COLORS: The warp and ground weft are Oregon Worsted's Willamette: #1625 Charcoal and #515 Black. The pattern wefts are Harrisville Singles: Rust and Camel.

E.P.I.: 24.

WARP COLOR ORDER FOR FABRIC #1:

gray (Charcoal)	12	12	12	12	12	= 48/repeat
rust (Rust Brown)	20	20	20	20		= 80/repeat
beige (Camel)		2	4	6	8	= 20/repeat

6-SHAFT DRAFT FOR FABRIC #1:

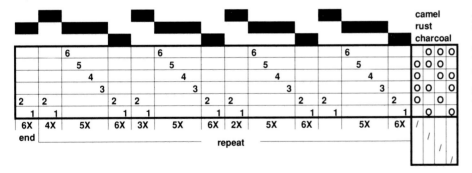

8-SHAFT DRAFT FOR FABRIC #1:

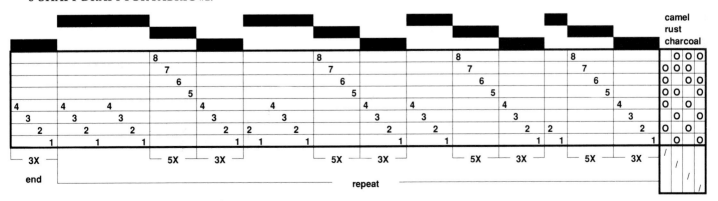

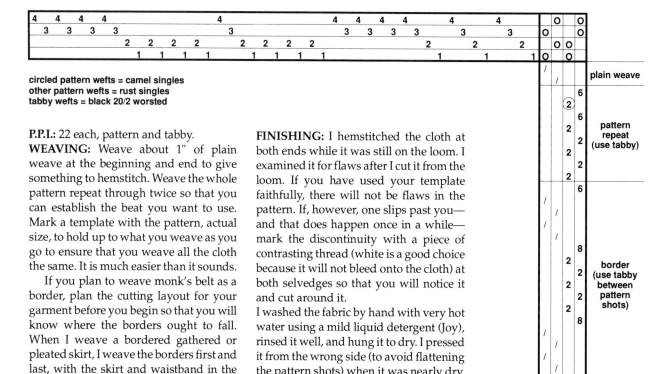

circled pattern wefts = camel singles
other pattern wefts = rust singles
tabby wefts = black 20/2 worsted

P.P.I.: 22 each, pattern and tabby.
WEAVING: Weave about 1" of plain weave at the beginning and end to give something to hemstitch. Weave the whole pattern repeat through twice so that you can establish the beat you want to use. Mark a template with the pattern, actual size, to hold up to what you weave as you go to ensure that you weave all the cloth the same. It is much easier than it sounds.

If you plan to weave monk's belt as a border, plan the cutting layout for your garment before you begin so that you will know where the borders ought to fall. When I weave a bordered gathered or pleated skirt, I weave the borders first and last, with the skirt and waistband in the middle. In any case, make and use a template for the borders so that they will match at the seams.

FINISHING: I hemstitched the cloth at both ends while it was still on the loom. I examined it for flaws after I cut it from the loom. If you have used your template faithfully, there will not be flaws in the pattern. If, however, one slips past you—and that does happen once in a while—mark the discontinuity with a piece of contrasting thread (white is a good choice because it will not bleed onto the cloth) at both selvedges so that you will notice it and cut around it.
I washed the fabric by hand with very hot water using a mild liquid detergent (Joy), rinsed it well, and hung it to dry. I pressed it from the wrong side (to avoid flattening the pattern shots) when it was nearly dry.

#3: Jacket Fabric   ❷ ❹

PROJECT NOTES: I designed this fabric for use as a jacket. It is about the weight of commercial tweed fabric, although a good deal softer than most tweeds. The high value contrast of the camel pinstripes with the gray/black background makes this fabric quite bold looking. It has been woven at the lower limit of the sett for plain-weave cloth and so is quite supple and not very bulky.

The pinstripes are easy to warp for weavers who warp from the front of the loom (that is, thread first). Those of us who beam our warps first can do it easily if we wind our warp using a warping paddle (4 gray and 1 camel) or use a small, fixed rigid heddle. A rigid heddle that is clamped in one spot does just the same thing as a warping paddle without having to carry the paddle in one's hands; making the cross is a simple matter of using the slots and holes in the heddle the same way you use the heddle to weave. (I am indebted to Harry P. Linder for this useful technique.)
FABRIC DESCRIPTION: Plain weave with warp stripes.
WARP & WEFT: 2-ply Shetland-style

wool at 2000 yd/lb: dark gray and camel warp, black weft.
YARN SOURCES & COLORS: These are Harrisville Shetland Style: Charcoal and Camel warp, Black weft.
E.P.I.: 12.
WARP COLOR ORDER: 4 gray (Charcoal), 1 camel. (End with 4 gray.)
DRAFT:
P.P.I.: 12.
WEAVING: As you might expect, this fabric is very easy to weave. Maintain an even beat as you work. Sometimes it helps, particularly with a dark-colored fabric like this, to look at the open spaces between the threads as you weave. Strive to make those spaces square rather than rectangular, and everything will go well.

You need to know that the black and Charcoal yarns crock, that is, the color comes off on your hands and on anything else that touches the yarns *until they are washed*. The excess dye washes off your hands, wears off your shuttles, and will

wash out of some fabrics. As I was winding the warp, I could see that my hands were turning black so when it came time to weave, I wore a dark-colored cotton apron. After I finished weaving this fabric (and fabric #4), I washed the apron. All of the black came off my apron (I had thought that dyes that worked on wool would not work on cotton), but I do not know if it will come off wool fabric or blended-fiber fabrics.

After the fabric had been washed, it no longer crocked. I tried hard to get the color to rub off on white cloth and it did not.
FINISHING: I hemstitched the fabric at both ends and then cut it from the loom and examined it for flaws. I washed it in very hot water using a mild liquid detergent (Joy). I used two detergent baths because the first one colored up a lot as the excess dye came out in the wash water. The second one showed almost no bleeding, and the rinse (twice is always a good idea) showed none at all. I hung the fabric to dry and pressed it when nearly dry.

I was concerned that the excess black dye might migrate to the camel yarns, changing their color. I am glad to say that the camel yarns are just the same color after washing as before, so that the color relationship between the charcoal/black and camel was retained.

#4: Plain Skirt Fabric ❷ ❹

PROJECT NOTES: Every collection of fabrics has to have something plain in it; this is the plain fabric in this collection. In fact, there is some color interest in this plain cloth: as is the case with every other cloth in this collection, the warp is gray (some are only partly gray) and the weft is black. There are several reasons that I designed the cloth this way. The first is that gray is supposed to be important this fall, taking over from unrelieved black. The second is that it is more interesting to look at a cloth that is gray and black than it is to look at an all-black one; the color appears richer. The next two reasons are very practical ones: gray/black photographs better than flat black, and it is easier on the eyes to thread gray than it is black.

Again, crocking of the yarns was a minor problem (see Weaving, fabric #3). The washed cloth does not crock at all, but reasonable care must be taken before the yarns have been washed. Above all, do not hesitate to use these yarns because crocking occurs; just take precautions to protect your clothes, and then wash the fabric after it is woven.

This fabric is about the weight of tweed, although much softer. I had in mind using it as a coat fabric. This and the pinstripe can be use in combination, one to trim the other, or one as a jacket and the other as a slim (lined) skirt.

FABRIC DESCRIPTION: Plain weave.
WARP & WEFT: 2-ply Shetland-style wool at 2000 yd/lb: dark gray warp and black weft.
YARN SOURCES & COLORS: These are Harrisville Shetland Style: Charcoal warp and Black weft.
E.P.I.: 12.
DRAFT:
P.P.I.: 12.
WEAVING: Wear your apron as you weave this easy-to-weave fabric. Watch the spaces between the threads (see fabric #3) to help to maintain an even beat.
FINISHING: Finish as directed for fabric #3.

#5: Striped Skirt Fabric ❹

PROJECT NOTES: This fabric was designed to give the illusion of having jaspé, or simple ikat, stripes. I wanted to give the illusion of ikat stripes without actually having to measure, tie, and dye the warp ends that are used to make the stripes. The fabric is plain so that the stripes are shown to best advantage. They are separated in the warp by two charcoal warp ends so that the impact of the fancy yarns is more dramatic.

A spinning wheel, a drop spindle, or even a spindle-type bobbin winder may be used to create the fancy yarn. It is easiest to use a spinning wheel. (If it were not, they never would have been invented!) If you treadle the same number of "beats" with each arm-long draw of both yarns, then the number of twists in the ply will be even everywhere.

If you use a drop spindle, keep an eye on the number of turns that build up so that the plying is even.

A hand-operated bobbin winder (the Swedish ones or the one Harrisville Designs makes will work) may be used to ply the yarns. First, fasten the yarns to the spindle, then hold an arm-span length of yarn with one hand while you turn the winder with the other. Let the spin go into the yarns; do not let them wind onto the spindle yet. When they are twisted enough (about 4 turns per inch looks nice), wind them onto the spindle and draw out another arm's length and repeat. This is like the technique for using a great wheel or walking wheel.

When you have spun your fancy yarn, make it into a skein and set the spin by wetting it thoroughly in warm water (a drop or two of detergent in the water will help). Allow the skein to dry under just enough tension to keep it from kinking, and then use it as you would any other yarn.

The stripes are put into the warp, so after you have made your fancy yarn and put it onto the loom with the other yarns, it is smooth sailing. The stripes are spaced so as to give a nice stripe for a soft skirt. If you wanted to make slacks, you might reduce the width of both the jaspé and the gray/black stripes. The fabric is lightweight, so you probably would want to line your slacks.

FABRIC DESCRIPTION: Plain weave with warp stripes.
WARP & WEFT: 20/2 wool worsted at 5600 yd/lb: gray.
PLIED WARP: Same as warp—dark gold, plied with 2-ply Shetland-style wool at 2000 yd/lb: rust.

YARN SOURCES & COLORS: The worsted is Oregon Worsted's Willamette: #1625 Charcoal and #280 Dark Gold. The 2-ply is Harrisville Shetland Style: Rust.
E.P.I.: 24. I used a 12-dent reed and put 2 ends in each dent. (The fancy yarn was always sleyed with one 20/2 yarn.)
WARP COLOR ORDER:

		repeat			
Charcoal	22	2	2	2	22
Fancy yarn		1	1	1	1

DRAFT:
P.P.I.: 24.
WEAVING: This fabric is very easy to weave and progresses quite rapidly. It is fun to see how the fancy yarn is caught by the weft so first it flashes red and then saffron gold.
FINISHING: Finish as directed for fabric #1.

SWATCH COLLECTION #11

pages 60–63

Fabrics #1–#5   ❹ ❽

PROJECT NOTES: Five different, fairly lightweight fabrics are woven on this warp of 20/2 natural pearl cotton with stripes of colored, slightly textured 8/2 cotton. These fabrics may be used for blouses without a lot of gathers, pleated or lightly gathered skirts or culottes, simple dresses, beach cover-ups or caftans. Consider using these fabrics together in one garment: the plaid could be used as a trim (perhaps a bias strip to bind neck and arms of a dress or top) for the striped fabric.

Eight shafts were used to design these fabrics, but four shafts will do any of them. Use the eight-shaft instructions if you want to weave all the fabrics on one warp. You can use the four-shaft instructions if you want to weave just one of them.

FABRIC DESCRIPTION: Fabric #1: plain weave with warp stripe. Fabric #2: plain weave, plaid. Fabric #3: plain weave with weft-faced broken twill bands. Fabric #4: skip-dented plain weave. Fabric #5: plain weave with inlays.

WARP & WEFT: 20/2 mercerized cotton at 8400 yd/lb: natural off-white.

WARP STRIPES, PLAID & INLAY WEFTS: 8/2 cotton at 3600 yd/lb: light peach, fleshy rose, light yellow, and mint.

YARN SOURCES & COLORS: The 20/2 cotton is UKI color #79 Natural. The 8/2s are UKI colors #41 Peach, #23 Rose, #31 Yellow, and #3 Mint Green.

E.P.I.: 30 for pearl cotton, 15 for 8/2 cotton. I used a 15-dent reed, sleying 2 ends of 20/2 per dent and 1 end of 8/2 per dent.

WARP COLOR ORDER:

			repeat				
Natural 20/2	12	12	12	12	12	12	12
Rose 8/2		2			2		
Peach 8/2			2			2	
Yellow 8/2				2			
Mint Green 8/2							2

P.P.I.: 30 (ground weft).

4-SHAFT DRAFTS: Note that Fabric #3 has 12 ends of natural between each pair of colored ends.

Circled numbers and slashes = 8/2 cotton.

Fabrics 1, 2, and 3

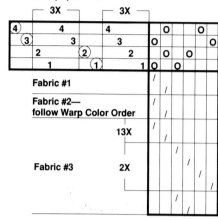

8-SHAFT DRAFTS: Note that 2 out of 12 ends of natural are removed and warp is resleyed in Fabric #3.

Circled numbers and slashes = 8/2 cotton

Fabrics 1 and 2

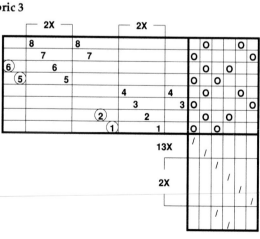

Fabric 3

Fabrics 4 and 5

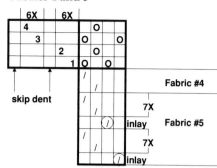

Fabrics 4 and 5

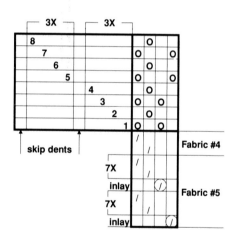

WEAVING: Fabric #1 is woven plain weave using just the 20/2 cotton in natural.

Fabric #2 is woven plain weave following the same order as the Warp Color Order. When you have woven a few repeats so that you can be sure that you have established a steady rhythm, mark a strip of cardboard to use as a weaving template. Use colored pencils or pens to show the color order to avoid mistakes. Be careful to keep an even beat so that you can match your plaids.

Fabric #3 is woven plain weave with broken-twill bands using the 20/2 cotton in natural. I chose broken twill because I wanted to show the colored warp stripes coming and going and the contrast of the lustrous twill stripes against the plain-weave ground. The twill line that appears in a straight-twill treadling would have been distracting.

For the eight-shaft version it was necessary to remove 2 ends in 12 of the 20/2 natural cotton, leaving 10 ends between each pair of 8/2 cotton. The warp was resleyed. When all 12 ends were used, there was a long, distracting skip across 4 ends. If the four-shaft version is used, there can be 12 ends between each pair of 8/2 ends. See the drafts, compare them, and thread accordingly.

Fabric #4 is woven plain weave with the 20/2 cotton in natural. The two ends of 20/2 removed to weave fabric #3 were put back into the warp again, and the ends of 8/2 were cut out. It was not necessary to resley because the ends of 8/2 left two empty dents and only one was needed for the replaced ends (see draft). This fabric has a very subtle stripe. If you prefer a more noticeable effect, you may wish to use the denting I used for the dolman top.

Fabric #5 is woven on the same warp as fabric #4 with no modifications. As you can see by examining the drafts, the warp is threaded and sleyed so that it is easy to inlay the colored wefts with regularity. The skipped dents show just where the inlaid wefts start and stop. The warp is threaded in two blocks (1, 2, 3, 4 and 5, 6, 7, 8 *or* 1, 2 and 3, 4) so that it is easy to lay in wefts in alternate blocks.

The wefts are inlaid in a twill pattern. A partial diagram is given for the sample shown here; I continued the diagonals in the same colors to the edge of the fabric. Many more variations are possible.

The inlay yarns were used double and cut into 1½" lengths. I found after washing, however, that the cut ends of the 8/2 fray a lot, so I used yarn butterflies to

Inlay diagram for Fabric 5:

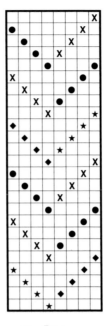

● = Rose
X = Peach
★ = Yellow
◆ = Mint Green

weave the inlaid portion of the yardage for the dolman top. A continuous inlay thread sheds less lint as it is washed and does not show from the front.

FINISHING: All swatches were hemstitched while still on the loom. Any flaws were corrected before they were machine washed in hot water. They were smoothed by hand after washing and then ironed while they were still damp.

Fabrics #6 & #7 ❹

PROJECT NOTES: I wanted to add to the collection a solid-colored fabric with a texture that came from its structure. The use of openwork is a natural one for spring/summer fabrics. I didn't want to weave it as leno, so I looked for a mock leno or canvas weave. I also wanted to preserve the possibility of weaving plain weave everywhere, so I was careful to select a mock leno based on a three-end unit. The draft is a modification of "Canvas weave spots", page 68 of *A Handweaver's Pattern Book* by Marguerite P. Davison.

These colorful, silky fabrics of 20/2 pearl cotton are suitable for dresses, skirts, or shirts. The mock-leno sections give the fabrics a more fragile and delicate appearance than they actually have. I machine washed the swatches you see here twice, full cycle, to be sure that the fabrics

would remain strong and not be damaged by further washing.

The striped fabric is woven with the striped areas sleyed three per dent with a skipped dent in between, which makes the stripes very open. The fabric with the squares was resleyed so that the plain-weave ground surrounding the squares would be the same above and below each square as it is on either side of them. The result is a less showy, more modest fabric.

FABRIC DESCRIPTION: Plain weave with mock-leno warp stripes or squares.
WARP & WEFT: 20/2 mercerized cotton at 8400 yd/lb: bright pink.
YARN SOURCES & COLORS: This 20/2 cotton is UKI color #71 Tahitian Pink.
E.P.I.: 40. Fabric #6 is sleyed 2 per dent in a 20-dent reed for plain-weave sections and 3, 0, 3, 0, etc., for mock-leno stripes. Fabric #7 is sleyed 2 per dent in a 20-dent reed throughout.
DRAFT:

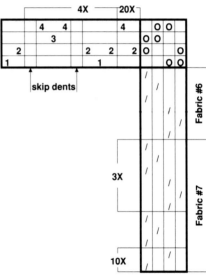

P.P.I.: 40.
WEAVING: Fabric #6 is woven according to the draft shown above. It is an easy one-shuttle weave with a short treadling repeat. I was concerned that the mock-leno portions of the warp would become looser as the warp was woven, but I did not have that trouble in a 3-yard warp. I am sure that if a very inelastic fiber such as linen were used, tension inequalities would result during weaving. If you plan to weave yards and yards of this fabric (for curtains?), use a second beam for the open stripes.

Fabric #7 has a longer repeat. The use of a template (a strip of cardboard on which the repeat is marked so that the repeat length may be checked) is highly recommended. Because there is so much plain weave, this warp is not as likely to develop loose areas.

FINISHING: I hemstitched the fabrics on the loom and examined them for flaws after cutting them from the loom. I machine washed them, full cycle, in hot water. I smoothed the fabrics by hand and then ironed them while damp.

Fabrics #8–#10 ❷ ❹

PROJECT NOTES: Designed to provide the "bottom weight" (slacks, shorts, tailored skirts) that is needed to balance this collection, these three fabrics are more alike than the others, but each has its own character. The first two are woven with a textured 8/2 cotton across an 8/2 cotton warp. The warp is a very bright pink; the first weft is a duller pink of almost the same value, which softens the warp color considerably. The second weft is the same texture in an orange of lighter value. The third weft varies only slightly in hue and value, but is lustrous and smooth and less than half the size of the warp yarn. It is 20/2 pearl cotton doubled on the bobbin to make the sizes of the warp and weft more nearly equal; a balanced cloth is achieved by adjusting the beat. The result is a cloth that plays a dull texture against a shiny one. It looks lively from a distance and is very interesting when observed up close.

FABRIC DESCRIPTION: Plain weave.

WARP: 8/2 cotton at 3600 yd/lb: rose.

WEFT: Fabric #8—same as warp: fleshy rose.

Fabric #9—same as warp: light peach.

Fabric #10—20/2 mercerized cotton at 8400 yd/lb, used doubled: pink.

YARN SOURCES & COLORS: These 8/2 cotton yarns are UKI colors. The warp is #24 Beauty Rose. The fleshy rose weft is #23 Rose; the light peach weft is #41 Peach. The 20/2 weft is UKI color #71 Tahitian Pink.

E.P.I.: 18.

DRAFT:

P.P.I.: 18.

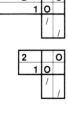

WEAVING: Fabric #8 is woven with a single shuttle. The friction of the slightly rough warp and weft requires a steady, moderate beat. An uneven beat will show streaks, even with colors as close in hue and value as this warp and weft.

Fabric #9 is also a single-shuttle weave. Because the warp and weft colors are further apart in hue and value, it is essential to beat evenly. The result is a very interesting fabric for all its simplicity—one which changes color as it moves.

Fabric #10 is the most challenging of this trio of fabrics to weave, but it is still easy. The first trick is doubling the yarn on the bobbin so that there won't be loops of yarn poking out of the finished fabric. The most difficult problem is the one I faced: one cone of yarn and no doubling equipment. I found it best to wind two bobbins equally full and then use them to create the doubled bobbin. (If the yarn sources are different, for example, one bobbin and one cone, the yarn comes off at different tensions and different rates.) When you wind the yarns from the two bobbins together onto a third one, use the fingers of one hand as a tension box: weave the threads over and under your fingers to even the tension.

When you have wound your bobbins perfectly, weave with restraint. This smooth yarn presents less friction in the shed, requiring a gentle beat. Furthermore, its size is smaller, even doubled, than that of the 8/2 yarn, so it will pack more easily. If you find yourself beating too hard, resley the warp to 20 e.p.i. The textural variation and light play on the surface of the cloth are well worth the bother. *Or* you may allow little loops to poke up through the cloth to "decorate" the surface by deliberately winding the bobbins with tight tension on one of the two threads. Sometimes what appears to be a problem can be seen, instead, as an asset.

FINISHING: See fabrics #6 and #7.

SWATCH COLLECTION #12

pages 64–67

#1: Suit Fabric ❹

PROJECT NOTES: I wanted to make a soft, fine tweed suitable for a jacket or jacket and skirt. I wanted some vertical emphasis, a slimming effect, and planned dark gray ends to mark the breaks in the twill direction. The weft reversals were planned to occur at a slightly longer interval so that rectangles rather than squares were produced for added vertical emphasis.

FABRIC DESCRIPTION: Broken point twill (dornick twill).

WARP & WEFT: 18-cut single-ply woolen yarn at 3600 yd/lb: gray, charcoal, and gray-blue.

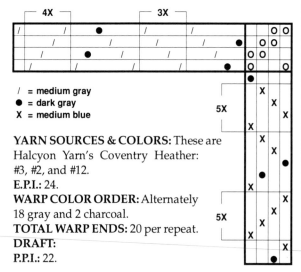

= medium gray
● = dark gray
X = medium blue

YARN SOURCES & COLORS: These are Halcyon Yarn's Coventry Heather: #3, #2, and #12.

E.P.I.: 24.

WARP COLOR ORDER: Alternately 18 gray and 2 charcoal.

TOTAL WARP ENDS: 20 per repeat.

DRAFT:

P.P.I.: 22.

TAKE-UP & SHRINKAGE: 12% in width and 9% in length.

WEAVING: The most important thing to remember when weaving a fabric with weft stripes is that the stripes must be the same width or they cannot be matched when the garment is made. I make a template from a strip of lightweight cardboard on which I mark the weft stripes with colored pencil. The colored pencil makes it easy to prevent errors when I work with several stripes that are all about the same width.

These yarns are highly twisted. In weaving 5 yards I had no frayed or broken ends, but the weft yarn tended to kink in the weaving. Don't pull the shuttle out to the side as it leaves the shed or it will reel out extra weft which will kink up instead of lying flat against the fell as it is beaten into place. Wind the bobbins carefully, pay attention to how you handle the shuttle, and keep a sharp eye on the fell so that you can correct kinks as they occur.

FINISHING: When the fabric is off the loom, hold it up to a strong light to find knots and kinks that need correcting. There is a lot of spinning oil in tweed yarns, so wash the fabric in moderately hot water with a generous amount of liquid detergent. Add a little liquid fabric softener in the third rinse and spin the fabric briefly. Press the fabric on both sides until it is dry to the touch.

#2: Plain Skirt Fabric ❹

PROJECT NOTES: This fabric was designed to complement the dornick twill described above and the granite weave.
FABRIC DESCRIPTION: 2/2 twill.
WARP & WEFT: 18-cut single-ply woolen yarn at 3600 yd/lb: gray-blue.
YARN SOURCES & COLORS: This is Halcyon Yarn's Coventry Heather: #12.
E.P.I.: 24.
DRAFT:
P.P.I.: 22.
WEAVING: This fabric is very easy to weave, but be sure to maintain an even beat to avoid streaking.
FINISHING: Same as for fabric #1.

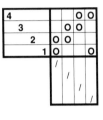

#3: Granite Weave Skirt Fabric ❹

PROJECT NOTES: Granite weave is a twill or crepe weave that produces a small overall pattern or figure that looks like granite. The simplest granite is the one I chose: a broken twill with a light color in one direction and a dark one in the other.
FABRIC DESCRIPTION: Granite weave (2/2 broken twill).
WARP & WEFT: 18-cut single-ply woolen yarn at 3600 yd/lb: gray and gray-blue (use one for warp and the other for weft).
YARN SOURCES & COLORS: These are Halcyon Yarn's Coventry Heather: #3 and #12.
E.P.I.: 24.
DRAFT:
P.P.I.: 20.
WEAVING: An even beat is important, but it is a little harder to overbeat a broken twill because where the twill changes directions the sheds are opposite and resist being beaten closely.
FINISHING: Same as for fabric #1.

#4: Dornick Twill Suit Fabric ❹

PROJECT NOTES: To create a very elegant cloth, I chose a fine Merino wool and

added a silk yarn in small amounts to bring a glint of light to an otherwise matte fabric. I was concerned that the Merino yarn might be more elastic than the silk. I wove and finished a couple of yards without seeing the silk yarns buckle in the finished cloth. However, if you use other yarns in this way, weave a generous sample to be sure.

This fabric is intended for skirt, suit, or even dress patterns which recommend gabardine.
FABRIC DESCRIPTION: Broken point twill (dornick twill).
WARP: 24/2 wool worsted at 6400 yd/lb: dark blue.

30/2 silk at 7250 yd/lb: blue.
WEFT: Same 24/2 wool worsted as warp: dark blue.
YARN SOURCES & COLORS: The worsted is Halcyon Yarn's 24/2 Merino: #2 navy. The silk is Gemstone Silk 30/2 from Halcyon Yarn: #12 Sapphire.
E.P.I.: 32.
WARP COLOR ORDER: Alternately 2 ends of silk and 26 ends of wool, beginning and ending with the silk.
TOTAL WARP ENDS: 28 per repeat.
DRAFT:

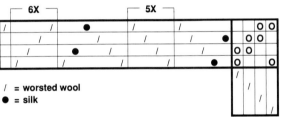

/ = worsted wool
● = silk

P.P.I.: 32.
TAKE-UP & SHRINKAGE: 9% in width and 8% in length.
WEAVING: I put silk ends at the selvedges because they are stronger than the wool and had no breakage. Establish a rhythm as you weave this fabric. If an edge end floats, try starting the treadling at a different point or starting the shuttle from the opposite side. If you like to use floating selvedges, use the silk ends.
FINISHING: Examine the cloth for flaws and correct them. Worsted yarns are spun without added spinning oil so washing does not require a lot of detergent. I use moderately hot water and less manipulation or agitation when I wash worsted than when I wash tweed fabrics. Rinse the fabric twice at the same temperature (fabric softener is optional), and spin briefly. Press the fabric before it is dry; use a press cloth to avoid putting a shine on the fabric.

#5: Striped Merino Suit Fabric ❽ ❹

PROJECT NOTES: This fabric began with an idea about a way to weave a cloth quickly with one color warp and one color weft and produce a striped fabric with the same weight everywhere. Warp-faced twill stripes on a plain-weave ground would produce fabrics with two weights: plain weave and twill, but weaving twill stripes side by side, warp-faced 1/3 then weft-faced 3/1, produces just the hand and appearance I wanted.

I chose two colors very similar in value and hue so that the stripes would be subtle and so that the weft picks that show in the warp-faced sections wouldn't be distracting and vice versa. I was surprised to find that the yarn which I thought was dull in texture has a subtle luster which this weave shows nicely. This fabric would be good for skirts, suits, and dresses.
FABRIC DESCRIPTION: 3/1 and 1/3 twill.
WARP & WEFT: 24/2 wool worsted at 6400 yd/lb: lavender-rose and dark red (use one for warp and the other for weft).
YARN SOURCES & COLORS: These are Halcyon Yarn's 24/2 Merino: #22 and #23.
E.P.I.: 32.
DRAFT: Note: The 4-shaft version does not have warp-faced stripes next to weft-faced stripes, but similar color play may be achieved by putting stripes into the warp, threading the warp as a dornick twill, and weaving it so that the fabric is warp-faced.

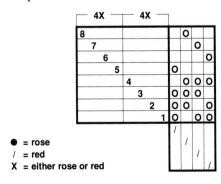

● = rose
/ = red
X = either rose or red

4-SHAFT VERSION:

P.P.I.: 32.

WEAVING: This fabric weaves quickly and easily. There was no warp breakage.
FINISHING: Same as for fabric #4.

#6: Jacket or Coat Fabric ❷ ❹

PROJECT NOTES: I wanted to add a slightly kicky fabric to this collection for textural contrast. The color of the fabric is the same as fabric #5 with the added sparkle of the lively red and orange flecks.

This tweed would be nice for a raglan-sleeved jacket or coat with padded shoulders. I like it teamed with the elegant blue worsted fabric as well as with the red worsted it matches.

The yarn is heavy enough that a plain-weave fabric has plenty of body and substance for a coat. A twill structure produces quite a heavy fabric. There is so much visual activity in the yarn itself that no structural interest is needed.
FABRIC DESCRIPTION: Plain weave.
WARP & WEFT: Singles wool tweed at 1700 yd/lb: dark red.
YARN SOURCES & COLORS: This is Surrey Tweeds from Halcyon Yarn: #13 (maroon with red flecks).
E.P.I.: 14.
DRAFT:
P.P.I.: 14.
TAKE-UP & SHRINK-AGE: 12% in width and 8% in length.
WEAVING: Weave the fabric to square. This yarn is tightly spun: see fabric #1 for advice.
FINISHING: See fabric #1. Full this fabric a little harder than the finer tweeds. When it is washed, it will track. If you choose to leave the tracking in, the fabric will be bumpier to the touch and look rather trendy. If you choose to take the tracking out as I did, steam press the fabric before it has dried while stretching it flat. Removing the tracking is work, but it isn't difficult.

SWATCH COLLECTION #13

pages 68–70

#1: Skirt or Dress Fabric ❷ ❹

PROJECT NOTES: This 100% silk fabric is woven in plain weave to make it lightweight. The texture of the yarn keeps it from sliding in the warp or weft direction, even at a relatively open sett.
FABRIC DESCRIPTION: Plain weave.
WARP & WEFT: Singles silk noil at 4400 yd/lb: natural.
YARN SOURCES & COLORS: The yarn originally used was Aurora Silk's Natural Tussah #105. You could substitute a comparable size of tussah silk such as Tussah Fine Singles at 4220 yd/lb from The Silk Tree or a blend such as 18/2 silk/rayon (50% tussah silk/50% bright rayon, blended) at 4500 yd/lb from Crystal Palace: #51783.
E.P.I.: 18 (sleyed 1, 2 in a 12-dent reed).
DRAFT:
P.P.I.: 18.
TAKE-UP & SHRINK-AGE: 17% in width and 10% in length.
WEAVING: Maintain an even beat and advance the warp frequently to minimize wear on the selvedges.
FINISHING: Hemstitch the fabric while it is still on the loom, note and correct any flaws after cutting it off the loom, and wash in moderately hot water with a mild liquid detergent. Rinse twice at the same temperature, and press the fabric while it is still quite damp.

#2: Top Fabric ❻

PROJECT NOTES: This silk/cotton fabric is woven of silk noils and shiny pearl cotton. It behaves like plain-weave cloth, which it very nearly is.
FABRIC DESCRIPTION: Overchecked plain weave with warp and weft floats.
WARP & WEFT: Singles silk noil at 4400 yd/lb: natural.

10/2 mercerized cotton at 4200 yd/lb: tan.
YARN SOURCES & COLORS: The silk is the same as that in fabric #1. The cotton is UKI color #96 Deep Beige.
E.P.I.: Silk 18, cotton 24 (in a 12-dent reed the silk is sleyed 1, 2 and the cotton 2 per dent).
WARP COLOR ORDER: See draft.
TOTAL WARP ENDS: 8 silk and 4 cotton per repeat.
DRAFT: below.
P.P.I.: Silk 18, cotton 24.
TAKE-UP & SHRINKAGE: 8-9% in width and length.
WEAVING: Weave to square. Use a template to ensure matching the check at seams.
FINISHING: The fabric was hemstitched on the loom, inspected for flaws when it was cut off, and washed in moderately hot water using mild detergent. It was rinsed twice at the same temperature and pressed while still damp.

#3: Jacket Fabric ❷ ❹

PROJECT NOTES: This 100% linen fabric was woven quickly and easily. The yarns are plied and are quite strong. I wetted the bobbins (plastic, not wooden or paper quills) with warm water after they were

DRAFT FOR FABRIC #2:

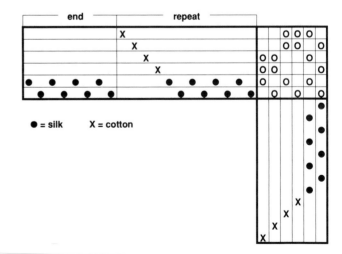

● = silk   X = cotton

126

wound to help soften the weft so that it would beat in more easily and prevent "overspinning" and snarling in boat shuttles. I held the bobbins under hot running water until their surfaces were wet all over. Because linen wicks quickly, it is not necessary to soak them. It is dry where I live; the cloth dried before it was wound onto the cloth beam. Do not wind damp cloth on the cloth beam because it will mildew.

FABRIC DESCRIPTION: Plain weave.
WARP & WEFT: 16/2 line linen at 2400 yd/lb: light gray, beige, and natural (dark grayed tan) for warp, and beige weft.
YARN SOURCES & COLORS: These are Halcyon Yarn's Newport Linen 16/2: colors #105, #106, and #102 warp, and #106 weft.
E.P.I.: 18 (sleyed 1, 2 in a 12-dent reed).
WARP COLOR ORDER:

light gray	1	1		= 2/repeat
beige		1	1	= 2/repeat
natural			1	1 = 2/repeat

DRAFT:
P.P.I.: 18.
TAKE-UP & SHRINKAGE: 8-10% in width and length.
WEAVING: Weave with an even, strong beat. Use a double beat; beat as the shed is being changed and after the new shed has been opened.
FINISHING: Hemstitch the cloth while it is on the loom. Wash it in very hot water with mild liquid detergent. Let the fabric soak for ten minutes or more, and then agitate it well to obliterate the reed marks, rinse well, and iron while it is still damp.

#4: Blouse Fabrics ❷ ❹

PROJECT NOTES: These fine cotton fabrics with tussah silk noil warp stripes in one and warp/weft stripes in the other are intended for a blouse but would be suitable for a skirt or dress. I was concerned that the rate of shrinkage between the two yarns might cause puckers or buckling in the cloth depending on which shrank more. The only way to be sure was to weave the fabric and wash it, so I did. If you choose to replace the tussah silk with 8/2 cotton, weave and wash a generous sample so that you can be sure there will be no problem.
FABRIC DESCRIPTION: Plain weave.
WARP & WEFT: 20/2 mercerized cotton at 8400 yd/lb: dark forest green.
Singles silk noil at 4400 yd/lb: natural.
YARN SOURCES & COLORS: The cotton is UKI color #98 Mountain. The silk is the same as that in fabric #1.
E.P.I.: Cotton 30, silk 15 (in a 15-dent reed the cotton is 2 per dent and the silk is 1 per dent).
WARP COLOR ORDER: below.
DRAFT:
P.P.I.: Cotton 30, silk 15.
TAKE-UP & SHRINKAGE: 6% in width and length.
WEFT COLOR ORDER: For the striped fabric, use the cotton weft alone. For the plaid fabric, follow the same order as the warp.
WEAVING: Weave with an even beat, striving for a balanced cloth. Make a template of lightweight cardboard to be sure that the plaid is squared and will match at the seams. Make the template by laying it on the warp and marking the silk ends on it.

FINISHING: Hemstitch the fabric while it is on the loom, inspect it for flaws when it is cut off, and wash in moderately hot water using a mild liquid detergent. Rinse twice at the same temperature, and iron while damp.

#5: Multipurpose Fabric ❷ ❹

PROJECT NOTES: This plain-weave fabric has a complex balanced stripe. It has a cotton warp and silk weft; the silk weft makes the fabric softer and more supple without changing its stability. The width of the stripe repeat in the finished fabric is 2⅞".
FABRIC DESCRIPTION: Plain weave.
WARP: 8/2 cotton at 3600 yd/lb: dark green, beige, light gray, and tan.
10/2 mercerized cotton at 4200 yd/lb: tan.
WEFT: Singles silk noil at 4400 yd/lb: natural.
YARN SOURCES & COLORS: The 8/2 cottons are UKI colors #12 Dark Green, #16 Polo Tan, #59 Silver, and #15 Beige. The 10/2 is UKI color #96 Deep Beige. The silk weft is the same as that in fabric #1.
E.P.I.: 20.
WARP COLOR ORDER: below.
DRAFT:
P.P.I.: 20.
TAKE-UP & SHRINKAGE: 15% in width and 5% in length.
WEAVING: Weave with an even beat. Advance the warp frequently because the 8/2 cotton is softly spun and subject to wear.
FINISHING: See fabric #4.

WARP COLOR ORDER FOR FABRIC #4:

				X						
cotton	20	16	12	8	6	4	4	4	20	= 74/repeat
silk		2	2	2	2	2	2	2	2	= 16/repeat

WARP COLOR ORDER FOR FABRIC #5:

					X							
dk. green (Dk. Green)	1	1	2	1	1		1	1	2	1	1	1 1 = 14/repeat
beige (Polo Tan)	6			6		6			6			= 24/repeat
lt. gray (Silver)			1	1	1	1						= 4/repeat
tan (Beige)		1	1	1	1		1	1	1	1		= 8/repeat
tan 10/2 (Deep Beige)			2	2	2	2	2			6		= 16/repeat

#6: Multipurpose Fabric ❷ ❹

PROJECT NOTES: This cotton and silk fabric is designed with an unbalanced (asymmetrical) stripe. I like to look at stripes like these, but they require special care in choosing a pattern and laying it out. A repeating two-end stripe of dark green forms a matrix into which two-end stripes of three other colors are set: three light (Silver), three medium (Polo Tan), and three dark (Beige). The width of the stripe repeat in the finished cloth is 1½".
FABRIC DESCRIPTION: Plain weave.
WARP: 8/2 cotton at 3600 yd/lb: dark green, beige, light gray, and tan.
WEFT: Singles silk noil at 4400 yd/lb: natural.
YARN SOURCES & COLORS: The 8/2 cottons are UKI colors #12 Dark Green, #16 Polo Tan, #59 Silver, and #15 Beige. The silk weft is the same as that in fabric #1.
E.P.I.: 20.
WARP COLOR ORDER: above right.
DRAFT:
P.P.I.: 18.
TAKE-UP & SHRINK-AGE: 14% in width and 6% in length.
WEAVING: Weave with an even beat, advancing the warp frequently .
FINISHING: See fabric #4.

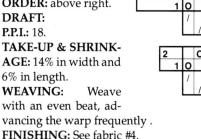

SWATCH COLLECTION #14

pages 72–75

#1: Jacket or Skirt Fabric ❷ ❹

PROJECT NOTES: This lively plain-weave fabric is the cornerstone of this swatch collection. The "action" is all in the yarn: dramatic flecks of black and red-violet on a blue ground. The warp and weft yarn is used in all but one of the fabrics in the rest of the collection.
FABRIC DESCRIPTION: Plain weave.
WARP & WEFT: Wool singles tweed at 2000 yd/lb: blue-violet tweed.
YARN SOURCES & COLORS: This is Harrisville Singles Tweed: True Blue.
E.P.I.: 15 (sleyed 1, 2 in a 10-dent reed).
DRAFT:
P.P.I.: 15.
TAKE-UP & SHRINK-AGE: 6% in width and length.

WEAVING: Use a moderate beat to produce a balanced cloth. Count the picks per inch to establish your beat.
FINISHING: Hemstitch fabric while it is on the loom. Find and correct any flaws. Wash in moderately hot water using a liquid detergent. Long lengths may require a second washing: tweed yarns have a fair amount of spinning oil. Rinse well. Steam press well on both sides before the fabric air dries completely.

#2: Vest Fabric ❹

PROJECT NOTES: One of the properties of the tweed yarn was exploited in the design of this fabric. The woolen-spun tweed yarn blooms and becomes slightly fluffy when it is washed. It is crammed into one dent and woven as one end, although threaded as four separate ends, and left unwoven at intervals in the cloth so that it spreads out to form ovals of tweed yarn on the surface of the cloth.
FABRIC DESCRIPTION: Plain weave with warp floats.
WARP & WEFT: 24/2 wool worsted at 6400 yd/lb: gray-blue (for warp and weft).
Wool singles tweed at 2000 yd/lb: blue-violet tweed (for warp only).
YARN SOURCES & COLORS: The worsted is 24/2 Merino Item 177 from Halcyon Yarn: #29 Gray-blue. The tweed is Harrisville Singles Tweed: True Blue.
E.P.I.: In a 12-dent reed, sley the worsted 2 per dent and the tweed 4 per dent.
WARP COLOR ORDER: 12 worsted and 4 tweed (see draft), ending with worsted.
DRAFT:

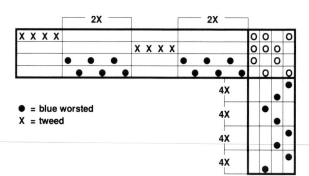

● = blue worsted
X = tweed

P.P.I.: 30.
TAKE-UP & SHRINKAGE: 7½% in width and 8% in length.
WEAVING: Maintain an even, firm beat. Advance the warp often to protect the selvedge ends.
FINISHING: Hemstitch fabric while it is on the loom. Find and correct any flaws. Wash to remove the spinning oil from the tweed and fluff it out. Use moderately hot water and mild liquid detergent; rinse well. Steam press from the back when nearly air dry.

#3: Jacket Fabric ❷ ❹

PROJECT NOTES: I had in mind designing a color-and-weave-effect fabric in which the tweed yarn made a pattern like the diagram of plain weave against a dark ground. I drew down the pattern and figured out how to thread and weave it.
FABRIC DESCRIPTION: Plain weave.
WARP & WEFT: 24/2 wool worsted at 6400 yd/lb: black.
Wool singles tweed at 2000 yd/lb: blue-violet tweed.
YARN SOURCES & COLORS: The worsted is 24/2 Merino Item 177 from Halcyon Yarn: #5 Black. The tweed is Harrisville Singles Tweed: True Blue.
E.P.I.: In a 15-dent reed, sley the worsted 2 per dent and the tweed 1 per dent.
WARP COLOR ORDER: 2 black worsted, 1 blue tweed (see draft).
DRAFT: on next page.
P.P.I.: 24.
TAKE-UP & SHRINKAGE: 6½% in width and length.
WEAVING: Use a moderate, even beat. The shuttle carrying the worsted yarn always starts on the same side because it is used for two shots, which helps to keep track of where you are. The shuttle carrying the tweed is used for single shots between the black shots, so it alternates sides. Watch the pattern as it goes so that you can catch any

errors as you make them; correcting flaws later is an experience worth avoiding.

FINISHING: Hemstitch the fabric while it is on the loom. Find and correct—or mark so you can cut around—flaws. Wash in moderately hot water with mild liquid detergent. Steam press well before it is completely air dry.

DRAFT FOR FABRIC #3:

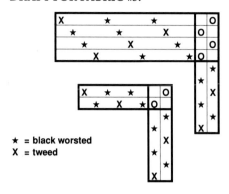

★ = black worsted
X = tweed

#4: Tunic-jacket Fabric ❹

PROJECT NOTES: This soft fabric is designed with three-pick warp floats so that each yarn in the warp comes to the surface to produce dotted lines on the surface of the fabric. The worsted yarns are used doubled throughout in both warp and weft.

FABRIC DESCRIPTION: Plain weave with warp floats.

WARP & WEFT: 24/2 wool worsted at 6400 yd/lb (used doubled): black (warp only) and gray-blue (warp and weft).

Wool singles tweed at 2000 yd/lb: blue-violet tweed (warp only).

YARN SOURCES & COLORS: The worsteds are 24/2 Merino Item 177 from Halcyon Yarn: #5 Black and #29 Gray-blue. The tweed is Harrisville Singles Tweed: True Blue.

E.P.I.: 18 (3 per dent in a 6-dent reed).

WARP COLOR ORDER: 1 doubled black worsted, 1 double blue worsted, 1 tweed (see draft).

DRAFT:

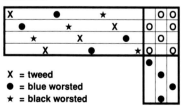

X = tweed
● = blue worsted
★ = black worsted

P.P.I.: 20.

TAKE-UP & SHRINKAGE: 12% in width and 11½% in length.

WEAVING: Use the gray-blue worsted, doubled, as weft. Strive for a light, even beat.

FINISHING: See fabric #3.

#5: Coat Fabric ❽

PROJECT NOTES: The colors in the tweed were picked up in fancy yarns, two loopy and two brushed mohairs. The structure is a variation on plain weave; each area weaves plain weave half the time and basket weave half the time.

The color arrangement in the fabric makes a series of overchecks that seem to be at different levels in the fabric because of their colors. The plaid is an uneven one and requires extra care in laying out the pattern pieces, but the results are interesting and well worth the effort.

The brushed mohair yarns tend to stick when some sheds are opened. Because the same colors are available in loop, you might want to consider replacing the mohair with loop. The loop may be brushed in the finishing process to make it resemble a brushed yarn. If you brush the fabric vigorously, all the loop yarns will be opened. The choice is yours.

FABRIC DESCRIPTION: Plain and basket weaves.

WARP & WEFT: Wool singles tweed at 2000 yd/lb: blue-violet tweed.

Mohair/wool loop at 1350 yd/lb: red-violet and blue-violet.

Mohair/wool brushed yarn at 1170 yd/lb: black and lavender.

YARN SOURCES & COLORS: The tweed is Harrisville Singles Tweed: True Blue. The loop is Victorian Bouclé (58% wool/30% mohair/12% nylon) Item 163 from Halcyon Yarn: #120 and #123. The brushed yarn is Victorian Brushed Mohair (70% mohair/25% wool/5% nylon) Item 164 from Halcyon Yarn: #134 and #124.

E.P.I.: 16 (2 per dent in an 8-dent reed).

WARP & WEFT COLOR ORDER: below.

DRAFT: below.

P.P.I.: 16.

TAKE-UP & SHRINKAGE: 10½% in width and 11% in length.

WEAVING: Use a moderate, even beat. Beat before and after each shot using brushed mohair and loop yarns. The brushed mohair in the warp tends to stick, making the sheds open reluctantly. This stickiness slows the weaving process. Watch carefully to avoid weaving errors. Use a template to keep the checks even.

FINISHING: See fabric #3. While steam pressing the fabric, brush it gently to raise the nap of the brushed mohair. If you brush vigorously, the loops in the wool loop will break, making those yarns fuzzy.

DRAFT FOR FABRIC #5:

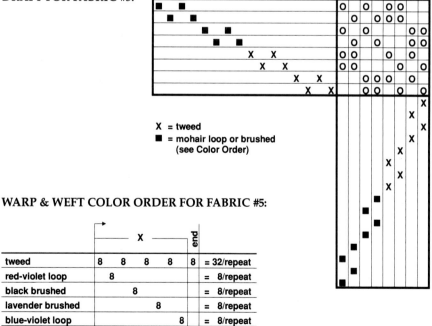

X = tweed
■ = mohair loop or brushed (see Color Order)

WARP & WEFT COLOR ORDER FOR FABRIC #5:

		X		end	
tweed	8	8	8	8	= 32/repeat
red-violet loop	8				= 8/repeat
black brushed		8			= 8/repeat
lavender brushed			8		= 8/repeat
blue-violet loop				8	= 8/repeat

#6: Dress Fabric

PROJECT NOTES: This dress fabric is made of fine pearl cotton. The colors are from the tweed. It is woven in a simple overcheck, a simplified version of the coat fabric. In the center of the large, blue squares are squares of canvas weave. This structure may be woven on just four shafts. Most of the warp is carried on shafts 1 and 2, so be sure that you have enough heddles on those shafts before you begin to thread. This fabric might also be woven in wool: use worsted wool so that the canvas weave opens up as it does here; in a woolen yarn, the structure will be blurred.

FABRIC DESCRIPTION: Plain and canvas weaves.

WARP & WEFT: 20/2 mercerized cotton at 8400 yd/lb: royal blue and red-violet.

YARN SOURCES & COLORS: These are UKI colors #16 Royal and #102 Magenta.

E.P.I.: 30 (3 per dent in a 10-dent reed). Be sure to sley the canvas-weave areas as the draft indicates (one adjacent dent will have only 2 ends).

DRAFT FOR FABRIC #6:

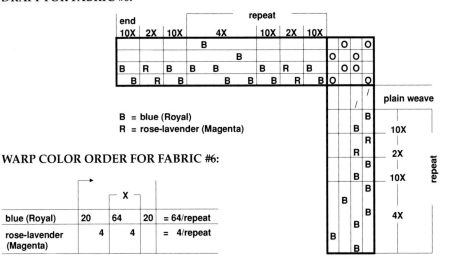

B = blue (Royal)
R = rose-lavender (Magenta)

WARP COLOR ORDER FOR FABRIC #6:

		X		
blue (Royal)	20	64	20	= 64/repeat
rose-lavender (Magenta)		4	4	= 4/repeat

P.P.I.: 30.

TAKE-UP & SHRINKAGE: 7% in width and 6% in length.

WEAVING: Advance the warp frequently to protect the selvedge threads; pearl cotton is softly twisted to make it more lustrous. The soft twist makes it more vulnerable to abrasion. Use a template to be sure that the squares in the fabric are square.

FINISHING: Hemstitch ends of fabric. Machine wash in moderately hot water. Iron while damp.

SWATCH COLLECTION #15
pages 76–80

#1: Skirt Fabric ❷ ❹

PROJECT NOTES: This fabric was designed using the stripe sequence of an old Guatemalan fabric. The original was an intense blue with fine red stripes. I have used a fine brown cotton in place of the blue with slightly heavier, textured gray yarn for the stripes. The original fabric is warp-faced and stiffer than this balanced-weave version.

FABRIC DESCRIPTION: Plain weave.

WARP & WEFT: 20/2 mercerized cotton at 8400 yd/lb: light brown (for both warp and weft).

8/2 unmercerized cotton at 3600 yd/lb: gray (for warp only).

YARN SOURCES & COLORS: The 20/2 warp and weft are UKI color #58 Spice. The 8/2 warp is UKI color #1 Grey.

E.P.I.: 30 (3 per dent in a 10-dent reed).

DRAFT:

P.P.I.: 30.

TAKE-UP & SHRINKAGE: 9% in width and length.

WEAVING: I had no trouble weaving this cloth. Sometimes pearl cotton like this frays and breaks at the selvedges. There are a number of things a weaver can do to avoid that trouble: first, wind the warp carefully and evenly, then advance the warp frequently by small amounts. Cotton is stronger when wet so use a plant mister to dampen the selvedges where they will pass through the heddles and the reed. I have found Magic Sizing® spray extremely helpful in strengthening weak selvedges when all else has failed: spray the unwoven warp and weave when it has dried. Aim carefully; the spray is messy and tedious to remove from loom parts.

FINISHING: Hemstitch the cloth on both ends while on the loom; inspect for flaws and correct them after cutting it from the loom; then machine wash, warm, and iron while damp.

#2: Dress Fabric ❷ ❹

PROJECT NOTES: This checked fabric is a liberal interpretation of a checked Guatemalan fabric. A fine 20/2 cotton is used for most of the cloth with a slightly heavier, slightly textured yarn used to outline the brown warp and weft stripes in the gray field. The textured yarn is the same color as the stripe, so it mainly adds textural interest and defines the edges of those stripes well.

FABRIC DESCRIPTION: Plain weave.

WARP & WEFT: 20/2 mercerized cotton at 8400 yd/lb: light brown and bluish gray.

8/2 unmercerized cotton at 3600 yd/lb: brown.

YARN SOURCES & COLORS: The 20/2 is UKI colors #58 Spice and #74 Birch. The 8/2 is UKI color #18 Light Brown.

E.P.I.: In a 10-dent reed, sley 3 ends 20/2 per dent and 1 end 8/2 with 1 end 20/2 in one dent.

WARP COLOR ORDER: on next page.

DRAFT:

WARP COLOR ORDER FOR FABRIC #1:

		repeat					end			
lt. brown (Spice) 20/2	16	16	16	4	4	4	16	16	16	= 60/repeat
gray (Grey) 8/2		2	2	2	2	2	2	2	2	= 12/repeat

WARP COLOR ORDER FOR FABRIC #2:

	repeat		end	
lt. brown (Spice) 20/2		4		= 4/repeat
greenish gray (Birch) 20/2	48		48	= 48/repeat
brown (Light Brown) 8/2	1		1	= 2/repeat

P.P.I.: 28.
TAKE-UP & SHRINKAGE: 9% in width and length.
WEFT COLOR ORDER:

lt. brown (Spice) 20/2		4
greenish gray (Birch) 20/2	44	
brown (Light Brown) 8/2	1	1

WEAVING: Mark and use a template to be sure that the checks are truly square. Strengthen the selvedge ends as described for fabric #1.
FINISHING: See fabric #1.

#3: Skirt Fabric   ❻ ❹

PROJECT NOTES: The stripes in this fabric are based on a Peruvian mantle from the central coast of Peru, probably Chancay, that I saw at the Dallas Museum of Art. I chose cotton in colors as close as possible to the natural pigmented and creamy white cotton in the original fabric. The gray cotton color forms a two-end border on either side of the brown cotton stripes on the creamy white field. The original textile was warp-faced plain weave; this one has warp-faced twill stripes on a plain-weave ground. The version shown requires six shafts.

The same fabric may be woven on four shafts by putting the stripes in the weft direction, where they become weft-faced stripes. If that option is chosen, a template must be used to ensure even spacing and stripe width. Four shuttles are required, one for each color. The warp color order becomes the weft color order, woven across a plain-colored warp.
FABRIC DESCRIPTION: 3/1 twill and plain weave.
WARP & WEFT: 20/2 mercerized cotton at 8400 yd/lb: natural off-white (for both warp and weft).

8/2 unmercerized cotton at 3600 yd/lb: gray, brown, and beige (for warp only).
YARN SOURCES & COLORS: The 20/2 warp and weft are UKI color #79 Natural. The 8/2 warps are UKI colors #1 Grey, #18 Light Brown, and #16 Polo Tan.
E.P.I.: In a 10-dent reed, sley the 20/2 at 3 per dent and the 8/2 at 2 per dent.

WARP COLOR ORDER FOR FABRIC #3:

	repeat			end	
off-white (Natural) 20/2	18	18		18	= 36/repeat
gray (Grey) 8/2	2	2	2	2	= 8/repeat
brown (Light Brown) 8/2	12				= 12/repeat
beige (Polo Tan) 8/2		12			= 12/repeat

DRAFT FOR FABRIC #3:

P.P.I.: 36.
TAKE-UP & SHRINKAGE: 9% in width and length.
WEAVING: See fabric #1. If this fabric is woven using four shafts, it is necessary to mark a template, a lightweight piece of cardboard, with the stripe colors and widths so that their spacing and their widths can be uniform throughout the cloth. It is more trouble to weave the fabric this way, but it is the only way to reproduce it on four shafts.
FINISHING: See fabric #1.

4-SHAFT VERSION:

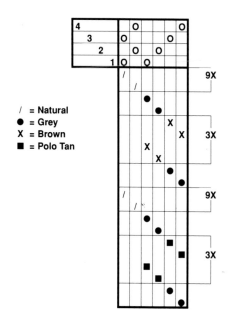

/ = Natural
● = Grey
X = Brown
■ = Polo Tan

#4: Vest Fabric   ❹

PROJECT NOTES: This fabric was designed for use in a vest. Its stripes are quite strong, so it ought to be used in small quantities. The gray supplemental warp stripes bordering the solid brown stripes are based on a Peruvian mantle. I wanted to produce a raised surface and permit the two gray yarns to float, first on the face and then on the back—the cloth is completely reversible—without compromising the structural integrity of the cloth. There is a plain-weave structure inside those warp float areas that adds stability. The areas with supplemental warp ends are very crowded in the reed. I had no trouble because of that crowding, but I do not recommend reed substitution.

FABRIC DESCRIPTION: Plain weave with supplemental warp stripes.
WARP & WEFT: 20/2 mercerized cotton at 8400 yd/lb: natural off-white (for both warp and weft).

8/2 unmercerized cotton at 3600 yd/lb: brown, light gray, and gray (for warp only).
YARN SOURCES & COLORS: The 20/2 warp and weft are UKI color #79 Natural.

The 8/2 warps are UKI colors #18 Light Brown, #59 Silver, and #1 Grey.
E.P.I.: In a 10-dent reed, sley the 20/2 at 3 per dent, the narrow brown stripes 2 per dent with 1 end of 20/2, the wider brown stripes at 2 per dent, and the supplemental warp stripes at 4 ends of 8/2 and 2 ends of 20/2 per dent.
WARP COLOR ORDER: on next page.
DRAFT: on next page.
P.P.I.: 32.
TAKE-UP & SHRINKAGE: 9% in width and length.
WEAVING: See fabric #1.
FINISHING: See fabric #1.

WARP COLOR ORDER FOR FABRIC #4:

			repeat								
	4X			6X	6X	6X	6X		4X		
off-white (Natural) 20/2	12	4	12	1	1	1	1	12	4	12	= 64/repeat
brown (Light Brown) 8/2	2	2				6		2	2		= 16/repeat
lt. gray (Silver) 8/2				1	1	1	1				= 24/repeat
gray (Grey) 8/2				1	1	1	1				= 24/repeat

DRAFT FOR FABRIC #4:

3X — 3X — 3X — 3X — 3X — 6X — 4X — 6X

/ = Natural   ● = Light Brown   X = Silver   ■ = Grey

#5: Blouse Fabric ❹

PROJECT NOTES: This fabric springs from a liberal interpretation of the texture of some brocaded areas I saw in some old Guatemalan huipils in the textile collections at the Dallas Museum of Art. The huipils were designed and woven on a very small scale, as clothing for *santos*, the effigies of saints used in Roman Catholic churches and carried in religious processions. Those brocaded areas did not make up allover patterns as this is; they did not extend from selvedge to selvedge as this does.

The fabric has slightly long floats and should be used in places where it won't be subject to abrasion or snagging: a yoke framing the face, perhaps, but not in a closely fitted sleeve or on a cuff. The draft permits the weaving of plain weave, or near plain weave with some ends doubled in the warp, so that the fabric for a complete blouse may be woven on one warp. The yoke may be either woven in or cut and sewn in. The mercerized cotton is very lustrous and pearly, providing a nice contrast to the matte finish of the unmercerized cotton wefts that make up the pattern.

FABRIC DESCRIPTION: Spider weave or linear zigzag.

WARP & GROUND WEFT: 20/2 mercerized cotton at 8400 yd/lb: natural off-white.

PATTERN WEFT: 8/2 unmercerized cotton at 3600 yd/lb: light gray.

YARN SOURCES & COLORS: The 20/2 is UKI color #79 Natural. The 8/2 is UKI color #59 Silver.

E.P.I.: 30 (3 per dent in a 10-dent reed).

DRAFT: below.

P.P.I.: 30 (ground 20/2).

TAKE-UP & SHRINKAGE: 9% in width and length.

WEAVING: When weaving this fabric, it is very important to put the 8/2 cotton into its sheds with a wide arc: there must be enough slack to allow the picks to move in the cloth as it is finished to form the patterns you see here. Do not be disappointed in the appearance of the cloth on the loom: washing is required to permit the pattern in the cloth to develop fully.

FINISHING: See fabric #1.

DRAFT FOR FABRIC #5:

/ = Natural 20/2   ● = Silver 8/2

SWATCH COLLECTION #16
pages 81–84

#1: Jacket/Coat Fabric ❹

PROJECT NOTES: This four-shaft twill fabric is intended for use as a jacket, sporty suit, or a coat. The fabric as it appears here is soft; for a very tailored cut, increase the sett from 12 e.p.i. to 15. The mohair/wool loop novelty yarn adds interesting surface texture to the fabric. At a closer sett, the loop will be slightly more subdued, appropriate for a more tailored look, and the repeat will be about 20% smaller.

FABRIC DESCRIPTION: 2/2 twill plaid.

WARP & WEFT: 2-ply wool at 1470 yd/lb: brick rose.

Wool/mohair loop at 1350 yd/lb: beige.

Singles wool tweed at 2000 yd/lb: light rose tweed.

YARN SOURCES & COLORS: The 2-ply is Victorian 2-Ply, Item 162, from Halcyon Yarn: #114. The loop is Halcyon's Victorian Bouclé (58% wool/30% mohair/12% nylon), Item 163: #102. The tweed is Harrisville Singles Tweed: Clay.

E.P.I.: 12 (see Project Notes).

WARP COLOR ORDER:

		X			
brick rose 2-ply	8		6	2	= 6/repeat
beige loop	6	6			= 12/repeat
lt. rose tweed		6			= 6/repeat

DRAFT: Follow Warp Color Order in threading and Weft Color Order in treadling.

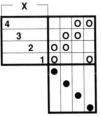

P.P.I.: 12 (or more if closer sett and harder beat).

WEFT COLOR ORDER:

		X	
brick rose 2-ply			6
beige loop	6	6	
lt. rose tweed		6	

TAKE-UP & SHRINKAGE: 10% in width and length.

WEAVING: The loop yarn is finer than the others and can be beaten in too closely if you are not careful. Use restraint—and a cardboard template marked with yarn changes—to square the fabric.

FINISHING: Hemstitch the fabric on both ends while it is on the loom. Inspect it for flaws when it has been cut from the loom. Hand wash in 100–110° F water using a mild liquid detergent (such as Joy), rinsing three times at the same temperature. Use a liquid fabric softener in the final rinse. Allow to air dry until just damp to the touch; steam press. Fluff the loops with your fingertips while the fabric is hot and steamy, to accentuate the loops. (Washing helps bring the loops to the surface.)

#2: Vest or Jacket Fabric ❸ ❴

PROJECT NOTES: This double-weave fabric is designed to be used for a close-fitting (not draped) bolero vest or a jacket. The vest could be constructed so that the stripes fall from the shoulder with the squares woven just above the hem as a border. For use as a jacket, the body might be squared with striped sleeves, or vice versa. Of course, because the stripe and square designs are woven on one threading, either could be chosen and used alone.

As shown, this fabric requires eight shafts. Another version with vertical stripes can be woven in four-shaft Bed-

ford cord, but that weave does not have the option of the squared border.

Although the Bedford cord would have to be lined, the double-cloth version is self-lining and may be used reversed as a trim for itself. The cord version is softer and lighter weight than the firm double weave.

FABRIC DESCRIPTION: 2-block double weave (a 4-shaft Bedford cord version is also given).

WARP & WEFT: Singles wool tweed at 1700 yd/lb: gray-brown and soft brick.

YARN SOURCES & COLORS: These are Halcyon's Surrey Tweeds, Item 160: #8 and #12.

E.P.I.: 32 (or 16 for Bedford cord).

WARP COLOR ORDER: Alternate ends of gray-brown and soft brick (or 24 ends gray-brown and 16 ends soft brick for Bedford cord)—see drafts.

DRAFTS:

DOUBLE WEAVE DRAFT:

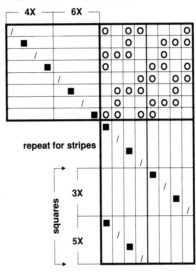

/ = soft brick   ■ = gray-brown

BEDFORD CORD DRAFT:

P.P.I.: 28 (14 in each layer) in double weave (or 14 in Bedford cord).

TAKE-UP & SHRINKAGE: 12% in width and 10% in length.

WEAVING: These yarns are tightly spun (to ensure their structural integrity), and they tend to kink. Watch carefully for kinks in the weft as you weave. (The use

of an end-feed shuttle helps them weave smoothly.)

I advanced the warp frequently by small amounts to avoid putting extra stress on selvedge warp ends. None of the warp ends broke in more than two yards of weaving, but it is a good idea to be careful with any singles woolen-spun yarn.

FINISHING: Hemstitch the fabric on the loom; inspect it for flaws and correct them before washing. There is a lot of spinning oil in this yarn, so more than one washing is necessary (see fabric #1). The Bedford cord draws up weftwise, but it can be pressed out—do not be alarmed!

#3: Dress or Suit Fabric ❴

PROJECT NOTES: This lightweight fabric was designed for use as a dress or light suit. The Merino yarn in the warp makes it smooth and buttery soft to the touch. The singles tweed is used as a decorative element in the cloth, weaving little squares of rosy red on a plain-weave ground. The tweed warp shows on the surface in an over 3, under 1 interlacement so that it is caught securely but stays mainly on the surface in the little squares. The floats on the back are not tied, so the dress must be lined.

FABRIC DESCRIPTION: Plain weave with supplemental warp.

WARP: Ground—12/2 wool worsted at 3200 yd/lb: beige.

Pattern—singles wool tweed at 1700 yd/lb: soft brick.

WEFT: 20/2 wool worsted at 5600 yd/lb: tan.

YARN SOURCES & COLORS: The worsted warp is 12/2 Merino, Item 156, from Halcyon Yarn: #10. The tweed pattern warp is Halcyon's Surrey Tweeds, Item 160: #12 soft brick. This weft was Oregon Worsted's Willamette in #3214 Blonde Beige, a discontinued color. You could substitute the same yarn in #133 Beige or a yarn of comparable size such as JaggerSpun's Heather 2/20 in the color of your choice.

E.P.I.: 20 ground (2 per dent in a 10-dent reed; in supplementary stripes, 2 ground and 2 pattern per dent, with 2 ground and 1 pattern at end of stripe).

WARP COLOR ORDER: on next page.

DRAFT: on next page.

P.P.I.: 24.

TAKE-UP & SHRINKAGE: 10% in width and length.

WEAVING: Weaving goes smoothly. The tweed yarns tend to cling, but because

		X						
beige 12/2 worsted	19	1	1	1	1	1	19	1	= 24/repeat
soft brick tweed		1	1	1	1	1			= 5/repeat

DRAFT FOR FABRIC #3:

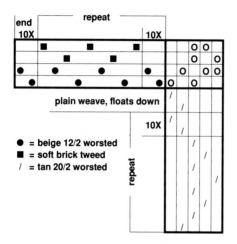

● = beige 12/2 worsted
■ = soft brick tweed
/ = tan 20/2 worsted

they are spaced out in the warp, they behave nicely. Their tendency to kink is controlled by the warp tension.

FINISHING: Hemstitch the fabric while it is on the loom; inspect it for flaws and correct them before washing.

I washed several versions of this fabric (see Finishing for fabric #1) and made a surprising discovery: when I put the fabric into the sudsy water and began to squeeze the water through it, it tracked dramatically. When I put it into the water and left it to soak and cool down, there was very little tracking. I drained the water and rewashed the fabric by squeezing very warm sudsy water through it without having severe tracking develop. I washed subsequent pieces that way, too, with the same results.

#4: Jacket, Coat, or Suit Fabric ❹

PROJECT NOTES: This fabric combines the neutral cool beige of the dress fabric and the soft rosy brick of all the preceding fabrics.

The structure is a simple four-shaft one in which stripes of 2/2 twill alternate with stripes of 2/2 basket weave. The sett is the same for both structures, so they are very compatible.

The colors are similar in value (lightness/darkness) but very different in hue. The tweed, with its flecks of brick, pink, and lavender, shows off in this environment, producing a very lively cloth which teams nicely with the dress fabric.

FABRIC DESCRIPTION: 2/2 twill and 2/2 basket weave.

WARP: 2-ply Shetland-style wool at 2000 yd/lb: light tan.

WEFT: Wool singles tweed at 2000 yd/lb: light rose tweed.

YARN SOURCES & COLORS: The warp is Harrisville Shetland Style: Lichen. The weft is Harrisville Singles Tweed: Clay.

E.P.I.: 16.

DRAFT: see below.

P.P.I.: 17.

TAKE-UP & SHRINKAGE: 10% in width and length.

WEAVING: This fabric is a pleasure to weave. Take care to beat so that a 45° angle is maintained in the twill areas.

FINISHING: Finish as for fabric #1.

#5: Skirt Fabric ❹

PROJECT NOTES: This soft, fairly lightweight fabric is well suited for use in a softly pleated or slightly flared skirt. The stripe is small in scale, making it appropriate even for petite figures.

The warp is several of the yarns used in other swatches of this collection. To show off all of them well, the fabric is woven in a 3/1 twill. This means that each warp yarn shows on the face of the fabric for three-fourths of its path.

FABRIC DESCRIPTION: 3/1 twill.

WARP & WEFT: 12/2 wool worsted at 3200 yd/lb: beige (warp only).

Singles wool tweed at 1700 yd/lb: soft brick (warp only).

20/2 wool worsted at 5600 yd/lb: tan (warp and weft).

2-ply wool at 1470 yd/lb: brick rose (warp only).

YARN SOURCES & COLORS: The 12/2 worsted warp is Merino, Item 156, from Halcyon Yarn: #10. The tweed warp is Halcyon's Surrey Tweeds, Item 160: #12. The 20/2 worsted warp and weft were Oregon Worsted's Willamette in #3214 Blonde Beige, a discontinued color (see note on fabric #3). The 2-ply warp is Victorian 2-Ply, Item 162, from Halcyon Yarn: #114.

E.P.I.: 20.

WARP COLOR ORDER: below.

DRAFT: Follow Warp Color Order in threading.

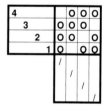

WARP COLOR ORDER FOR FABRIC #5:

		X		
beige 12/2 worsted	1	1		= 2/repeat
soft brick tweed singles	1	1		= 2/repeat
tan 20/2 worsted		1	1	= 2/repeat
brick rose 2-ply			1	= 1/repeat

DRAFT FOR FABRIC #4:

P.P.I.: 20.

TAKE-UP & SHRINKAGE: 12% in width and length.

WEAVING: Take care not to beat the cloth too hard. The warp floats ought to be about ⅛" long (that's easy to watch where the heavy brick rose wool shows). As with all yardage weaving, work on an easy, regular rhythm and everything else will take care of itself. I always allow about 6" at the beginning of the warp to get my loom and my body "tuned up" to the cloth at hand.

FINISHING: Finish as for fabric #1. Press mostly from the back, the weft-dominant side. The fabric tends to curl toward the back a bit, but it can be persuaded out of that tendency as it is pressed.

SWATCH COLLECTION #17

pages 85–88

#1: Skirt or Dress Fabric ❽ ❻ ❹

PROJECT NOTES: This fabric is intended to show off the color play between the cooler, darker blue-violet and the lighter, warmer rose and peach colors. The yarns in the alternating stripes are, by turns, woven as a single cord and then interlaced in a 2/2 basket structure of warp floats.

The structure of this reversible fabric is very simple—plain weave with two-end stripes. It requires six shafts (but if eight are available, you can thread the plain-weave ground on four shafts instead of two). If only four shafts are available, you can weave a variation in which the areas of basket weave are lined up all across the cloth instead of being offset.

8-SHAFT DRAFT FOR FABRIC #1:

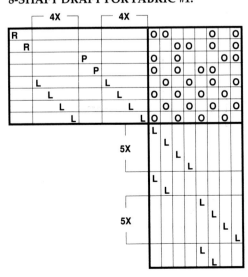

FABRIC DESCRIPTION: Plain weave with basket and corded stripes.

WARP: Ground—20/2 mercerized cotton at 8400 yd/lb: blue-violet.

Stripes—8/2 unmercerized cotton at 3600 yd/lb: light peach.

WEFT: Same as ground warp: blue-violet.

YARN SOURCES & COLORS: This 20/2 is from Robison-Anton: Violet Bloom. You could substitute UKI color #81 Grotto. The 8/2 is UKI colors #41 Peach and #23 Rose.

E.P.I.: In a 10-dent reed, sley the ground triple (30 e.p.i.) and the stripes double (20 e.p.i.).

WARP COLOR ORDER: 16 ground, 2 peach 8/2, 16 ground, 2 rose (see drafts).

DRAFTS: below.

P.P.I.: 30.

TAKE-UP & SHRINKAGE: 8% in width and 7% in length.

WEAVING: Although its luster is irresistible, this 20/2 cotton has a very soft twist and tends to break easily. (Either replace it with comparable yarn from another source or use utmost care. To prevent breakage, mist the warp or use a spray sizing, advance the warp frequently by small intervals, wind your bobbins carefully, and do not "handle" the selvedges.) The draft is easy to weave, as it uses only one shuttle.

FINISHING: Wash the mended, hem-stitched fabric in moderately hot water, rinsing twice; spin briefly and iron while damp.

#2: Vest or Jacket Fabric ❹

PROJECT NOTES: This fabric was designed to show off the lovely luster of the cotton yarns and play the colors off each other. Two shuttles alternate, making progress slower than in the one-shuttle

6-SHAFT DRAFT FOR FABRIC #1:

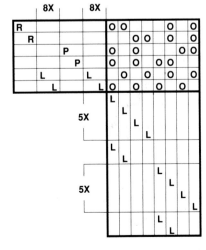

fabrics, but it is the way to produce the warpwise columns of color.

FABRIC DESCRIPTION: Plain weave with weft floats.

WARP & WEFT: 20/2 mercerized cotton at 8400 yd/lb: blue-violet and peach.

YARN SOURCES & COLORS: These are 20/2 from Robison-Anton: Violet Bloom and Orange Ice. You could substitute UKI colors #81 Grotto and #115 Peach.

E.P.I.: 30.

WARP COLOR ORDER: 92 blue-violet followed by 92 peach.

DRAFT:

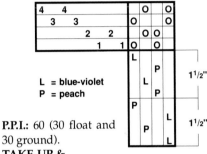

L = blue-violet
P = peach

P.P.I.: 60 (30 float and 30 ground).

TAKE-UP &
SHRINKAGE: 7% in width and length.

WEAVING: When using these yarns, I found the violet ends were more tender, noticeably more softly spun than the orange ends—they broke when stressed. My suggestions for fabric #1 apply here, too.

The cloth is easy to weave, although slow because two shuttles are used. Make a template out of a piece of cardboard and mark it to show where the color changes take place so that the fabric can be matched at the seams when it is cut and sewn.

FINISHING: Finish as for fabric #1. Iron in the weft direction to avoid distorting the weft floats.

4-SHAFT DRAFT FOR FABRIC #1:

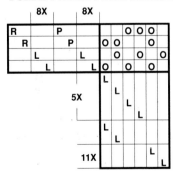

L = blue-violet 20/2
R = flesh rose 8/2
P = light peach 8/2

#3: Skirt Fabric

PROJECT NOTES: This fabric uses all three colors for this collection (blue-violet, rose, and peach) in a simple structure, log cabin plain weave. The warp and weft both alternate cool/warm and fine/heavy.

FABRIC DESCRIPTION: Plain weave.

WARP: Fine—30/2 mercerized cotton at 12,600 yd/lb: blue-violet.

Heavy—8/2 unmercerized cotton at 3600 yd/lb: light peach.

WEFT: Fine—same as fine warp: blue-violet.

Heavy—8/2 unmercerized cotton at 3600 yd/lb: flesh rose.

YARN SOURCES & COLORS: The fine warp and weft are Madeira 30/2 Pearly Perle from Cotton Clouds: #783. The heavy warp and weft are 8/2 cotton in UKI colors #41 Peach warp and #23 Rose weft.

E.P.I.: 30 (1 fine and 1 heavy per dent in a 15-dent reed).

WARP COLOR ORDER: see draft.

DRAFT:

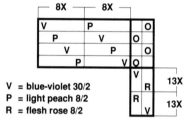

V = blue-violet 30/2
P = light peach 8/2
R = flesh rose 8/2

P.P.I.: 26 (13 each fine and heavy).

TAKE-UP & SHRINKAGE: 9% in width and 12% in length.

WEAVING: This fine cotton is very strong (perhaps a good substitute for the 20/2 used in fabric #2)—I had no breakage.

FINISHING: Finish as for fabric #1.

#4: Dress Fabric

PROJECT NOTES: I wanted to show off the extraordinary luster of the cottons that make up this fabric. The orange threads float over and under the fabric, gleaming where they catch the light and then disappearing into a plain-weave ground. Warning: The floats are relatively short (just over 1/8"), but they will snag if exposed to a lot of abrasion.

FABRIC DESCRIPTION: Plain weave with supplementary warp floats.

WARP: Ground—30/2 mercerized cotton at 12,600 yd/lb: blue-violet.

Supplementary floats—20/2 mercerized cotton at 8400 yd/lb: orange.

WEFT: Same as ground warp: blue-violet.

YARN SOURCES & COLORS: The 30/2 blue-violet is the same as that used in fabric #3. The 20/2 warp is also a Madeira yarn, Mini Pearly Perle 20/2: #588.

E.P.I.: In a 20-dent reed, sley ground warp double (40) and float areas triple (60).

WARP COLOR ORDER: see draft.

DRAFT:

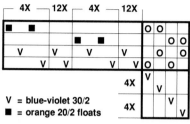

V = blue-violet 30/2
■ = orange 20/2 floats

P.P.I.: 40.

TAKE-UP & SHRINKAGE: 10% in width and 8% in length.

WEAVING: I found this one-shuttle structure easy to weave, and had no breakage with these yarns. Sometimes the floating supplementary warp ends do not present a smooth edge when they change from the face to the back or vice versa; if that happens, slip a tapestry needle under the floats and pop them into place.

FINISHING: Same as for previous fabrics.

#1: Skirt Fabric

PROJECT NOTES: This slightly iridescent, buttery soft Merino fabric was designed for use in a soft, slightly shirred skirt. There are tick-weave stripes on a plain ground. The blue-violet weft crossing the plain rust areas makes those stripes iridescent.

Soft fabrics like this one are best suited to loose fitting, unconstructed (not tailored) styles. Exploit the flowing softness in a style that allows movement.

FABRIC DESCRIPTION: Plain weave.

WARP & WEFT: 18/2 wool worsted at 5040 yd/lb: rust (warp only) and blue-violet (warp and weft).

YARN SOURCES & COLORS: These are JaggerSpun's Superfine Merino 18/2: Copper warp and Iris warp and weft.

E.P.I.: 18.

WARP COLOR ORDER:

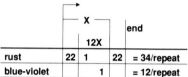

	X		end	
		12X		
rust	22	1	22	= 34/repeat
blue-violet		1		= 12/repeat

DRAFT:

P.P.I.: 18.

TAKE-UP & SHRINKAGE: 12% in width and length.

WEAVING: In spite of their softness, these yarns are not tender—I had no broken warp ends.

It is important to use a very even beat any time one color crosses another, as in this fabric.

FINISHING: I hemstitched the cloth on the loom; then I corrected the flaws. I washed the fabric in almost hot water with a mild liquid detergent (Joy); I rinsed it well and pressed the cloth while it was still barely damp.

#2: Jacket Fabric

PROJECT NOTES: This soft Merino wool fabric is plain weave with an overcheck of singles tweed. The overcheck is woven 3/1 twill in the warp direction and 1/3 twill in the weft direction so that the tweed lies on the surface of the cloth.

This fabric is light enough to be tailored into a jacket. It passes the "fold test".

(When you want to make a jacket or coat with a notched lapel, fold the fabric to make four layers, as there would be at the notch in the collar. If the fold is awkward and thick, the cloth is not well suited to that use.)

FABRIC DESCRIPTION: Plain weave with 3/1 and 1/3 twill overcheck.

WARP & WEFT: Ground—18/2 wool worsted at 5040 yd/lb: rust.

Twill overcheck—wool singles tweed at 2000 yd/lb: rose tweed.

YARN SOURCES & COLORS: The worsted ground is JaggerSpun's Superfine Merino 18/2: Copper. The tweed is Harrisville Singles Tweed: Rose Agate.

E.P.I.: 20 (2 per dent in a 10-dent reed).

WARP COLOR ORDER:

	X		
rust (Copper) 18/2	32	32	= 32/repeat
rose (Rose Agate) tweed		6	= 6/repeat

DRAFT:

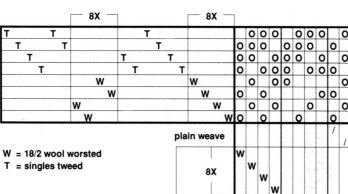

W = 18/2 wool worsted
T = singles tweed

P.P.I.: 20.

TAKE-UP & SHRINKAGE: 10% in width and length.

WEAVING: Strive for an even beat. It is important to weave the squares so that they are either actually square or clearly rectangular (because "nearly square" areas will be visually displeasing). It is helpful to make a cardboard template—mark a lightweight piece of cardboard with the repeat size you want, and compare the web with it as you go.

FINISHING: Finish as for fabric #1.

#3: Skirt Fabric ❻

PROJECT NOTES: This fabric plays dull against lustrous in yarns of two closely related colors. The warp is a wool/silk blend and the weft is silk. Textural differences are subdued in the plain weave areas and highlighted in the knotlike areas of warp and weft floats.

The weight of this cloth makes it well suited as a jacket fabric; like fabric #2, it passes the fold test.

FABRIC DESCRIPTION: Plain weave with warp and weft floats.

WARP: 18/2 wool/silk at 5040 yd/lb: rust.

WEFT: 12/2 silk at 3300* yd/lb: rust.

YARN SOURCES & COLORS: The warp is JaggerSpun's Zephyr (50% wool/50% silk) 18/2: Copper. The weft is Halcyon's Gemstone Silk 12/2 at 2970* yd/lb: Tiger's Eye.

E.P.I.: 20.

DRAFT: on next page.

P.P.I.: 18.

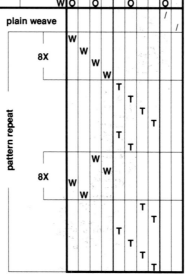

plain weave

pattern repeat

TAKE-UP & SHRINKAGE: 10% in width and length.

WEAVING: I had no breakage problems. If you are frequently plagued by broken warps, reverse the roles of the yarns in this fabric and use the silk (which has a higher tensile strength) for the warp and the wool/silk for weft.

Take care not to beat quite as firmly in the areas where the "knots" are woven, as it is easy to pack those areas more tightly than the plain-weave bands.

FINISHING: Finish like fabric #1.

*See General Instructions for yardage notes.

#4: Sweater Fabric ❻

PROJECT NOTES: This cuddly, stretchy, highly insulating, soft waffle-weave fabric is just right for a sweaterlike jacket. The structure gives it a lot of depth and good insulating properties because of the trapped air in the cells. The structure draws in when it is taken from the loom and even more when washed, so that a lot of natural stretch is built right in. I used wool, the most elastic and resilient natural fiber, to create an even stretchier fabric.

There are three kinds and colors of yarn in this waffle, used in such a way that they make the cells appear even deeper. The woolen-spun yarn is used on the surface because it has less tendency to snag than the others. There is the surprise of a little blue-violet "eye" at the bottom of each cell. A smaller version of this structure can be constructed on four shafts, but the effect isn't as dramatic.

When constructing a garment from this fabric, do not stretch or pull the fabric as the pieces are laid out and cut—treat it like a very springy knit.

FABRIC DESCRIPTION: 6-shaft waffle weave.

WARP & WEFT: Wool singles tweed at 2000 yd/lb: rose tweed (for cell outlines).

18/2 wool worsted at 5040 yd/lb: rust and blue-violet (for cell sides and center).

YARN SOURCES & COLORS: The tweed is Harrisville Singles Tweed: Rose Agate. The worsteds are JaggerSpun's Superfine Merino 18/2: Copper and Iris.

E.P.I.: 20 (even though it crowds the tweed yarn).

WARP & WEFT COLOR ORDERS: See draft (3 tweed, 4 rust, and 3 blue-violet per warp repeat).

DRAFT: (on next page). This draft weaves the fabric face down.

P.P.I.: 22.

TAKE-UP & SHRINKAGE: 22% in width

DRAFT FOR FABRIC #3:

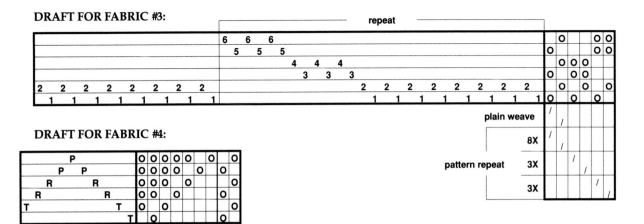

DRAFT FOR FABRIC #4:

T = singles tweed
R = rust 2/18 worsted
P = blue-violet 2/18 worsted

and 12% in length (from measurement of relaxed cloth).

WEAVING: Keep an even beat. The selvedges are naturally a little messy, but if you are careful not to draw them in, they will be all right. If you weave the cells so that they are just a little longer than they are wide (under tension), they will be square when the fabric is relaxed and washed.

FINISHING: Hemstitch while the cloth is on the loom, then wash to remove the spinning oil. I pressed the fabric while it was damp to flatten it a bit, then shook it to bring it to full three-dimensionality again, and let it air dry. The depth of the waffle weave is an important aspect of the cloth and should be retained. Be sure when using the cloth to keep the tweed face as the right side.

SWATCH COLLECTION #19

pages 92–95

Note: All four of these fabrics use 16/1 linen at about 5450-5500 yd/lb or 16/2 linen at 2420-2720 yd/lb, in off-white, tan, and dark blue. These are all Bockens linen from Glimåkra Looms 'n Yarns. The off-white is Half-Bleached, the tan is Natural, and the blue is color #136.

#1: Top Fabric   ❹

PROJECT NOTES: This classic fabric is woven in Bronson lace to form a checkerboard in the cloth. Each square of lace is five units wide and high.

I have designed this cloth with plain-weave selvedges, because the lace weave does not produce stable edges automatically. All other areas of the warp have equal take-up because the blocks balance each other, but the plain-weave selvedges will have different take-up. They must be beamed separately, weighted instead of beamed, or replaced by simple floating selvedge threads.

I would like to see this fabric made into a loose-fitting T-shirt shape—the fewer seams, the better the design.

FABRIC DESCRIPTION: Two-block Bronson lace.
WARP & WEFT: 16/1 linen: half-bleached (see opening note).
E.P.I.: 30.
DRAFT: at right.
P.P.I.: 28.
TAKE-UP & SHRINKAGE: 8% in width and length.
WEAVING: Wind your

bobbins carefully, and weave with a firm beat to square.
FINISHING: Hemstitch and correct any flaws. Wash in hot water with laundry detergent. Manipulate the fabric well to remove reed marks. Squeeze out the water, tumble the fabric in the dryer briefly (air only) to shake out the wrinkles, then iron until dry. If you want a softer fabric, machine dry it until it is just damp, and then iron it. I found that tumbling the ironed fabric and re-ironing it softened it further.

#2: Jacket Fabric   ❽

PROJECT NOTES: This weave requires eight shafts, four for each block. Drafts are given for two other four-shaft versions. One of them makes crosswise bands of plain and basket weaves; the other contrasts the weaves in lengthwise stripes. The cloth in basket-weave areas is not as firm as in the plain weave—in this eight-shaft version, that is no problem because

DRAFT FOR FABRIC #1:

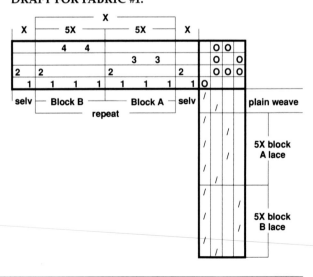

the squares alternate and balance each other. But in the lengthwise-striped version, the stripes must be beamed separately because the take-up of each structure is different.

Because two successive weft picks go into the same shed in the basket-weave sections, the selvedges must be handled specially. If more shafts are available, thread an extra four ends 9, 10, 9, 10 at each selvedge (and add these to the tie-up). Otherwise, use a floating selvedge thread on each edge.

FABRIC DESCRIPTION: Plain weave and 2/2 basket weave.

WARP: 16/2 linen: natural (see opening note).

WEFT: 16/2 linen: dark blue (see opening note).

DRAFTS FOR FABRIC #2:

B (5X)	A (5X)

(threading and tie-up draft for fabric #2)

plain weave

5X (block A plain weave, block B basket weave)

5X (Block A basket weave, block B plain weave)

Thread selvedges on additional shafts or use floating selvedges (see text).

FOUR-SHAFT VERSION FOR WEFT-WISE BANDS: Use floating selvedges.

(four-shaft draft)

10X (plain weave)

5X (2/2 basket weave)

FOUR-SHAFT VERSION FOR WARP-WISE STRIPES:

5X plain	5X basket

(four-shaft draft)

repeat

E.P.I.: 20.
P.P.I.: 20.
TAKE-UP & SHRINKAGE: 10% in width and length.
WEAVING: This cloth weaves up easily. Mark a strip of cardboard as a template, and use it to ensure that the blocks are all woven the same length so that your checkerboard will be even.
FINISHING: Same as fabric #1.

#3: Shirt, Jacket, or Skirt Fabric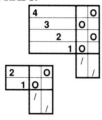

PROJECT NOTES: This checked fabric is very simple, a classic design, and the sheerest in this collection. It is constructed like a gingham except that the pairs of colors in the warp and weft directions are not the same. I like the interplay of natural and half-bleached linen with the indigo blue.

FABRIC DESCRIPTION: Checked plain weave.

WARP & WEFT: 16/1 linen: 14-end stripes of half-bleached and dark blue in the warp, 14-pick bands of natural and dark blue in the weft (see opening note).

E.P.I.: 27.

DRAFT:

(draft for fabric #3)

P.P.I.: 25.
TAKE-UP & SHRINKAGE: 7% in width and length.
WEAVING: If working with fine singles linen worries you, keep the warp slightly damp (which strengthens the yarn). I had no trouble with breakage except when a shed didn't open properly and my heavy, end-feed shuttle struck the errant ends "bang-on" and broke them.

Use an even beat, and mark a strip of cardboard with the repeat length to measure, to ensure that you can match the check.
FINISHING: Same as for fabric #1.

#4: Jacket Fabric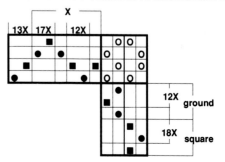

PROJECT NOTES: This somewhat heavier jacket fabric is the boldest of the collection. Squares of horizontal lines are framed by a background of vertical lines (while the back of the fabric is opposite— squares of verticals on a horizontally lined ground). The structure is very nearly plain weave.

In designing this cloth, I made a sketch of the look I wanted and then did a thread-by-thread color-and-weave-effect drawdown to derive the warp and weft color orders, the threading, the tie-up, and the treadling necessary to produce the six-shaft cloth you see here. A draft is also included for a nearly identical four-shaft version.

Because this structure is plain weave nearly throughout the cloth, this is a stable, smooth fabric that shows off linen nicely.

FABRIC DESCRIPTION: Near-plain weave with color effect (similar to shadow weave).

WARP & WEFT: 16/2 linen: alternating ends of natural and dark blue in the warp, and alternating picks of the same two colors in the weft (see opening note).

E.P.I.: 20.
P.P.I.: 20.

DRAFTS FOR FABRIC #4:

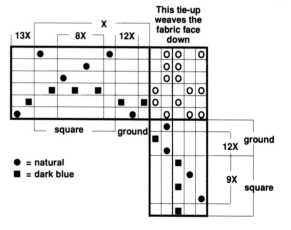

This tie-up weaves the fabric face down

● = natural
■ = dark blue

FOUR-SHAFT VERSION FOR FABRIC #4:

(four-shaft draft)

TAKE-UP & SHRINKAGE: 10% in width and length.

WEAVING: This fabric was easy to weave but requires two shuttles that alternate. I had no problems with breakage or fraying.

FINISHING: Same as for fabric #1.

SWATCH COLLECTION #20

pages 96–99

#1: Suit Fabric   ❹

PROJECT NOTES: This is a Katharine Hepburn sort of fabric—tailored, elegant, and very "finished" looking. It is firm and fairly lightweight, suitable for slacks, a tailored jacket, or a suit.

FABRIC DESCRIPTION: 2/2 twill.

WARP & WEFT: 20/2 wool worsted at 5600 yd/lb: dark brown and gray.

YARN SOURCES & COLORS: These are Oregon Worsted's Willamette: #341 Tobacco and #1625 Charcoal.

E.P.I.: 27.

WARP COLOR ORDER:

WEFT COLOR ORDER:		X	
dark brown	40		40
gray		2	

2 dark brown,
38 gray.

DRAFT:
P.P.I.: 26.
TAKE-UP & SHRINKAGE: 7½% in width and 9% in length.

4				O	O
3			O	O	
2		O	O		
1	O				O

WEAVING: Mark the warp stripes on a strip of cardboard. As you weave, change the weft colors as indicated on this strip. Because there is a little more loss in the warp direction, I include the width of my pencil mark in the length of the ground color, in this case gray. I found I needed 38 shots of gray and 2 shots of brown to square the pattern.

Establishing an even beat is crucial when the warp and weft are different colors. Allow yourself about 5" extra warp to use to establish the rhythm.

FINISHING: Hemstitch the fabric while it is on the loom. Correct any flaws before washing. Soak the fabric in very warm water for half an hour or longer. Wash, using a mild liquid detergent such as Joy. Rinse three times, using a liquid fabric softener in the second rinse. Spin briefly to extract water, hang to air dry. While it is slightly damp, press the fabric on both sides until it feels dry. Hang to complete drying.

#2: Jacket Fabric   ❽

PROJECT NOTES: This undulating twill fabric is rich looking and interesting at several distances. From far off it appears to be subtly striped; a closer look reveals the curvaceous twill lines.

The sett is a little denser than what an ordinary twill requires. The areas of longer floats tend to become mushy unless the overall sett is increased slightly. Because of the nature of the structure, the drape of the fabric is not compromised by a firmer sett.

Any twill may be used to create the undulating lines. This is an eight-shaft twill, chosen because its three-shaft weft float creates a more dramatic cloth. (Note that in an undulating twill, a three-shaft float becomes longer than three ends because of the threading.)

Twills may be made to undulate either through the threading or the treadling. This one has a complex threading and simple treadling so that the weaving progresses quickly, rhythmically, and easily.

Be sure that your pattern does not rule out an obvious diagonal!

FABRIC DESCRIPTION: 8-shaft undulating twill.

WARP: 2-ply Shetland-style wool at 2000 yd/lb: gray-brown.

WEFT: Wool singles tweed at 2000 yd/lb: dark red tweed.

YARN SOURCES & COLORS: The warp is Harrisville Shetland Style: Hickory. The weft is Harrisville Singles Tweed: Burgundy.

E.P.I.: 18.

P.P.I.: 15.

TAKE-UP & SHRINKAGE: 15% in width and 12% in length.

WEAVING: No special selvedges, either threaded or floating, are necessary to preserve a good edge. The treadling is simple, and only one shuttle is required so the work goes quickly.

FINISHING: Same as for fabric #1.

#3: Dress Fabric   ❻

PROJECT NOTES: This pearl cotton fabric is intended to be made into a classic shirtwaist dress. The brown areas are woven plain weave; the red and gray stripes are warp-faced twill. Warp-faced twill stripes on a plain-weave ground rise up out of the plane of the cloth, strengthening their visual impact.

FABRIC DESCRIPTION: 3/1 twill and plain weave.

WARP & WEFT: 20/2 cotton at 8400 yd/lb: brown (for plain-weave warp and weft), and dark red and gray (for twill warp stripes).

YARN SOURCES & COLORS: These are UKI colors #86 Sequoia, #32 Lipstick, and #19 Medium Grey.

E.P.I.: In a 15-dent reed, sley the brown at 2 per dent, the red 2, 3, 2, 3, and the gray/brown area at 3 per dent.

WARP COLOR ORDER: on next page.

DRAFT: on next page.

P.P.I.: 28.

TAKE-UP & SHRINKAGE: 7% in width and length.

WEAVING: The draft is given for weaving the fabric right side up (I like to look

DRAFT FOR FABRIC #2:

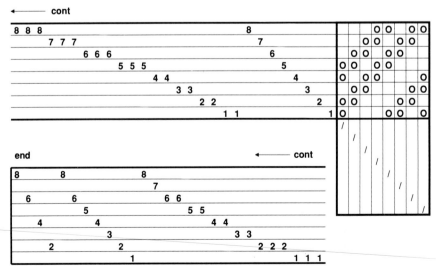

at the right side). If you prefer a lighter treadle load, lift the *other* shafts (for example, 2 and 6 where 1, 3, 4, and 5 are indicated).

FINISHING: Same as for fabric #1, except that two rinses will suffice.

WARP COLOR ORDER FOR FABRIC #3:

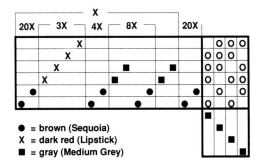

| | | X | | | |
		8X			
brown (Sequoia)	40	2	8	40	= 64/repeat
dk. red (Lipstick)				12	= 12/repeat
gray (Medium Grey)		2	2		= 18/repeat

DRAFT FOR FABRIC #3:

20X	3X	4X	8X	X	20X			
		X				O	O	O
		X				O	O	O
	X		■		■	O	O	O
	X		■		■	O		O O
●		●	●		●	O		O
●		●	●		●	O	O	
						■		
							■	
								■
								■

- ● = brown (Sequoia)
- X = dark red (Lipstick)
- ■ = gray (Medium Grey)

PROJECT NOTES: This woolen twill fabric was designed for a coat. Either a straight cut or a flared one will do. The vertical stripes, alternating dark brown with light grayed brown, produce a strong vertical line. That line is cut at even intervals by a streak of rich red. The structure is twill, the lightest way I could think of to produce strong vertical stripes.

FABRIC DESCRIPTION: 3/1 and 1/3 twill stripes.

WARP: 2-ply Shetland-style wool at 2000 yd/lb: gray-tan.

WEFT: Main—wool singles at 2000 yd/lb: medium brown.

Bands—wool singles tweed at 2000 yd/lb: dark red tweed.

YARN SOURCES & COLORS: The warp is Harrisville Shetland Style: Suede. The main weft is Harrisville Singles: Chocolate. The band weft is Harrisville Singles Tweed: Burgundy.

E.P.I.: 16.

DRAFT:

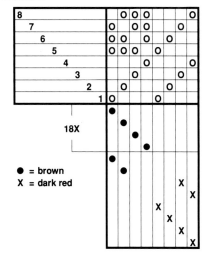

P.P.I.: 17.

TAKE-UP & SHRINKAGE: 8½% in width and 6½% in length.

WEAVING: Mark a strip of cardboard with the distance between red stripes and follow it to ensure that the pattern will match at the seams. Establish an even beat. I wove about 4½" of brown and 6 shots of red per repeat.

FINISHING: Same as for fabric #1.

INDEX